FORCE AND FEAR AS INVALIDATING MARRIAGE: THE ELEMENT OF INJUSTICE

THE CATHOLIC UNIVERSITY OF AMERICA
CANON LAW STUDIES
No. 310

Force and Fear as Invalidating Marriage: The Element of Injustice

BY

REV. JOSIAH G. CHATHAM, PH.B., S.T.L., J.C.L.
PRIEST OF THE DIOCESE OF NATCHEZ

A DISSERTATION

SUBMITTED TO THE FACULTY OF THE SCHOOL OF CANON LAW OF THE CATHOLIC UNIVERSITY OF AMERICA IN PARTIAL FULFILLMENT OF THE REQUIREMENTS FOR THE DEGREE OF DOCTOR OF CANON LAW

THE CATHOLIC UNIVERSITY OF AMERICA
WASHINGTON, D. C.
1950

NIHIL OBSTAT:

LUDOVICUS MOTRY, S.T.D., J.C.D.

Censor Deputatus

Washingtonii, die XIII febr. 1950.

IMPRIMATUR:

RICARDUS O. GEROW, S.T.D.

Episcopus Natchetensis

Jackson, Mississippi, die XV febr. 1950.

MURRAY & HEISTER

WASHINGTON, D. C.

PRINTED BY

TIMES AND NEWS PUBLISHING CO.

GETTYSBURG, PA., U. S. A.

Dedicated To
THE MOST REV. RICHARD O. GEROW, S.T.D.,
Bishop of Natchez
And To
MY MOTHER AND FATHER

TABLE OF CONTENTS

PAGE

FOREWORD xiii

PART ONE

HISTORICAL SYNOPSIS

CHAPTER

I. ROMAN LAW (527-565) 3

Article I. Matrimonial Coercion 3
Article II. The Law on *Vis-Metus* 4
Article III. The Qualification of Coercion 6
Article IV. The Obligation to Marry as Arising *ex Delicto* 8

II. THE DECREE OF GRATIAN (*ca.* 1140) 9

Article I. Matrimonial Coercion 9
Article II. The Obligation to Marry as Arising *ex Delicto* 13

III. THE *Compilationes Antiquae* (1190-1226) AND THE DECRETALS (1234-1317) 16

Article I. Matrimonial Coercion in the Decretals 16

Article II. Evolution of the Law on Force-Fear: Qualifications 19

§ 1. *Gravity of Force-Fear* 20
§ 2. *Extrinsic Origin of Fear* 21
§ 3. *Causal Relationship Between Coercion and Marriage* 21
§ 4. *The Injustice of Matrimonial Coercion* 22
§ 5. *The Obligation to Marry as Arising from Contract* 22
§ 6. *The Obligation to Marry as Arising ex Delicto* 23

Article III. The Source of Invalidity 25

TABLE OF CONTENTS (Continued)

CHAPTER PAGE

IV. Canonical Science from Rufinus (*circa* 1157-1159) to the Council of Trent (1545-1563) 27

Article I. Terminology and Distinctions 27

Article II. The Injustice of Coercion in Marriage 30

§ 1. *Culpa Praecedens* 31

§ 2. *Matrimonial Coercion After Delict* 31

1. First class: emphasis upon exceptional cases, in which coercion could be used to cause marriage 32

2. Second class: emphasis upon the general rule, that marriage which was the result of coercion was to be deemed invalid 34

§ 3. *Matrimonial Coercion in View of Previous Contract* 36

§ 4. *Metus Iniuste Incussus* 39

§ 5. *The Courts and the Justice of Coercion* 42

Article III. The Source of Invalidity 43

V. Saint Thomas Aquinas (1225-1274) 51

Article I. Concepts, Distinctions, Use of Terms 51

Article II. The Injustice of Matrimonial Coercion and the Obligation to Marry as Arising *ex Delicto* and *ex Contractu* 53

Article III. The Source of Invalidity 54

VI. Dominicus Soto (1494-1560) 59

Article I. Terminology and Distinctions 59

Article II. The Source of Invalidity 60

§ 1. *Opinion of Those Who Ascribed the Invalidating Effects of Coercion in Marriage to the Natural Law* 60

§ 2. *Opinion of Those Who Ascribed the Invalidating Effects of Coercion in Marriage to the Positive Law* 62

Article III. The Injustice of Matrimonial Coercion 63

TABLE OF CONTENTS (Continued)

CHAPTER PAGE

VII. CANONICAL SCIENCE FROM THE COUNCIL OF TRENT TO THE CODE OF CANON LAW 66

Article I. Terminology 66

Article II. Summary Statements Concerning the Law on Coercion in Marriage 68

Article III. Relationship Between the Intention of the Person Who Causes Fear in the Victim, and the Marriage Which Is the Result of Such Fear: *Metus Directe Incussus vs. Metus Indirecte Incussus* 71

Article IV. The Justice and the Injustice of Fear .. 76

§ 1. *The Problem; Manner of Treatment* 76
§ 2. *Distinctive Opinions on the Justice and the Injustice of Fear in Marriage* 77
§ 3. *The Distinction Between "Metus Iniustus Quoad Substantiam" and "Metus Iniustus Quoad Modum Tantum"* 79
§ 4. *Fear Which Was Considered Just* 81
§ 5. *Fear Which Was Considered Unjust* 84

Article V. The Justice and the Injustice of Force and Fear in Cases of Seduction 86

§ 1. *The Problem* 86
§ 2. *Terms* 87
§ 3. *Presumptions* 88
§ 4. *Circumstances in Which the Man Had No Obligation Either to Marry the Woman or to Endow Her* 89
§ 5. *Circumstances in Which the Seducer Was Entitled to the Alternative Either of Marrying or of Endowing the Seduced Woman* 92
§ 6. *Circumstances in Which the Seducer Was Obliged to Marry the Woman Without Benefit of Alternative* 93

Article VI. The Source of the Invalidating Effects of Fear 95

TABLE OF CONTENTS (Continued)

PART TWO

CANONICAL COMMENTARY

CHAPTER PAGE

VIII. COMMENTARY ON CANON 1087: THE *Iniuste Incussus* AND OTHER SPECIAL POINTS ... 101

Article I. The Right to Matrimonial Liberty and the *Ratio Canonica* of Canon 1087 ... 101

Article II. Force and Fear: Concepts and Divisions ... 104

Article III. The Scope of Canon 1087 ... 108

Article IV. The Relationship of Canon 1087 to the Pre-Code Law ... 109

Article V. Metus Iniuste Incussus ... 112

§ 1. *Under the Law of the Code "Metus Iniustus Quoad Modum Tantum" Suffices to Invalidate Marriage* ... 112
§ 2. *Relationship of the Injustice of Fear to the Intention of the Person Who Inflicts It* ... 115
§ 3. *Metus Iniustus Quoad Substantiam* ... 117
§ 4. *Material Injustice Suffices to Invalidate Marriage* ... 120
§ 5. *Metus Iniustus Quoad Modum* ... 120
§ 6. *Special Problem Cases* ... 123
§ 7. *Coercion in View of Espousals* ... 126

Article VI. The Special Question of the Justice and the Injustice of Coercion in Cases of Seduction ... 127

§ 1. *The Problem* ... 127
§ 2. *The Concept of "Stuprum"* ... 127
§ 3. *General Obligation of the Seducer "in Foro Conscientiae"* ... 128
§ 4. *Circumstances in Which the Seducer Has No Obligation in Conscience Either to Endow or to Marry the Woman* ... 129

TABLE OF CONTENTS (Continued)

CHAPTER PAGE

§ 5. *Circumstances in Which, According to Some Authors, the Seducer Has the Obligation in Conscience to Marry the Woman Without Benefit of Alternative* 130
§ 6. *Circumstances in Which Even the Seducer Who Has Promised Marriage Is Not Obliged in Conscience to Marry the Woman* 131
§ 7. *The Obligation in Conscience of a Seducer Who Lacks the Means to Endow the Woman* 132
§ 8. *The Justice and the Injustice of Action Against a Seducer in the Ecclesiastical Courts* 133
§ 9. *Just and Unjust Coercion in the Secular Courts* 138
§ 10. *The Justice and the Injustice of Action by Private Persons; Threats of Accusation* 142

Article VII. The Qualification: *A Quo Ut Quis Se Liberet, Cogatur Eligere Matrimonium* 145

§ 1. *The Problem* 145
§ 2. *Opinion of Those Who Hold That Only "Metus Directe Incussus" Invalidates Marriage* 145
§ 3. *Refutation of the Arguments Proposed in Support of the Opinion Which Requires "Metus Directe Incussus"* 148
§ 4. *The Opinion of Those Who Do Not Require That the Fear Be "Directe Incussus"* 150
Practical Summary 154

IX. The Source of the Invalidating Effects of Force-Fear upon Marriage 157
Observations 158

Conclusions 160

Bibliography 162

Abbreviations 167

Biographical Note 168

Index 169

Canon Law Studies 173

FOREWORD

Much has been written and much still needs to be written about force and fear in marriage. When Sangmeister wrote his dissertation on the topic in 1932 (*Force and Fear as Precluding Matrimonial Consent,* The Catholic University of America Canon Law Studies, n. 80, Washington, D. C.: The Catholic University of America, 1932) four points, in particular, were still in dispute: 1. the scope of canon 1087—whether or not it embraces *vis physica* as well as *vis moralis* or *metus;* 2. whether *metus iniustus quoad modum tantum* invalidates marriage; 3. whether *metus indirecte incussus* invalidates marriage, a problem which is closely related to the meaning of the *a quo ut quis se liberet* of canon 1087; 4. the source of the invalidating effects of force and fear as described in canon 1087—whether invalidity derives from the natural law or only from the positive law. Besides these unsolved problems there was the vexing question of the justice of the use of coercion especially after the commission of the delict of *stuprum,* which seemed almost to defy a clear and adequate treatment.

The purpose of this thesis is to re-examine these problems, especially the problem of the justice and the injustice of matrimonial coercion. In this examination the historical development of the various problems will be briefly traced with special emphasis upon the periods which were touched upon only briefly by Sangmeister. An instance in point is the period from the Council of Trent to the Code of Canon Law. Another example is the re-evaluation of the opinion of Saint Thomas on the source of the invalidating effects of coercion upon marriage in the light of the recent research of Lottin on *Le Droit Naturel chez Saint Thomas d'Aquin et ses Predecesseurs* (2. ed., Bruges: Charles Beyaert, 1931).

In the historical synopsis the problem of force and fear in marriage has been treated in all its aspects as contained in Roman Law, in the Decree of Gratian and in the Decretals. This should serve to place the particular problems considered in this study in their proper setting. In tracing the doctrinal development subsequent to the Decretals only those aspects of force and fear have been discussed which form the special subject of this study as outlined above.

Since 1932 the Rota has published a wealth of material on the subject. Inasmuch as the *Decisiones* of the Rota are published only about ten years after they are actually rendered, and since the first decade after the publication of the Code still found the majority of cases concerned with marriages that had been contracted prior to 1918, it is only now that the Rota decisions offer an abundance of material precisely on canon 1087.

In citing the *Decisiones* of the Rota, cases which are concerned with marriages contracted before 1918 have been used in the study of the pre-Code Law though they were published after the Code. In the commentary on canon 1087 only those decisions have been used which deal with marriages contracted since the Code of Canon Law went into effect. This procedure should be helpful in delineating clearly the modification of the law introduced by canon 1087.

The text has been equipped with copious cross-references. Thus, in the commentary, references are given to the pertinent parts of the historical section. In this way the necessity of a summary of the historical synopsis seems to be eliminated.

The writer of this dissertation is happy to have occasion to express his gratitude to his Bishop, the Most Rev. Richard O. Gerow, S.T.D., Bishop of Natchez, for the opportunity of making advanced studies in Canon Law. At the same time the writer wishes to acknowledge his indebtedness and abiding sense of appreciation to the members of the Faculty of the School of Canon Law of The Catholic University of America, not only for their guidance and instruction during the preparing of this modest study, but also for the aid and inspiration which they have afforded him in many other ways as well. A final but special word of thanks is due by the writer to his devoted sister, Ann Caroline Chatham, for her generous assistance in having this dissertation printed.

PART ONE

Historical Synopsis

CHAPTER I

ROMAN LAW (527-565)

ARTICLE I. MATRIMONIAL COERCION

Canonists of the Middle Ages attributed a special authority to Roman Law in the matter of force-fear. For example, Tancred (circa 1226) wrote:

> Bazianus dixit — cuius opinionem amplector — quod iuramentum metu seu vi extortum neminem obligat, (cum) tamquam divina voce pretor edixerit quod metus causa factum erit, ratum non habebo.[1]

In the period after Gratian, canonists were influenced especially by the law of Justinian (527-565).[2] For this reason a brief chapter will be devoted to the Justinian Law on force-fear. No attempt at exhaustive presentation or interpretation will be made. The general lines of Justinian's treatment will be sketched, and typical passages quoted in order to illustrate the principles and spirit of Roman Law.[3]

---

[1] Quoted from Stephan Kuttner, *Kanonistische Schuldlehre von Gratian bis auf die Dekretalen Gregors IX, Studi e Testi n.* 64 (Città del Vaticano: Biblioteca Apostolica Vaticana, 1935), pp. 327-328 (hereafter cited *Kanonistische Schuldlehre*). For a more general observation on the influence of Roman Law upon Canon Law in the Middle Ages, cf. A. Esmein, *Le Mariage en Droit Canonique* (2 vols., Vol. I, 2. ed., mise à jour par R. Génestal, Paris: Librairie du Recueil Sirey, 1929), I, 92-93 (hereafter cited Esmein-Génestal, *Le Mariage*); A. Van Hove, *Commentarium Lovaniense in Codicem Iuris Canonici,* Vol. I, Tom. I, *Prolegomena* (2. ed., Mechliniae, Romae: H. Dessain, 1945), pp. 524-527 (hereafter cited *Prolegomena*).

[2] Van Hove, *Prolegomena,* pp. 457-467.

[3] The *Codex* is quoted from: *Corpus Iuris Civilis,* Vol. II, *Codex Iustinianus* (ed. stereotypa decima, recognovit et retractavit Paulus Krueger, Berolini: apud Weidmannos, 1929); the *Digest* is quoted from: *Digesta Iustiniani Augusti* (2 vols., recognovit, adsumpto in operis societatem Paulo

Roman Law enunciated the principle that consent was of the essence of marriage.[4] It therefore forbade coercion in marriage, using such phrases as: *ne filium quidem familias invitum ad ducendum uxorem cogi legum disciplina permittit.*[5]

Any marriage entered into contrary to this prohibition of the use of coercion was invalid: *si adversus ea quae diximus aliqui coierunt, nec vir, nec uxor, nec nuptiae, nec matrimonium, nec dos intelligitur. . . .*[6]

ARTICLE II. THE LAW ON *Vis-Metus*

It was in complete independence of its treatment of marriage that Roman Law enunciated the principles on force-fear that were later to be adopted by the canonists. Force and fear were propounded as a juridical fact giving rise to the *restitutio in integrum,* whereby the pretor rescinded a state of affairs and returned things to their original status.[7]

Force was thus defined: *vis autem est maioris rei impetus, qui repelli non potest.*[8] So defined, *vis* clearly excluded any voluntary

---

Kruegero, Th. Mommsen, Berolini: apud Weidmannos, 1870); the *Institutes* are quoted from: *Corpus Iuris Civilis,* Vol. I, *Institutiones* (ed. stereotypa quinta decima, recognovit Theodorus Mommsen, retractavit Paulus Krueger, Berolini: apud Weidmannos, 1928).

[4] D. (50, 17) 30: "Ulpianus . . .: Nuptiae non concubitus sed consensus facit." Cf. also D. (23, 1) 4; D. (23, 1) 11. It must be recalled, however, that this consent was non-contractual in nature, and was expressed in the *affectio maritalis* or social acceptance of each other by the consorts as man and wife. Cf. Biondo Biondi, *Istituzioni di Diritto Romano* (Milano: A. Giuffre, 1946), pp. 437-438 (hereafter cited *Diritto Romano*).

[5] C. (5, 4) 12. Cf. also: C. (5, 4) 14; D. (23, 1) 13; D. (23, 1) 21. At the same time, however, Roman Law insisted upon the concurrence of parental consent as a condition of validity.—D. (23, 2) 2; D. (23, 1) 12; D. (23, 1) 22.

[6] I. (1, 10) 12. In spite of this ruling, Sangmeister holds that, under Roman Law, marriage entered into under coercion was valid but rescissible.—Joseph V. Sangmeister, *Force and Fear as Precluding Matrimonial Consent,* The Catholic University of America Canon Law Studies, n. 80 (Washington, D. C.: The Catholic University of America, 1932), p. 33 (hereafter cited *Force and Fear*).

[7] D. (4, 2) 1, sq.

[8] D. (4, 2) 2.

action on the part of the subject moved: the response to such propulsion was a purely passive, physical, mechanical reaction.

Metus, on the other hand, was defined as follows: *metus est instantis vel futuri periculi causa mentis trepidatio.*[9] Such trepidation clearly affected the will, but not to such an extent as necessarily to exclude its co-operation. The idea of this reluctant though active co-operation of the will was expressed in the phrase: *coactus volui.*[10]

Having thus laid down distinct definitions for *force* on the one hand and *fear* on the other, Roman Law then proceeded to observe that whenever grave force is brought to bear upon a person, this person reacts from a motive of fear: *quodcumque vi atroci fit, id metu quoque fieri videtur.*[11] Consequently, in the matter of terminology, the entire phrase *vis metusve* was expressed by the simple term *metus,* and the terms *vis* and *metus* became interchangeable for all practical purposes: *olim edicebatur 'quod vi metusve causa' . . . sed postea detracta est vis mentio. . . .*[12]

The practical result was that though the definition of *vis,* in its full rigor, could apply only to such force as completely eliminated an act of the will on the part of the victim, in practice the term came to be used especially to signify a force compatible also with the reluctant co-operation of the will of the victim. In other words, for all practical purposes *vis physica* was eliminated from consideration, and the terms *vis* and *metus* were used interchangeably to signify such force as does not completely

---

[9] D. (4, 2) 1.

[10] D. (4, 2) 21: "Si metu coactus adii hereditatem puto me heredem effici, quia quamvis si liber essem noluissem, tamen coactus volui. . . ."

[11] D. (4, 2) 1. It is to be noted that Roman Law by saying in effect: *ubi vis, ibi metus,* thus moved the problem of determining the degree of mental disturbance into the open. Fear was to be measured by the force from which it arose. Implicit in this principle was the idea that only such fear as arose *from without* gave title to the *restitutio in integrum.*

[12] D. (4, 2) 1. Cf. Orio Giacchi, *La Violenza nel Negozio Giuridico Canonico* (Milano: Giuffre, 1937), pp. 9-10; Giuseppe Dossetti, *La Violenza nel Matrimonio in Diritto Canonico* (Milano: Società Editrice "Vita e Pensiero," 1943), pp. 66-68 (hereafter cited *La Violenza nel Matrimonio*).

destroy the co-operation of the will. To convey this idea, the term *metus* was generally preferred, and was used alone in this sense.

Thus the Roman Law terminology on force-fear was rather complicated. This state of affairs was to cause no small confusion in the writings of the canonists of subsequent periods.

ARTICLE III. THE QUALIFICATION OF COERCION

In Roman Law not every experience of coercion entitled the victim to a *restitutio in integrum.* Gravity was required, indeed such gravity as could rightly be considered sufficient to sway a *very resolute* man: *metum autem non vani hominis, sed qui merito et in homine constantissimo cadat. . . .*[13]

This qualification was to be considerably mitigated in the Decretal Law, in which the norm of the *homo constans* was to be substituted.[14]

In order to give title to the *restitutio in integrum,* it was postulated that the fear arose from an outside agent: *sufficit enim hoc docere metum sibi illatum. . . .*[15] Since fear that arose purely from one's conscience or imagination could not be said to be "inflicted," an extrinsic origin was clearly implied in the law. Furthermore, the employment of coercion had a distinctively penal note which led to the added inference that the agent producing the fear was required to be a person capable of delictual imputability.[16]

A causal relationship was required between the coercion and the status of affairs which the victim wished to have rescinded through the action of the pretor. This appears in numerous phrases such as: *si quis vi compulsus aliquid facit, per hoc edictum restituatur.*[17]

Finally, the coercion had to be tainted with a note of injustice if it was to give title to the *restitutio in integrum*:

> Sed vim accipimus . . . quae adversus bonos mores fiat, non eam quam magistratus recte intulit, scilicet iure

[13] D. (4, 2) 6. Cf. also: D. (4, 2) 3; D. (47, 10) 7; D. (4, 2) 4; D. (4, 2) 5; D. (4, 2) 7; D. (4, 2) 8; C. (2, 18) 9.

[14] Cf., e.g., c. 15, X, *de sponsalibus et matrimoniis,* IV, 1.

[15] D. (4, 2) 14.

[16] D. (4, 2) 12.

[17] D. (4, 2) 3; D. (4, 2) 14.

> licito et iure honoris quem sustinet. Ceterum si per iniuriam quid fecit populi Romani magistratus vel provinciae praeses, Pomponius scribit hoc edictum locum habere. . . .[18]

It is to be noted that recourse to the proper public authority for the purpose of bringing coercion to bear against another established a presumption that no injustice was done: *Is qui iure publico utitur non videtur iniuriae faciendae causa facere*: *iuris enim executio non habet iniuriam.*[19]

It would be an exaggeration, however, to contend that Roman Law was entirely clear on the question of the injustice of force-fear.

On the one hand, certain texts seem to indicate that if the victim of coercion had been the culpable cause of the coercion, no relief could be sought by means of recourse to the pretor:

> Si mulier contra patronum suum ingrata facta sciens se ingratam, cum de suo statu periclitabatur, aliquid patrono dederit vel promiserit, ne in servitutem redigatur: cessat edictum quia hunc sibi metum infert.[20]

This is a clear case of *culpa praecedens* eliding the possibility of recourse to the pretor for redress against coercion.

On the other hand, this rule seems to be contradicted, and action admitted in spite of the existence of *culpa praecedens*:

> . . . si quis in adulterio deprehensus [fuerit]. . . . Pomponius . . . recte scribit posse eum ad hoc edictum pertinere, timuit enim vel mortem vel vincula . . . sed potuerunt vel non iure occidi, et ideo iustus [that is, meeting the requirements of the law in order to entitle the victim to the *restitutio in integrum*] fuerit metus. . . .[21]

---

[18] D. (4, 2) 3. Cf. also: D. (4, 2) 12; D. (48, 7) 7.

[19] D. (47, 10) 13; more directly in D. (50, 17) 155: "Non videtur vim facere qui iure suo utitur et ordinaria actione experitur." Cf. also: D. (50, 17) 55; D. (50, 17) 116.

[20] D. (4, 2) 21.

[21] D. (4, 2) 7. Actually there is no contradiction here. The text seems to mean that the fear was substantially justified, though the *manner* of infliction feared was unjust. Reference to the *manner* of infliction is clear also in D. (4, 2) 3, cited above in note 18.

The purpose here is merely to point out that Roman Law was complex in its treatment of the element of injustice and *culpa praecedens* in the matter of force-fear. This complexity has followed canonical science down to the present day and its evolution will be studied at length in subsequent chapters.

ARTICLE IV. OBLIGATION TO MARRY AS ARISING *ex Delicto*

Roman Law recognized contract and delict as being the two sources of obligations.[22]

This principle was later to be applied by the canonists as the legal and moral basis for justifying the use of coercion in order to effect a marriage: if a man had assumed an obligation to marry either by contracting to do so, or by committing some delict which could be repaired only through marriage, then it was possible that coercion to bring the marriage about could be justified in such cases. The Canon Law on this point will be studied in subsequent chapters.

Suffice it here to say that this canonical attitude could not be reconciled with the principles and the spirit of the Roman Law, according to which marriage consisted in an *affectio maritalis,* which could not even be conceived as being the product of coercion under any circumstances.[23] Consequently delicts which might give rise to an obligation to marry under a legal system, such as Canon Law, which considered marriage as a contract, could, in Roman Law, give rise only to a purely criminal action or to a so-called mixed action (requiring both restitution and a penalty) without any possible consideration of an obligation to contract marriage.[24]

---

[22] I. (3, 13) 2.

[23] Cf. R. W. Leage, *Roman Private Law* (2. ed., by C. H. Ziegler, London: Macmillan, 1942), pp. 133 and 138; Max Radin, *Handbook of Roman Law,* Hornbook Series (Saint Paul: West Publishing Co., 1927), p. 115.

[24] Cf. I. (3, 13) 18.

CHAPTER II

THE DECREE OF GRATIAN (*ca.* 1140)

ARTICLE I. MATRIMONIAL COERCION

From the positive point of view, Gratian based his defense of matrimonial freedom upon the words of Saint Paul: *Cui vult nubat, tantum in Domino.*[1]

Negatively, Gratian ruled definitely and firmly against coercion in marriage, using the same Pauline text as the basis of his argument:

> Quod autem aliqua non sit cogenda nubere alicui, Ambrosius testatur super epistolam I ad Corinthios: "Nubat cui vult: tantum in Domino;" id est, quem sibi aptum putaverit, illi nubat; quia invitae nuptiae solent malos proventus habere. . . .[2]

Having thus stated his position against coercion in marriage, Gratian applied his principle in the rubric which follows immediately after the above-quoted *dictum*: a girl is not to be coerced into marrying a man to whom she has never given her consent, even though her father has sworn that she would marry

---

[1] I Cor. 7, 39—*dictum* of Gratian to c. 1, C. XXXI, q. 2; cf. also *palea,* c. 38, C. XXVII, q. 1. The *Decretum Gratiani* (ca. 1140), originally entitled *Concordia Discordantium Canonum,* will be quoted from the *Corpus Iuris Canonici* (ed. Lipsisensis secunda, 2 vols., post Aemilii Ludovici Richteri curas instruxit Aemilius Friedberg, 1879-1881; ed. anastatice repetita, Lipsiae: Tauchnitz, 1928). Cf. Van Hove, *Prolegomena,* pp. 339-348. Van Hove has the following to say concerning the Decree: "Decretum Gratiani nunquam fuit approbatum ab Ecclesia ut Codex authenticus iuris . . . neque . . . consuetudine collectio ut talis fuit approbata. Attamen . . . plures textus . . . immo quaedam dicta . . . vim legis universalis obtinuerunt. . . ."—*Op. cit.,* pp. 345-346.

[2] *Dictum,* c. 1, C. XXXI, q. 2; cf. also c. 16, C. XXXII, q. 2.

him. Gratian quoted Urban II (1088-1099) as his authority for this conclusion.[3]

Continuing his appeal to the authority of Urban II, Gratian quoted a letter of this Pope to Sancho, King of Aragon (1063-1094), prefacing the excerpt with a *dictum* which clearly rules against coercion in marriage:

> Quorum unum futurum est corpus, unus debet esse et animus: atque ideo nulla invita est copulanda alicui.[4]

In the fourth canon of the same question Gratian then adduced an excerpt from a letter of Pope Nicholas I (858-867) which treated of the famous case of Lothair II, King of Lorraine (855-869), whose marriage to Theutberga took place in 855 or 856.[5] The details of Lothair's case are not evident in Gratian's reference, but a reading of the papal correspondence indicates that, among many charges and countercharges, Lothair claimed that he had been coerced into the marriage. The important point for this study is Gratian's conclusion: *His auctoritatibus evidenter ostenditur, quod nisi libera voluntate nulla est copulanda alicui.*[6]

In the midst of this clear canonical doctrine which ruled against coercion in marriage two difficulties appear. A *palea* attributed to Pope Hormisdas (514-523) states that a father may not give an adult son in marriage, but that he may give a minor son in marriage without consideration of the will of the child.[7] Since

---

[3] Rubric and c. 1, C. XXXI, q. 2; Philippus Jaffé, *Regesta Pontificum Romanorum ab condita Ecclesia ad annum post Christum natum MCXCVIII* (2. ed., 2 toms. in 1 vol., correctam et auctam auspiciis Gulielmi Wattenbach curaverunt F. Kaltenbrunner, P. Ewald, S. Löenfeld, Lipsiae: 1885-1888), n. 5382 (hereafter cited Jaffé).

[4] *Dictum,* c. 3, C. XXXI, q. 2; cf. Jaffé, n. 5399.

[5] Jaffé, n. 2726. Cf. Le Bras, "Mariage à l'Epoque Carolingienne," *Dictionnaire de Théologie Catholique* (15 vols. in 30, Paris: Mabillion-Marletta, 1903—), tome 9, 2 partie, col. 2118, sq. Material on this case is also reported in Jaffé, nn. 2697-2702; 2707; 2723; 2725; 2726; 2729; 2748-2751; 2753; 2870; 2873.

[6] *Dictum* after c. 4, C. XXXI, q. 2.

[7] *Palea,* c. 2, C. XXXI, q. 2. According to Thiel the decretal is spurious.—A. Thiel, *Epistolae Romanorum Pontificum Genuinae et quae ad eos scriptae sunt a S. Hilario usque ad S. Hormisdam* (Brunsbergae, 1868), p. 1006. It

the canon is a *palea,* it is safe to say that it did not appear in the original text of Gratian's work. This view is strengthened by the fact that the *palea* interrupts a series of quotations which Gratian made from the work of Urban II. Furthermore, the text does not appear in all the codices.[8] The true mind of Gratian appears rather in the phrase: . . . *qui pueris dant puellas in cunabulis, et e converso, nihil faciunt. . . .*[9]

It must be admitted, however, that the presence of this *palea* is indicative of a canonical problem of the twelfth century.[10] The problem expressed in this text will be seen in its proper perspective in a later chapter.[11]

Another difficulty appears in Gratian's treatment of the binding force of oaths taken under conditions of coercion.[12] The case is as follows: a certain Ubaldus, moved by a fear of death which apparently arose from certain threats, swore that he would marry his concubine and eject his mother and brothers from his house without supporting them. The oath to the detriment of his family was held to be invalid, but concerning the oath that he would marry the following comment was made: *matrimonium sit in Deo firmum et stabile.*[13]

This text was widely discussed by the decretists and decretalists who proposed a number of explanations, as will be seen in subsequent chapters.[14] Whatever interpretation is placed upon the

---

should be noted here that *paleae* were additions made by Gratian's students, either during the lifetime of the Master or at a later date. They were so called after Paucapalea (circa 1150), the first to add glosses to the Decree. Cf. Van Hove, *Prolegomena,* p. 341; Esmein-Génestal, *Le Mariage,* I, 126, in note.

[8] Cf. critical paraphernalia of Friedberg, *Corpus Iuris Canonici,* at this text.

[9] C. un., C. XXX, q. 2.

[10] Cf. Sangmeister, *Force and Fear,* p. 50, in note.

[11] *Infra,* p. 49, note 80.

[12] C. 22, C. XXII, q. 4. In his *dictum* Gratian attributed this canon to Saint Augustine. Berardi, however, was of the opinion that this canon was not the work of Saint Augustine.—Carolus Sebastianus Berardus, *Gratiani Canones Genuini ab Apocryphis Discreti* (4 vols., Venetiis, 1777), Vol. IV, pars III, p. 216.

[13] C. 22, C. XXII, q. 4.

[14] Cf. *infra,* p. 31, note 10; p. 31, note 13; p. 33, note 22; p. 35, note 32; p. 35, note 34; p. 39, note 53; p. 41, note 61. Note that the decretalists gener-

text, it is immediately evident that this text is closely related to the problem of the obligation to marry as arising from previous crime and from previous contract.

Though Gratian defended the child against parental coercion, as has been seen above, he did require the concurrence of the consent of the parents for the marriage of their children.[15] This parental consent seems to have been required as a condition for the validity of the marriage.[16]

According to the *Decree* of Gratian, marriages which were the result of coercion were invalid.[17]

In ruling against coercion in marriage the *Decree* had taken the following stand:

> Quod autem aliqua non est cogenda nubere alicui, Ambrosius testatur . . . quem sibi aptum putaverit, illi nubat, quia invitae nuptiae solent malos proventus habere. . . .[18]

In this expression Gratian seemed to indicate that forced marriages would be, or at least could be, of themselves valid, but that they were forbidden by law because of their dangerous consequences. This constitutes an argument that the view according to which the invalidating effects of coercion in marriage derive from the positive law is consistent with the teaching of the *Decree.*

Gratian did not offer any distinct treatment of force-fear. As regards his terminology on coercion, he used a variety of terms in the many passages wherein coercion came up for incidental consideration: *violentia, vis, timor, metus, necessitas, periculum, invitus, coactus, compulsus, reclamans, repugnans, renitens,*

---

ally treated this case in their comment on c. 2, X, *de his quae vi metusve causa fiunt,* I, 40.

[15] C. 16, C. XXXII, q. 2; c. un., C. XXXII, q. 3. Cf. also *palea,* c. 38, C. XXVII, q. 1.

[16] Jean Dauvillier, *Le Mariage dans le Droit Classique de l'Eglise, depuis le Décret de Gratien (1140) jusqu'à la Mort de Clement V (1314)* (Paris: Librairie du Recueil Sirey, 1933), p. 192 hereafter cited *Le Mariage dans le Droit Classique*) ; Esmein-Génestal, *Le Mariage,* I, 173.

[17] C. 1, C. XXXI, q. 2; c. 3, C. XXXI, q. 2.

[18] *Dictum,* c. 1, C. XXXI, q. 2.

dolens.[19] There is no positive indication that Gratian depended upon Roman Law for terms or concepts. Furthermore, Gratian spoke of coercion without any reference to the necessity of its being qualified as in Roman Law: grave, from without, unjust, having a causal relationship.

A philosophical study of the implicit existence of these qualities in the concrete cases reported in the *Decree* would serve little purpose here. Only one point need be mentioned, namely, Gratian's rather oblique reference to the idea of *culpa praecedens.* The reference is called "oblique" because the point in question is one of delictual imputability, and not one of the effect of coercion upon the validity of an act. The text is as follows:

> Si quis insaniens aliquem occiderit, si ad sanam mentem pervenerit, levis ei penitentia imponenda est.[20]

To this text Gratian added the following comment: *Sed hoc forte de eo intelligitur, quem propria culpa ad furorem perduxit.*[21]

ARTICLE II. THE OBLIGATION TO MARRY AS ARISING *ex Delicto*

Gratian did not treat of the question of an obligation to marry as arising *ex delicto.* However, he discussed the delict of *stuprum* (deflowering of a virgin), and the question of *raptus* (abduction). It will be useful to review briefly Gratian's treatment of these two topics, since later canonists and theologians came to consider *stuprum* as a possible source of the obligation to marry (*ex delicto*), and, historically, *raptus* was closely connected with the question of coercion in marriage.

Stuprum, according to Gratian, was the illicit deflowering of a virgin under the following conditions: the parties were not engaged to marry; the virgin consented to the action; her father did not make an accusation of *iniuria* immediately upon receiving knowledge of the affair.[22] Violence, therefore, was not used against the

---

[19] Cf. Dossetti, *La Violenza nel Matrimonio,* p. 68, where an annotated analysis of the terminology in the *Decree* is to be found.

[20] C. 12, C. XV, q. 1.

[21] *Ibidem, dictum* of Gratian.

[22] "Struprum autem est proprie virginum illicita defloratio, quando videlicet non precedente coniugali pactione utriusque voluntate virgo corrumpitur,

woman; neither was violence done to her parents. Violence was not inflicted upon the virgin, for the action was committed *utriusque voluntate*. Neither was violence done to the parents, for the father did not take criminal action when he became informed of the situation. Under these circumstances it is not surprising that Gratian did not attach any special obligation in the way of restitution to the commission of *stuprum*.

Raptus was committed when a girl was taken by violence from her father's house in order to be deflowered and then taken in marriage. The violence was directed either against the girl or against her parents, or against both girl and parents.[23]

Raptus was a crime to which the death penalty was attached: *hic morte mulctatur*.[24] If the guilty party escaped death, he was nevertheless bound to public penance.[25]

No mention was made of an obligation to marry the girl because of the crime committed against her; rather, there was a prohibition against such a marriage: *Raptor in uxorem raptam ducere non valet*.[26] This prohibition, however, was based upon the necessity of doing public penance, and upon the fact that coercion was present in the abduction. The penance having been completed[27] and the girl and her parents having given their consent, the prohibition against the marriage immediately ceased.[28]

From this it is quite evident that *raptus* was not treated as a

---

patre iniuriam ad animum statim post cognitionem non revocante."—*Dictum*, c. 3, C. XXXVI, q. 1.

[23] "Raptus admittitur, cum puella a domo patris violenter ducitur, ut corrupta in uxorem habeatur, sive puellae solummodo, sive parentibus tantum, sive utrisque vis illata constiterit. . . ."—*Dictum*, c. 3, C. XXXI, q. 1. Cf. also c. 48, C. XXVII, q. 2.

[24] *Dictum* after c. 3, C. XXXVI, q. 1. Gratian here is evidently making reference to the penalties constituted in the Roman Law.—Cf. e.g., D. (48, 5) 20.

[25] *Dictum after* c. 8, C. XXXVI, q. 2.

[26] *Dictum* after c. 8, C. XXXVI, q. 2.

[27] ". . . legitime igitur post peractam penitentiam raptor poterit sibi copulare quam rapuit, nisi pater puellae illam raptori detrahere voluerit."—*Dictum* after c. 8, C. XXXVI, q. 2. Cf. also c. 32, C. XXVII, q. 2.

[28] C. 1, C. XXXVI, q. 2; *dictum*, c. 7, C. XXXVI, q. 2; cc. 8-9, C. XXXVI, q. 2; *dictum*, c. 11, C. XXXVI, q. 2.

distinct impediment in the *Decree* of Gratian. Marriage was forbidden in instances of abduction because of the impediment of public penance and because of the coercion involved.[29]

It can only be concluded that in the *Decree* of Gratian there was nothing which justified the use of coercion to cause a man to marry the woman whom he had seduced. Gratian did not make any mention of an obligation to marry as arising *ex delicto*.[30]

---

[29] Abduction as a matrimonial impediment has a long and involved history. In 845 the Council of Meaux reaffirmed abduction as a distinct diriment impediment.—Cf. Bartholomew Francis L. Fair, *The Impediment of Abduction*, The Catholic University of America Canon Law Studies, n. 194 (Washington, D. C.: The Catholic University of America Press, 1944), pp. 6-7. During the period from Gratian to the Council of Trent, abduction was treated rather as a species of coercion.—Fair, *op. cit.*, pp. 10-11; Sangmeister, *Force and Fear*, pp. 64-65. The Council of Trent restored abduction as a distinct impediment.—Concilium Tridentinum, sess. XXIV, *de ref. matrim.*, c. 6.—H. J. Schroeder, *Canons and Decrees of the Council of Trent* (St. Louis-London: Herder, 1941), p. 458. The Code of Canon Law, in canon 1074, adopted the ruling of the Council of Trent. Cf. also Dauvillier, *Le Mariage dans le Droit Classique*, p. 160; Esmein-Génestal, *Le Mariage*, I, 434-437. Gasparri, on the other hand, affirmed that the *Decree* of Gratian established a permanent prohibition against marriage between abductor and abducted, a conclusion which seems to be entirely unwarranted by the perfectly clear text of the Decree.—P. Gasparri, *Tractatus Canonicum de Matrimonio* (ed. nova ad mentem Codicis I.C., 2 vols., Civitate Vaticana: Typus Polyglottis Vaticanis, 1932), I, n. 635 (hereafter cited *De Matrimonio*). The studies cited in this note indicate that Gratian's teaching on *raptus* was generally adopted and prevailed until the Council of Trent.

[30] Cf., however, the case of Ubaldus, c. 22, C. XXII, q. 4—*supra*, p. 11, notes 12-13. According to Rufinus (circa 1177-1179), Joannes Faventinus (circa 1171) and Simon (circa 1177-1179) this may have been a case in which coercion was justified by reason of the previous delict of Ubaldus.—Cf. Kuttner, *Kanonistische Schuldlehre*, pp. 332-333.

CHAPTER III

The *Compilationes Antiquae* (1190-1226) and the Decretals (1234-1317)

ARTICLE I. MATRIMONIAL COERCION IN THE DECRETALS[1]

The positive basis in the Decretals for ruling against the use of coercion in marriage was the principle that consent is of the essence of marriage: *matrimonium autem assensu solo contrahitur.*[2] This principle was reinforced by the specific requirement that marriage was to be perfectly free: *ubi de ipso quaeritur plena debet libertate gaudere.*[3] Judges, therefore, were enjoined to take the necessary action to protect matrimonial liberty.[4]

---

[1] The *Compilationes* and the Decretals will be referred to under the one term "Decretals."

[2] C. 14, X, *de sponsalibus et matrimoniis,* IV, 1 (c. 19, Comp. I, h.t., IV, 1). The Decretals are quoted from the *Corpus Iuris Canonici* (complete reference, *supra,* p. 9, note 1). As to the *Compilationes Antiquae,* no material has been used from the Compilatio IV. The first three *Compilationes* are cited from the: *Antiquae Collectiones Decretalium* (ed. Antonii Augustini, Ilirìae: 1571). For the *Compilatio V* the work of Cironius has been used: *Compilatio* V, *studio Innocentii Cironii in lucem data* (Tolosae: 1645). Concerning the authorship, date of compilation, authority of the *Compilationes,* cf. Van Hove, *Prolegomena,* pp. 355-357; Stephan Kuttner, *Repertorium der Kanonistik (1140-1243), Studie Testi,* n. 71 (Città del Vaticano: Biblioteca Apostolica Vaticana, 1937), pp. 322 ff. For similar information concerning the Decretals, cf. Van Hove, *Prolegomena,* pp. 357-368.

As the material of the *Compilationes,* with few exceptions, is repeated in the Decretals, the Decretals will be cited first, because of their pre-eminence, and cross references will be given to the *Compilationes,* in parentheses. When words or phrases are dropped from the Decretal text, these will be supplied, in brackets, from the *Compilationes,* if they contribute to a clearer understanding of the text or otherwise have real significance.

[3] C. 14, X, *de sponsalibus et matrimoniis,* IV, 1 (c. 19, Comp. I, *h.t.,* IV, 1); cf. also rubric and c. 29, X, *h.t.,* IV, 1; August Potthast, *Regesta Pontificum Romanorum, MCXCVIII ad MCCCIV* (2 vols., Berolini: 1874-1875), n. 9660 (hereafter cited Potthast); c. 17, X, *de sponsalibus et matrimoniis,* IV, 1 (c. 12, Comp. I, *h.t.,* IV, 1); Jaffé, n. 15192.

[4] ". . . si timetur inferri violentia puellae, de cuius matrimonio agitur, debet

In order to safeguard matrimonial liberty, the Decretals ruled against the use of coercion in marriage. Alexander III (1159-1181) wrote to the Bishop of Pavia:

> Cum locum non habet consensus ubi metus, vel coactio intercedit, necesse est, ubi assensus cuiusquam requiritur, coactionis materia repellatur, matrimonium autem assensu solo contrahitur, et ubi de ipso quaeritur plena debet securitate gaudere; cuius est animus indagandus, ne per timorem dicat sibi placere, quod odit, et sequatur exitus qui de invitis solent nuptiis provenire.[5]

Parents were permitted to give their children in marriage, but this action of the parents required the confirmation of the child for validity both as to *sponsalia* and as to marriage itself.[6]

Another text of Alexander III to the Bishop of Bath further illustrated this point:

> . . . ante nubiles annos coniugalem consensum non habent, usque ad legitimam aetatem expectare tenentur, et tunc aut confirmetur matrimonium, aut, si simul esse noluerint, separentur; nisi carnalis commixtio ante intervenerit. . . .[7]

The *carnalis commixtio* simply established the legal presumption that the parties had given their personal consent to the union.[8]

---

iudex sibi providere locum tutum. . . ."—Summary before c. 14, X, *de sponsalibus et matrimoniis,* IV, 1.

[5] C. 14, X, *de sponsalibus et matrimoniis,* IV, 1 (c. 19, Comp. I, *h.t.,* IV, 1). In similar words Lucius III (1181-1185) made the same ruling.—C. 17, X, *h.t.,* IV, 1 (c. 12, Comp. I, *h.t.,* IV, 1) ; Jaffé, n. 15192. The text of Lucius closes with these words: *quum coactiones difficiles soleant exitus habere.* Cf. also, c. 29, X, *h.t.,* IV, 1 ; Potthast, n. 9660.

[6] Summary to text and text of Alexander III to the Bishop of York—c. 5, X, *de desponsatione impuberum,* IV, 2 (c. 6, Comp. I, *h.t.,* IV, 2) ; Jaffé, n. 13887. Also, Alexander III to the Bishop of Bath—c. 7, X, *de desponsatione impuberum,* IV, 2 (c. 9, Comp. 1, *h.t.,* IV, 2) ; Jaffé, n. 13767.

[7] C. 8, X, *de desponsatione impuberum,* IV, 2 (c. 10, Comp. I, *h.t.,* IV, 2) ; Jaffé, n. 13765. Cf. also rubric before c. 21, X, *de sponsalibus et matrimoniis,* IV, 1, and cap. un., *de desponsatione impuberum,* IV, 2, in VI°.

[8] C. 9, X, *de desponsatione impuberum,* IV, 2 (c. 12, Comp. I, *h.t.,* IV, 2) ;

Two difficulties occur in the Decretal defense of matrimonial liberty:

1. The text falsely attributed to Pope Hormisdas (514-523), which had found its way into the Decree of Gratian (*palea,* c. 2, C. XXXI, q. 2—*supra,* pp. 10-11, notes 7-8), was likewise included in the Decretals. According to this text, the parents were permitted to contract *sponsalia* for their minor children, apparently without regard for the will of the children.[9]

2. A decretal attributed to Pope Nicholas I (858-867) was reported. According to it the parents were permitted to give their children in marriage for the sake of public peace: *pro bono pacis.*[10]

The presence of these two texts in the Decretals is undeniably the reflection of practical canonical problems of the era. These problems will be viewed in their proper perspective in a later chapter.[11]

That under certain circumstances coercion had the effect of invalidating marriage is clearly indicated in a number of texts. For example, a text of Alexander III:

> . . . qui minori aetate desponsantur [traduntur et coniunguntur et . . . divortium postulant minorem allegantes aetatem, aut vim sibi a parentibus factam] . . . se possunt per illatam violentiam excusare, nisi post violentiam consensus accedat.[12]

The invalidity of marriages which were the result of coercion is apparent also in the texts cited below in Article II, § 1, of this Chapter, where the gravity of the coercion is discussed.

Jaffé, n. 13969; c. 30, X, *de sponsalibus et matrimoniis,* IV, 1; Potthast, n. 9661.

[9] C. 1, X, *de desponsatione impuberum,* IV, 2 (c. 2, Comp. I, *h.t.,* IV, 2). Cf. *supra,* pp. 10-11, notes 7 and 8, where this text is discussed.

[10] C. 2, X, *de desponsatione impuberum,* IV, 2 (c. 4, Comp. I, *h.t.,* IV, 2).

[11] Cf. *infra,* p. 49, note 80.

[12] C. 9, X, *de desponsatione impuberum,* IV, 2 (c. 12. Comp. I, *h.t.,* IV, 2); Jaffé, n. 13969. Cf. also c. 2, X, *de eo qui duxit in matrimonium quam polluit per adulterium,* IV, 7 (c. 2, Comp. I, *h.t.,* IV, 7); Jaffé, n. 13967; c. 5, X, *re regulis iuris,* V, 41 (c. 4, Comp. I, *h.t.,* V, 37; Jaffé, n. 13959; Reg. 64, R.J. in VI°.

One may properly note that in the Decretals, as in Gratian, abduction was considered as a species of coercion. Thus Innocent III (1198-1216) wrote: *rapta puella legitime contrahat cum raptore si prior dissensio transeat postmodum in consensum. . . .*[13]

The Decretals definitely adopted the Roman Law *vis-metus* terminology. Thus the following phrases were used: *metu illato compulsas . . . animo dissentirent . . . metus qui potuit cadere in constantem virum;*[14] *invitum coegit . . . metu coactus qui posset in virum constantem cadere;*[15] *per vim;*[16] *vim sibi factam . . . per illatam violentiam.*[17]

ARTICLE II. EVOLUTION OF THE LAW ON FORCE-FEAR: QUALIFICATIONS

Not only did the Decretals adopt the Roman Law terminology on force-fear, but they also began the process of assimilating Roman Law jurisprudence on the subject by specifying that force-fear had to be definitely qualified if it was to invalidate marriage. In this way the Decretals did something which Roman Law itself had not done; they applied the Roman jurisprudence on force-fear to the contract of marriage.[18]

It appears that Alexander III (1159-1181) was the first Pope to adopt Roman Law terminology in the matter of force-fear.[19] The first compiler to introduce a special title in *de his, quae vi metusve causa fiunt* was Bernard of Pavia (1188-1192) in the *Compilatio I.*[20] In this short title of the *Compilatio I* there was no specific treatment of marriage. However, elsewhere in the collection Bernard adduced texts in which the application of a

---

[13] C. 7, X, *de ràptoribus, incendiariis et violatoribus ecclesiarum,* V, 17 (c. un., Comp. III, *de raptoribus,* V, 9) ; Potthast, n. 1066.

[14] C. 28, X, *de sponsalibus et matrimoniis,* IV, 1 (c. 2, Comp. V, *h.t.,* IV, 1).

[15] C. 15, X, *de sponsalibus et matrimoniis,* IV, 1 (c. 2, Comp. II, *h.t.,* IV, 1).

[16] C. 21, X, *de sponsalibus et matrimoniis,* IV, 1 (c. 7, Comp. II, *h.t.,* IV, 1).

[17] C. 9, X, *de desponsatione impuberum,* IV, 2 (c. 12, Comp. 1, *h.t.,* IV, 2).

[18] *Vide supra,* p. 4, note 7.

[19] E.g., c. 6, X, *de sponsalibus et matrimoniis,* IV, 1 (c. 5, Comp. I, *h.t.,* IV, 1) ; Jaffé, n. 14235.

[20] Lib. I, tit, 30, *de his, quae vi metusve causa fiunt.*

force-fear jurisprudence was made specifically to the treatment of marriage.[21]

This point in the history of Canon Law marks the proper beginning of the development of a true canonical science on force-fear in marriage. Alexander III realized the necessity of such a scientific development when he wrote the words: *de muliere quae est invita tradita viro et detenta, quum inter vim et vim sit differentia . . . nihil certum inde tibi possumus respondere.*[22]

§ 1. *Gravity of Force-Fear*

Alexander III ruled that only such coercion invalidated marriage as sufficed to sway a resolute man: *qui posset in virum constantem cadere.*[23] In so doing he considerably mitigated the rigor of Roman Law which had required a coercion sufficient to move a *homo constantissimus.*[24]

Honorius III (1216-1227) used the same distinction:

> . . . Illis, quae benedictione accepta mox a sponsis aufugiunt ante carnis copulam subsecutam, asserentes, se nunquam in illos veraciter consensisse, sed metu illato compulsas, verba protulisse consensus licet animo dissentirent non statim est audientia deneganda de illato metu est cum diligentia inquirendum; et, si talis metus inveniatur illatus, qui potuit cadere in constantem virum erunt . . . audiendae.[25]

The teaching of the Decretals on the gravity of coercion is summarized in one phrase: . . . *Tenent sponsalia de praesenti, nisi per metum, qui potuisset cadere in constantem virum contracta sint.*[26]

---

[21] Cf., e.g., c. 5, Comp. I, *de sponsalibus et matrimoniis,* IV, 1.

[22] C. 6, X, *de sponsalibus et matrimoniis,* IV, 1 (c. 5, Comp. I, *h.t.,* IV, 1); Jaffé, n. 14235.

[23] C. 15, X, *de sponsalibus et matrimoniis,* IV, 1 (c. 2, Comp. II, *h.t.,* IV, 1); Jaffé, n. 15723.

[24] D. (4, 2) 6.

[25] C. 28, X, *re sponsalibus et matrimoniis,* IV, 1 (c. 2, Comp. V, *h.t.,* IV, 1); Potthast, n. 6106.

[26] Summary before c. 15, X, *de sponsalibus et matrimoniis,* IV, 1.

§ 2. *Extrinsic Origin of Fear*

As had been the case in Roman Law,[27] so also in the Decretals the requirement that the coercion arise from a free agent, extrinsic to the subject suffering the coercion, was expressed in the statement that *the force must be "inflicted," the fear must be "inflicted."* Only such fear had the effect of invalidating marriage. One finds the following phrases, for example, in which the idea is clearly expressed: *si constiterit quod . . . tanta vis illata fuerit . . . ;*[28] . . . *si talis metus inveniatur illatus . . . ;*[29] . . . *se possunt per illatam vim excusare. . . .*[30]

§ 3. *Causal Relationship Between Coercion and Marriage*

A number of phrases in the Decretals indicate the necessity of a causal relationship between the coercion and the marriage if the latter was to be considered invalid. The coercion had to cause the marriage. Two phrases of Alexander III serve to illustrate the point: *ne per timorem dicat sibi placere;*[31] *nisi metu coactus.*[32] In both these phrases the instrumentality of the fear (*per timorem; metu*) is expressed.

A phrase of Honorius III is perhaps more emphatic: *metu illato compulsas verba protulisse consensus, licet animo dissentirent.*[33]

Again, the point is summarized succinctly: *tenent sponsalia de praesenti, nisi per metum . . . contracta sint.*[34]

It may be noted that while a causal relation between the coercion and the marriage was postulated if the coercion was to have an invalidating effect, there seems to be no implication in the dispositive part of the texts that the agent inflicting the coercion

---

[27] *Vide supra,* p. 6, notes 15-16.

[28] C. 2, X, *de eo qui duxit in matrimonium quam polluit per adulterium,* IV, 7 (c. 2, Comp. I, *h.t.,* IV, 7).

[29] C. 2 Comp. V, *h.t.,* IV, 1.

[30] C. 9, X, *de desponsatione impuberum,* IV, 2 (c. 12, Comp. I, *h.t.,* IV, 2).

[31] C. 14, X, *de sponsalibus et matrimoniis,* IV, 1 (c. 19, Comp. I, *h.t.,* IV, 1).

[32] C. 15, X, *h.t.,* IV, 1 (c. 2, Comp. II, *h.t.,* IV, 1).

[33] C. 28, X, *h.t.,* IV, 1 (c. 2, Comp. V, *h.t.,* IV, 1).

[34] Summary to c. 15, X, *h.t.,* IV, 1.

must have had specifically in mind the purpose of bringing the marriage about.[85]

§ 4. *The Injustice of Matrimonial Coercion*

The injustice of the use of coercion was not expressly treated in the Decretals. This point was to be the object of a later process of doctrinal evolution. However, the various factors which were to serve as the basis of the scientific treatment of the element of injustice in coercion are found in the Decretal texts. These texts will be indicated in the present chapter, and a more detailed study will be left to the chapter on canonical science from Rufinus to the Council of Trent.

§ 5. *The Obligation to Marry as Arising from Contract*

One of the factors which served as a basis for a new jurisprudence on the injustice of coercion in marriage was the consideration of the consequences of the obligation to marry as assumed by a person who made a contract of espousals. It is not necessary here to enter into a discussion of the nature and form of espousals, though one may well indicate that the three types most commonly mentioned were 1) the simple promise to marry, 2) espousals in a stricter sense of the word (*sponsalia*), and 3) a promise to marry or espousals confirmed by an oath.

The Decretals considered the obligation arising from espousals as a very serious matter, and went so far in certain texts as to seem to approve the use of coercive measures for effecting the celebration of marriage on the basis of the obligation assumed in virtue of a previous contract.[86]

However, the Decretal Law on this particular point was not

---

[85] Concerning this point, cf. Franciscus Roberti, "De Metu Indirecto quoad Negotia Iuridica, praesertim Matrimonium," *Apollinaris* (Romae, 1928—), X (1938), 557-561; M. Wyszynski, "Utrum Metus Indirecte Incussus Dirimere Possit Matrimonium," *Jus Pontificium* (Romae, 1921-1940), X (1930), 193-200; XI (1931), pp. 42-51; XII (1932), 43-52; XII (1932), 122-127; XIII (1933), 52-63.

[86] Cf., e.g., cc. 10-22, X, *de sponsalibus et matrimoniis,* IV, 1 (c. 1, Comp. III, *h.t.,* IV, 1); c. 9, Comp. I, *de sponsalibus et matrimoniis,* IV, 1.

without its difficulties. In one text that was to become quite famous, Lucius III apparently denied the lawfulness of the use of coercion even after a sworn promise to marry: *mulier quae se nupturam iuravit . . . monenda est potius quam cogenda. . .*[37]

It may be useful to note here that in general the decretalists interpreted the phrase *monenda potius quam cogenda* as meaning *prius monenda et postea cogenda.*[38]

The decretalists, in placing such an interpretation upon this text, insisted that coercion could justly be used for the effecting of marriage because of the obligation previously assumed. This discussion will be seen in a later chapter.[39]

§ 6. *The Obligation to Marry as Arising ex Delicto*

Another factor as found in the Decretals, which was to serve as a basis for the scientific treatment of injustice in matrimonial coercion, was the principle that the commission of crime was a source of obligation, and that in certain crimes this obligation was closely connected with marriage.

Two such crimes were mentioned in the Decretals: deceit (*dolus*) and seduction (*stuprum* or *seductio*), and these deserve a word of further explanation.[40]

The case of *dolus* is as follows: a certain married man left his wife and took up habitation with another woman without informing her of his marital status. His wife died, and the man wished to abandon the woman whom he had deceived. The conclusion of the Decretal was that he could not be permitted to separate from the woman: *ad petitionem viri non sunt aliquatenus separandi.*[41] In this conclusion the decretalists were to see an obli-

[37] C. 17, X, *de sponsalibus et matrimoniis,* IV, 1 (c. 12, Comp. I, *h.t.,* IV, 1); Jaffé, n. 15192.

[38] Cf., e.g., *Decretales Gregorii IX una cum glossis* (Romae: 1582) ad *cap. cit.* s.v. *cum libera.* Latest research places the date of the final text of the *glossa ordinaria* between the years 1263-1266.—Cf. S. Kuttner-Beryl Smalley, "The Glossa Ordinaria to the Gregorian Decretals," *The English Historical Review* (London, 1886—), LX (1945), 97-105.

[39] *Infra,* pp. 36-39, notes 40-52.

[40] Cf. references immediately below.

[41] C. 1, X, *de eo qui duxit in matrimonium quam polluit per adulterium,* IV, 7.

gation to marry as arising *ex dolo* and were to discuss the degree of coercion that might be used in such a case in order to cause the man to marry the woman.[42]

As a basis for its law on seduction (*seductio* or *stuprum*) the Decretals drew up the Old Testament.[43]

As this Decretal text is of great importance, it will be quoted at some length, together with the summary which prefaces it:

> Stuprans virginem tenetur eam dotare et ducere in uxorem, et, si non vult cum ea contrahere, ultra dotem corporaliter castigabitur. Hoc dicitur cum capitulo sequenti. Si seduxerit quis virginem nondum desponsatam dormieritque cum ea, dotabit eam, et habebit uxorem. Si vero pater virginis dare noluerit, reddet pecuniam iuxta modum dotis, quam virgines accipere consueverunt.[44]

In this text it is seen that an obligation to marry was considered as arising from the crime of seduction. The obligation, however, was not absolute, but admitted an alternative solution which may be expressed as follows:

1. Either endow the virgin and take her in marriage, or,
2. Endow the virgin and accept corporal punishment.

Actually, this alternative appears in the summary to the canon which calls also upon the text of the following canon:

> Gregorius Sipontino Episcopo. Pervenit ad nos, quod Felix nepos tuus quamdam virginem . . . stupro decepit. Quod si verum est, quamvis . . . esset de lege poena plectendus, nos . . . aliquatenus legis duritiem mollientes, hoc modo disponimus, ut aut quam stupravit uxorem habeat, aut . . . si renuendum putaverit, . . . corporaliter

[42] Cf. *infra*, p. 33, note 19; p. 34, note 23; p. 35, note 33; p. 36, note 37.

[43] Exodus, 22, 16-17. The two terms *seductio* and *stuprum* are rendered by the word *seduction* in this dissertation. Authors generally do not distinguish carefully between *seductio* and *stuprum*, though, properly considered, *stuprum* implies the violation of a virgin through the use of force, while *seductio* is the violation of a virgin by means of fraud, deceit, persuasion. Cf. *infra*, pp. 86-88, notes 86-95. Gratian's peculiar use of the term *stuprum* has been seen above, p. 13, note 22.

[44] Summary and c. 1, X, *de adulteriis et stupro*, V, 16 (c. 1, Comp. I, *h.t.*, V, 13).

> castigatus, excommunicatusque in monasterio in quo agat penitentiam, retrudatur. . . .[45]

It is important to observe the severity of the punishments prescribed. Without doubt the contemplation of corporal punishment, excommunication, and confinement, were of sufficient gravity to affect even a resolute man. Yet, the law proposed these punishments as the alternative to marriage. The evolution of a canonical jurisprudence on the injustice of coercion in marriage is to be found largely in commentaries upon these two texts of the Decretals, the discussion of which continues to the present day.[46]

ARTICLE III. THE SOURCE OF INVALIDITY

1. It has been seen above that in ruling against the use of coercion in marriage the Decretals assigned as their reason the evil effects consequent upon such marriages: *ne . . . sequantur exitus, qui de invitis solent nuptiis provenire; quum coactiones difficiles solent exitus habere.*[47]

2. It has also been seen that the Decretals permitted the infliction of severe penalties upon the perpetrators of certain crimes. These penalties were sufficient to sway a constant man. Because of the gravity of the penalties it must be concluded that they caused serious trepidation of mind to the culprit. Yet marriage contracted in this state of mind was quite evidently considered valid in the Decretals.

The conclusion to be drawn from these facts is that the decretals considered the invalidating effects of coercion to arise merely from the positive law, which could be set aside for the proportionate cause, as in the instance of crime. If the invalidating effects of grave coercion had been considered in the Decretals as arising

---

[45] C. 2, X, *de adulteriis et stupro,* V, 16 (c. 2, Comp. I, *h.t.,* V, 13). In order to understand the radical departure from Roman Law, cf. *supra,* p. 8, notes 23-24.

[46] Cf. *infra,* p. 33, notes 20-21; p. 34, notes 24-26; p. 35, notes 33-34.

[47] *Supra,* p. 17, note 5.

from the natural law, no such exceptions could have been admitted.[48]

3. It also appears that the Decretals admitted the use of coercion in order to effect the marriage of a person who had engaged himself to enter marriage. If the Decretals had considered the invalidating effects of coercion as deriving from the natural law, this could not have been admitted.[49]

4. It may be noted, too, that in weighing the gravity of coercion the Decretals established as the primary consideration an extrinsic, objective norm with only a secondary consideration of the actual *state of mind and will* of the victim of coercion: that fear was grave *qui posset in virum constantem cadere.*[50] If the Decretals had considered the invalidating effects of coercion as arising purely from the natural law, it would have been necessary to put more emphasis on the purely internal, subjective state of mind of the person suffering the coercion, for it was precisely in this that the natural law would have been operative in determining the factor of the validity of the marriage.

To this it may be objected that the judge could deal only with externals, and therefore the establishment of an external norm to serve as the basis of a legal presumption could not be interpreted as indication that this external norm (coercion great enough to affect a resolute man) invalidated in virtue of the positive law, which recognized it solely as the practical basis for a sound presumption. The objection is a weighty one, but at the same time it must be observed that the whole tendency of the Decretals (and of subsequent law and interpretation) seems to have been to move the whole problem out into the open, objective order of things, where it could be regulated in terms of the positive law.

---

[48] Cf. *infra,* pp. 43-50.

[49] Cf. *supra,* pp. 22-23, notes 36-39.

[50] Cf. *supra,* p. 20, notes 23-26.

CHAPTER IV

Canonical Science from Rufinus (*circa* 1157-1159) to the Council of Trent (1545-1563)

ARTICLE I. TERMINOLOGY AND DISTINCTIONS

In the period of canonical science immediately after Gratian, certain fundamental divisions of coercion were worked out and precise definitions were formed corresponding to these divisions. The following authors of *Summae* were representative of the period: Rufinus (1157-1159), Joannes Faventinus (*post* 1171), Sicardus (*circa* 1179-1181), and Huguccio (1188).[1]

It will be sufficient here to summarize from the texts quoted by Kuttner.

Coercion (*coactio*) was either violent (*violenta*) or moderate (*modica*). Violent coercion was subdivided into *absolute or passive coercion* and *conditional or active coercion.*

Absolute or passive coercion existed when the victim was simply propelled by an outside active agent without giving any consent whatsoever.

Conditional or active coercion existed when the victim was confronted with some danger or peril which served as a conditioning agent prompting the victim to act, so that the victim willed to act from a motive to fear in order to avoid the danger or peril with which he was faced.[2]

---

[1] The doctrine of Rufinus, Joannes Faventinus and Sicardus is found in their respective *Summae,* ad c. 1, C. XXII, q. 5; of Huguccio, in his *Summa,* ad c. 118 *de consecratione,* D. 4. For quotations of all pertinent texts cf. Kuttner, *Kanonistische Schuldlehre,* pp. 301-306.

[2] "Sciendum est ergo quod coactio duplex est, modica scilicet et violenta; violenta absoluta est sive passiva, quae est per attractionem, ut fiat, cui coactus nulla ratione consentiat, ut si alicuius manus super aram ydolorum ad turificandum violenter poneretur; conditionalis vel activa est, quae habet fieri aliqua conditione periculosa presentis vel futuri facti instanter proposita ut si aliquis iratus gutturi tuo gladium poneret. . . ."—Rufinus, *Summa, loc cit.,* apud Kuttner, *op. cit., loc. cit.*

This doctrine may be expressed in the following diagram.

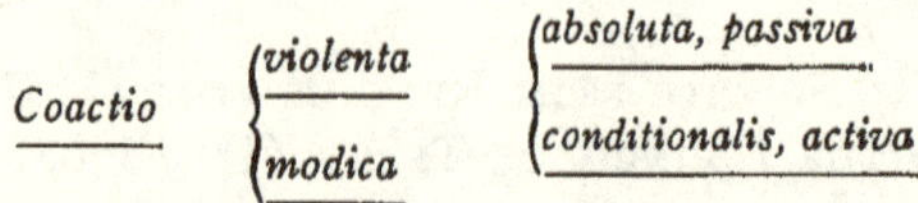

This division was not to endure, however. A careful examination of all available material from Bernard of Pavia (1198) to Panormitanus (died 1453) reveals that another plan was almost universally adopted, a plan more akin to one that might be constructed from the *Digest*. In spite of a certain inconsistency in terminology, a definite pattern of thought emerged in this period. It may be expressed in the following diagram:

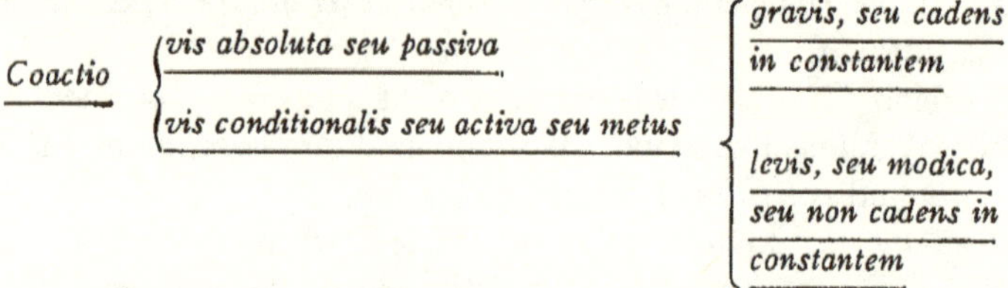

Though this division differed from that of the earlier authors, the concepts remained the same. *Vis absoluta seu passiva* took its definition from the Roman Law definition of *vis*: *vis autem est maioris rei impetus, qui repelli non potest.*[3] In absolute violence the reaction of the victim was purely passive and mechanical without any voluntary response whatsoever. Such violence invalidated marriage in every case.[4]

---

[3] D. (4, 2) 2.

[4] Bernardus Papiensis, *Summa ad Comp. I* (1198), ad I, 30, *de his, quae vi metusve causa fiunt* (apud Kuttner, *op. cit.*, pp. 308-309); *Decretum Gratiani una cum glossis* (1245) (2 vols., Venetiis, 1605), ad c. 22, C. XXII, q. 4, s.v. *matrimonium;* likewise ad c. 3, C. XXXI, q. 2, s.v. *neptis; glossa ordinaria* ad c. 5, X, *de his, quae vi metusve causa fiunt,* I, 40, s.v. *sacris, casus;* Hostiensis, *Commentaria in Quinque Decretalium Libros* (1270-1271) (2 vols., Venetiis, 1581), lib. I, tit. [40] *de his, quae vi metusve causa fiunt,* c. 2 (*abbas*), n. 7; *op. cit.*, lib. IV, tit. [1] *de sponsalibus et matrimoniis,* c. 14 (*cum locum*), n. 3 *in fine; ibidem,* c. 6 (*de muliere*), s.v. *invita* and

The manner in which Roman Law came practically to identify *vis conditionalis* with *metus* has already been seen.[5] The canonical science of this period adopted the same practice. *Vis conditionalis* was frequently referred to simply as *metus,* in fact the term *metus* was generally preferred. In its relationship to marriage the almost universal opinion of the period was that fear invalidated marriage if it was such as would sway a constant man. In the evaluation of the gravity of fear the attention was directed more to a consideration of the force which caused it than to the subjective effects of the fear upon the victim. Slight or moderate fear was not considered by any author of the period as invalidating marriage.[6]

Joannes Andreae and Panormitanus both taught that *vis absoluta seu passiva* was practically eliminated from the discussion of force-fear in marriage, so that only *vis conditionalis* was to be considered. However, it would be impossible to state definitely that some of the cases discussed in the canonical literature of the entire period were not cases of *vis absoluta.*[7] The

---

inter vim et vim; Joannes Andreae, *In VI Libros Decretalium Novella Commentaria* (1338) (6 vols. Venetiis: 1581), lib. I, tit. [40] *de his, quae vi metusve causa fiunt,* c. 4 (*ad audentiam*), n. 4; *ibidem,* c. 5 (*sacris*), n. 15; Parnormitanus, *Commentaria in Quinque Libros Decretalium* (*circa* 1445) (5 vols. Venetiis: 1588), lib. I, tit. [40] *de his, quae vi metusve causa fiunt,* c. 4 (*ad audientiam*), n. 2. Hereafter the works of Hostiensis, Joannes Andreae and Parnormitanus will be cited by the name of the author.

[5] *Supra,* p. 5, notes 11-12.

[6] Bernardus Papiensis, *op. cit., loc. cit.; glossa ordinaria* ad c. 4, C. XXXI, q. 2, s.v. *reprehensibilem; op. cit.,* ad c. 22, C. XXII, q. 4, s.v. *matrimonium; op. cit.,* ad c. 1, C. XXXI, q. 2, *casus; glossa ordinaria* ad X, *de sponsalibus et matrimoniis,* IV, 1, c. 10, s.v. *compellas; ibidem,* ad c. 28, s.v. *consultatione, casus;* Hostiensis, lib. I, tit. [40] *de his, quae vi metusve causa fiunt,* c. 2 (*abbas*), nn. 3, 4, 7; lib. IV, tit. [1] *de sponsalibus et matrimoniis,* c. 14 (*cum locum*), n. 3; Joannes Andreae, lib. IV, tit [1] *de sponsalibus et matrimoniis,* c. 6 (*de muliere*), n. 1; *ibidem,* c. 14 (*cum locum*), n. 3; Panormitanus, lib. IV, tit. [1] *de sponsalibus et matrimoniis,* c. 6 (*de muliere*), n. 2; *ibidem,* c. 15 (*veniens*), *casus* et n. 5.

[7] Joannes Andreae, lib. IV, tit. [1] *de sponsalibus et matrimoniis,* c. 30, n. 3: ". . . absoluta oppressio non potest esse in persona viri . . . licet conditionalis intervenire possit. . . ." Panormitanus, lib. I, tit. [40] *de his, quae vi metusve causa fiunt,* c. 4, n. 2: ". . . duplex est vis . . . quaedam est

terms *vis* (without further qualification) and *metus* and various combinations of both were used without great discrimination. In almost every case it is quite clear from the context that *vis conditionalis* (*metus cadens in virum constantem*) was under discussion. At other times, however, it is possible that *vis absoluta* was not excluded from the discussion. The point has little practical value, and, in view of the variety of the terms used, an annotated analysis becomes too intricate to attempt without necessity.

As a final point concerning the terminology, it should be noted that *metus gravis* was sometimes referred to in this period as *metus iustus*. It pointed to fear which, *under the law,* invalidated marriage or entitled the wronged party to a *restitutio in integrum.*[8]

ARTICLE II. THE INJUSTICE OF COERCION IN MARRIAGE

Canonical science of the period from Rufinus to the Council of Trent subjected to its scrutiny a number of special cases in which it seemed that the use of coercion in order to effect marriage might be justified. These cases were suggested by certain texts of the Decree of Gratian and of the Decretals.[9]

In connection with these texts, three questions, especially, were proposed for solution:

1. If a person by his own fault (*culpa praecedens*) had placed

---

prorsus contraria voluntati, cum quis ligatis manibus et pedibus baptizatur, vel compellitur communicare excommunicato in ecclesia, et de ista non fit mentio in isto titulo. . . ."

[8] Benencasa (1206) ad C. XXII, q. 5—apud Kuttner, *Kanonistische Schuldlehre,* p. 310; Joannes Teutonicus (1245-1246) ad c. 3, Comp. III, *de his, quae vi metusve causa fiunt,* I, 23, s.v. *violentiam,* apud Kuttner, *op. cit., loc. cit.;* Joannes Andreae, lib. I, tit. [40] *de his, quae vi metusve causa fiunt,* c. 2 (*abbas*), n. 2; *ibidem,* c. 5 (*sacris*), nn. 7-8, 17-18; Panormitanus, lib. I, tit. [40] *h.t.,* c. 1 (*perlatum*), n. 1 a; *ibidem,* c. 2 (*abbas*), nn. 1-3.

[9] C. 22, C. XXII, q. 4—a case of possible *culpa praecedens*—*supra,* p. 11, notes 12-13; c. 1, X, *de eo qui duxit in matrimonium quam polluit per adulterium,* IV, 7—a case of *dolus*—*supra,* pp. 23-24, notes 41-42; cc. 1-2, X, *de adulteriis et stupro,* V. 16—concerning the obligation to marry as arising *ex delicto stupri*—*supra,* pp. 24-25, notes 43-46; cc. 10-22 (especially c. 17), X, *de sponsalibus et matrimoniis,* IV, 1—concerning the obligation arising *ex contractu,*—*supra,* pp. 22-23, notes 36-39.

himself in a position in which coercion was brought to bear upon him, did such coercion invalidate the resultant marriage?

2. If a man had injured the rights of a woman by deceit (*dolus*) or seduction (*seductio, stuprum*), could coercion be used to cause him to marry the woman?

3. If by means of canonical engagement (*sponsalia*) a person had assumed the obligation of marrying, could coercion be used for the purpose of bringing about the promised marriage?

§ 1. *Culpa Praecedens*

It was generally admitted by the decretists and the decretalists that a person was responsible for actions performed under coercion if he had been the culpable cause of the coercion:
cion:

Rufinus: . . . *nunquam imputatur nisi quis suo delicto in huius coactionis angustias venerit.*[10]

Benencasa: *habet exceptionem contra petentem, . . . nisi quis sua culpa ad hoc prestandum sit compulsus. . . .*[11]

Joannes Andreae: *regulariter non excusat metus, cum culpa praecedit. . . .*[12]

Panormitanus: ". . . ea quae fiunt per metum, regulariter tenent, dummodo sine culpa sua quis incidat in metum . . . si culpa sua incidit in metum, tenent gesta et non competit aliquod remedium metum passo."[13]

§ 2. *Matrimonial Coercion After Previous Delict*

For the application of the foregoing principle to marriage, the problem became more complex. In spite of certain differences of opinion and variation of terminology, a general pattern of thought emerged in this period. It may be outlined as follows:

1. As a general rule, a person was not bound to the juridical

---

[10] *Summa,* ad c. 1, C. XXII, q. 5—*apud* Kuttner, *Kanonistische Schuldlehre,* p. 304.

[11] Ad c. 2, Comp. I, *de his, quae vi metusve causa fiunt,* I, 30—*apud* Kuttner, *op. cit.,* p. 313.

[12] Lib. I, tit. [40] *de his, quae vi metusve causa fiunt,* c. 6 (*cum dilectus*), n. 9.

[13] Lib. I, tit. [40] *h.t.,* c. 2 (*abbas*), n. 7.

consequences of actions which he performed under properly qualified coercion. Depending upon the nature of these actions, they were either null from the very beginning (the source of this nullity is not discussed here) or subject to being rescinded by the proper authority.

2. As an exception to this rule, if the coercion was the result of one's own serious fault, one was bound to the juridical consequences of one's actions though they were performed under coercion.

3. As a general rule, coercion could not be used to cause a person to marry. If a duly qualified coercion was employed, the marriage was invalid.

4. Even though the coercion was incurred because of one's own previous fault, the marriage contracted under coercion was as a general rule invalid.[14]

5. The foregoing rule admitted of exceptions, however, and in the instance of certain delicts or crimes a person could be coerced into marriage, and the marriage which was the result of such coercion was held to be valid.[15]

With so many modifications of general norms, it was inevitable that a certain confusion should result in the canonical literature of a period in which canonists began the first serious work of developing a jurisprudence. It seems possible to group the canonists of the period into two classes: the one emphasizing that there were exceptional cases in which, after the commission of a delict, *coercion could be used for the purpose of effecting marriage,* and the other emphasizing the general rule that *marriage which was the result of coercion was to be deemed invalid.* Neither class remained entirely free from apparent contradictions.

1. First class: emphasis upon exceptional cases, in which coercion could be used to cause marriage

---

[14] This rule did not remain undisputed.—Cf. authors cited in notes 16-26 and in § 4 of this article.

[15] The tenor of the majority of the texts quoted in § 2 seems to indicate that this represents the more common approach to the problem of the justice and injustice of coercion in this period. In § 4 it is seen that another approach, which attempted to put the problem on a broader and more theoretical basis, was also at work.

Certain expressions of some of the early decretalists of this period seem to put them into this class. Thus Rufinus (1157-1159): *quia sua gravi culpa incidit in hanc necessitatem, merito teneatur eam accipere quam prius coactus iuraverat. . . .*[16] Stephanus (circa 1160), Joannes Faventinus (post 1171) and Simon de Bisignano (1177-1179) expressed themselves in a similar fashion.[17]

Several passages in the work of Hostiensis emphasized the fact that coercion could be used in marriage in certain cases ". . . propter delictum praecedens cogitur quis ad matrimonium . . . nam debet ecclesia corrigere peccatorem peccantem . . . et hoc debet fieri per censuram excommunicationis."[18] In treating the case of a man who had deceived a woman with whom he cohabited by permitting her to believe that he was single, and who wished to leave this woman after the death of his true wife, Hostiensis made this comment: *Quod si vir non vult consentire? Ad consentiendum est per ecclesiam compellendus. . . .*[19] With regard to the delict of seduction, Hostiensis specifically pointed out that this was an exceptional case in which coercion could be used: *hic est specialis casus in quo quis cogitur ad matrimonium contrahendum. . . .*[20] He added immediately, however, that the culprit was to be given the alternative of endowing the woman, and that if he was incapable of endowing her, and did not wish to marry her, he had the added alternative of accepting punishment.[21]

Elsewhere Hostiensis pointed out that, as a rule, coercion could not be used in marriage, even in cases in which a party had been guilty of some transgression:

> Excipiuntur tamen casus in quibus, etsi quis in metum culpa sua inciderit, subvenitur. Primo in matrimonio, et est ratio, quia requirit animi libertatem. . . .[22]

[16] Heinrich Singer, *Die Summa Decretorum des Magister Rufinus* (Paderborn: 1902), ad c. 22, C. XXII, q. 4.

[17] Cf. Kuttner, *op. cit.*, pp. 332-333.

[18] Lib. IV, tit. [1] *de sponsalibus et matrimoniis*, c. 17 (*requisivit*), n. 1.

[19] Lib. IV, tit. [7] *de eo qui dixit in matrimonium quam polluit per adulterium*, c. 1 (*propositum*), *in principio*.

[20] Lib. V, tit [16] *de adulteriis et stupro*, c. 1 (*si seduxerit*), n. 2.

[21] *Ibidem*, n. 3; *ibidem*, c. 2 (*pervenit ad nos*), s.v. *corporaliter*.

[22] Lib. 1, tit. [40] *de his, quae vi metusve causa fiunt*, c. 2 (*abbas*), nn. 10-11.

Joannes Andreae emphasized the exceptional cases in which in view of a previous delict coercion could be used in marriage. In regard to the case of deceit, he quoted Hostiensis with approval.[23] He also pointed to the fact of seduction as constituting a special case in which the use of coercion was warranted.[24] Concerning seduction he made the observation that, though seduction could be committed only against a virgin, the violated woman was presumed to have been a virgin and the burden of proof to the contrary rested with the seducer.[25] He was frank in admitting that coercion was used for the specific purpose of causing marriage: *Dicebat T. quod gravis poena imponebatur, ut illius metu illam duceret in uxorem.*[26]

2. Second class: emphasis upon the general rule, that marriage which was the result of coercion was to be deemed invalid

Gilbertus (*ante* 1204),[27] Albertus (*ante* 1215)[28] and Joannes Teutonicus (*post* 1215)[29] are to be listed among those who emphasized the general principle that coercion could not be used in marriage.

Huguccio (+ 1210) permitted the use of coercion against a man who, under coercion brought about by his own fault, had taken an oath to marry a woman. He qualified his statement, however, by saying that the coercive measures should cease if the man refused to change his mind (*si de nolente non fit volens*). Huguccio's general attitude indicates that he permitted the use of only mild coercive measures in any case.[30]

---

[23] Joannes Andreae, lib. IV, tit. [7] *de eo qui duxit in matrimonium quam polluit per adulterium*, c. 3 (c. 1, *propositum*), n. 3—*supra*, p. 33, note 19.

[24] Lib. V, tit. [16] *de adulteriis et stupro*, c. 1 (*si seduxerit*), n. 9.

[25] *Ibidem*, n. 2.

[26] *Ibidem*, c. 2 (*pervenit*), nn. 1-2.

[27] C. 1, *Comp. Gilberti*, IV, 1 (c. 2, Comp. II, *de sponsalibus et matrimoniis*, IV, 1)—*apud* Kuttner, *Kanonistische Schuldlehre*, p. 313.

[28] Ad c. 1, Comp. III, *de his, quae vi metusve causa fiunt*, I, 23—*apud* Kuttner, *op. cit.*, *loc. cit.*

[29] Ad c. 1, Comp. III, *de his, quae vi metusve causa fiunt*, I, 23— *apud* Kuttner, *op. cit.*, *loc. cit.*

[30] "Prius est admonenda, et postea aliquantulum cogenda, ut dicit Huguccio." —*Glossa ordinaria* ad c. 1, C. XXXI, q. 2.

The *glossa ordinaria* to the Decree of Gratian was more emphatic: *etiam licet culpa alicuius praecesserit metum, tamen ille metus excusat eum a matrimonio ut extra* c. *veniens* [c. 15, X, *de sponsalibus et matrimonio,* IV, 1]. . . .[31]

The *glossa ordinaria* to the Gregorian Decretals stated the general rule in these terms: *qualiscumque metus interveniat culpa sua vel sine culpa, matrimonium contractum per metum non tenet.* . . .[32] The *glossa* admitted, however, that there were exceptions to this rule: *Item propter delictum praecedens quandoque quis compellitur ad matrimonium.* . . .[33] Nevertheless, the *glossa* furnished some reason for the view that even in these exceptional cases only mild coercive measures could be used to bring about a marriage. Thus, in explaining the validity of the marriage of a man who had been coerced into marriage (after having previously caused himself to be coerced into taking an oath to marry), the *glossa* remarked: *ibi non intervenit iustus metus, qui possit cadere in constantem virum. . . . Vel dicas . . . matrimonium sit firmum et stabile . . . non ponitur praeceptive sed consultive.* . . .[34]

The general rule forbidding the use of coercion in marriage was quoted by Panormitanus from the *glossa ordinaria.*[35] Panormitanus insisted upon this, for he was convinced that fear was opposed to the unity, indissolubility and primary purpose of marriage: *nam metus repugnat omnibus tribus bonis matrimonii, ideo ab omni coactione debet esse liberum.*[36]

Nevertheless he justified the use of coercion in an instance of the delict of *dolus,* though in this case he based his opinion rather upon the fact that a previous promise had been made to marry

---

[31] Ad c. 1, C. XXXI, q. 2, s.v. *quod autem.*

[32] Ad c. 2, X, *de his, quae vi metusve causa fiunt,* I, 40, s.v. *coactus.*

[33] Ad c. 17, X, *de sponsalibus et matrimoniis,* IV, 1, s.v. *cum libera.* In this case the admitted exception consisted in the delict of *dolus,* and a cross reference was made to c. 1, X, *de eo qui duxit in matrimonium quam polluit per adulterium,* IV, 7, to illustrate the point.

[34] Ad c. 2, X, *de his, quae vi metusve causa fiunt,* I, 40, s.v. *coactus;* cross reference to c. 22, C. XXII, q. 4.

[35] Panormitanus, lib. I, tit. [40] *de his, quae vi metusve causa fiunt,* c. 2 (*abbas*), n. 8.

[36] Lib. IV, tit. [1] *de sponsalibus et matrimoniis,* c. 15 (*veniens*), n. 8b.

than upon the fact that a delict had been committed: *ratione promissionis vir compellitur ad contrahendum.*[37]

Another exception was admitted by Panormitanus in cases of seduction. Coercion could be used in order to cause a seducer to marry the woman whom he had violated. Limitations were placed upon the exception, however, in that the seducer was to be given the alternative expressed as follows:

1. To endow the seduced virgin and to marry her, or,

2. If the seducer does not wish to marry the woman, to endow her and accept corporal punishment for his crime.[38]

Panormitanus also pointed out:

1. That the violated woman was presumed by the law to have been a virgin, and

2. That she was presumed to have been deceived by her seducer.

As regards both these points, the burden of proof to the contrary was thrown upon the man.[39]

The foregoing discussion, though not exhaustive, serves as a representative view of the general trends of canonical science during the period from Gratian to the Council of Trent on the complex question of the lawfulness of the use of coercion in marriage in instances of previous delict. Attention is now turned to the question of the lawfulness of the use of coercion for effecting marriage in consequence of previous contract.

§ 3. *Matrimonial Coercion in View of Previous Contract*

The *glossa ordinaria* to the *Decree* of Gratian permitted the use of mild coercive measures to cause the marriage of those who had made the contract of espousal (*sponsalia de futuro*). It provided, however, that the unwilling party was to be given the alternative of entering religion.[40]

---

[37] Lib. IV, tit. [7] *de eo qui duxit in matrimonium quam polluit per adulterium*, c. 1 (*propositum*), n. 4.

[38] "Stuprans virginem tenetur eam dotare, et duxere in uxorem: et si non vult cum ea contrahere, ultra dotem corporaliter castigabitur."—Lib. V, tit. [16] *de adulteriis et stupro*, c. 1 (*si seduxerit*), n. 1; ". . . deflorans virginem compellitur omnino contrahere cum ea: sed si non vult contrahere, punitur. . . ."—*Ibidem*, c. 2 (*pervenit*), n. 1.

[39] *Ibidem*, c. 1 (*si seduxerit*), n. 2 and n. 5.

[40] Ad c. 1, C. XXXI, q. 2, ad s.v. *quod autem, casus*.

The *glossa ordinaria* to the Decretals of Gregory IX gave two explanations of a decretal text which seemed to require coercion in the instance of sworn espousals, but provided for the relaxation of the rule for a reasonable cause:[41]

1. According to the strict letter of the law the Church could use coercion in this case, but a more merciful course could be followed and the coercion relaxed because of the danger that evil effects would arise from the marirage;

2. *Vis conditionalis* (grave fear, moral force) was to be used in order to cause the delinquent to change his mind and to enter marriage voluntarily. Absolute force, however, could not be used.

Both of these explanations were then rejected by the *glossa,* which concluded that there could be employed that degree of coercion which the circumstances required in order effectively to bring the person to marriage: "Sed neutra solutio videtur sufficere, quia iste mortaliter peccat veniendo contra iuramentum, ergo potest compelli finaliter, 24, q. 3 *tam sacerdotes,* et c. *ecce autem crimina. . . .*"[42]

That the *glossa* expected that such extreme measures would fall somewhat short of absolute physical violence is evidenced by the later comment that, though persons who had made a sworn promise to marry were to be compelled, coercion could, nevertheless, be relaxed in the face of absolute resistance because of the dire effects that otherwise might reasonably be expected.[43]

Hostiensis understood that the canons permitted the Church to use coercive measures against a person who refused to marry after he had made a sworn promise to do so. At the same time he permitted the relaxation of this law for a cause whose reasonableness was to be determined by the judge.[44]

According to Joannes Andreae, if a reasonable cause existed, such as the danger of homicide or adultery, a judge was justified

---

[41] C. 10, X, *de sponsalibus et matrimoniis,* IV, 1.

[42] *Glossa ordinaria* ad C. 10, X, *de sponsalibus et matrimoniis,* IV, 1, s.v. *compellas.*

[43] Ad c. 2, X, *h.t.,* IV, 1, s.v. *inducendi* and *noluerint.* Cf. also *ibidem,* c. 17, s.v. *requisivit, casus.*

[44] Lib. IV, tit. [1] *de sponsalibus et matrimoniis,* c. 17 (*requisivit*), nn. 4 and 7. Cf. also *ibidem,* c. 2 (*praeterea*), n. 8.

in not using coercion to induce a person to marry, in spite of the fact that such a person had made a sworn promise to do so.[45] If, however, no such reasonable cause existed, the judge was to use grave coercive measures (*causative distringet*) after having first warned the party of the obligation to marry.[46]

When a person had freely entered into an engagement to marry, the marriage could not be attacked in court on the grounds that it had been contracted under conditions of grave coercion (*oppressio conditionalis*).[47]

The last author to be considered on this point is Panormitanus. His doctrine appears to involve a real contradiction. On the one hand, he seems to permit the use of coercion not only in the case of sworn espousals, but also in the case of a simple promise to marry:

> . . . quia . . . haec compulsio fiat ratione peccati, ecclesia compellit non solum iurantem, sed etiam pactum nudum facientem. . . .[48]

Again, he is content simply to state that it is not licit for a person not to marry after having sworn to do so: *ubi sponsalia sunt iurata, non est licitum alteri ab eis resilire.*[49] Finally, he takes a position directly opposed to what he has already stated:

> . . . infero, quod si is, qui sponte contrahit sponsalia de futuro compellatur metu ad contrahendum matrimonium per verba de praesenti, quod tale matrimonium non teneat.[50]

---

[45] Lib. IV, tit. [1] *de sponsalibus et matrimoniis*, c. 10 (*ex litteris*), n. 12; *ibidem*, c. 17, n. 2.

[46] *Loc. cit.;* also tit. [2] *de desponsatione impuberum*, c. 7 (*de illis*), n. 4.

[47] Lib. IV, tit. [1] *de sponsalibus et matrimoniis*, c. 30 (*si qui*), n. 3.

[48] Lib. IV, tit. [1] *de sponsalibus et matrimoniis*, c. 10 (*ex litteris*), n. 3; *ibidem*, n. 4: *compellat per excommunicationem; ibidem*, n. 5: *et compellitur quis praecise ad factum, maxime, qui hic non potest solvi interesse. . . .*

[49] *Ibidem*, c. 22 (*sicut ex litteris*), n. 22.

[50] *Ibidem*, c. 17 (*requisivit*), n. 2; cf. also *ibidem*, c. 29 (*Gemma*), n. 4. The same indecision is manifested by Panormitanus in his discussion of the admissibility of justly inflicted fear.—Cf. *infra*, p. 42, note 65.

§ 4. *Metus Iniuste Incussus*

The term *metus iustus* was frequently used throughout this period simply in the sense of a *metus gravis* or a *metus cadens in virum constantem.* In this sense there is no reference to the justice or injustice of the coercion. The meaning is: "fear of sufficient gravity to invalidate or to render rescissible according to law."[51] This peculiarity of terminology one must keep in mind in order to avoid confusion. With this noted the attention of the reader is now directed to the *justice* and *injustice* of coercion in the proper sense of the words.

It has been seen in the first three sections of this article that the canonists from Gratian to the Council of Trent generally treated the justice and injustice of coercion in a very concrete way by admitting the use of coercion in certain cases, namely, as an exception to a general rule. Cases specifically treated in this fashion were *dolus, seductio, stuprum* and *sponsalia.*[52]

At the same time, however, efforts were being made to reach a synthesis, an expression of the law in more general and abstract terms. Instances of this effort may be seen in such statements as:

Rufinus: *quia sua gravi culpa incidit in hanc necessitatem, merito teneatur eam accipere quam prius coactus iuraverat. . . .*[53]

Hostiensis: *propter delictum praecedens cogitur quis ad matrimonium . . . nam debet ecclesia corrigere peccatorem peccantem. . . .*[54] While such statements were certainly subject to fur-

[51] Benencasa (+ 1206), ad pr. C. XXII, q. 5—*apud* Kuttner, *Kanonistische Schuldlehre,* p. 310; Joannes Teutonicus (+ 1245-1246), ad c. 3, Comp. III, *de his, quae vi metusve causa fiunt,* I, 23, s.v. *violentiam,—loc. cit.; glossa ordinaria* ad C. 6, X, *de his, quae vi metusve causa fiunt,* I, 40, s.v. *violentia;* Hostiensis, lib. I, tit. [40] *h.t.,* c. 2 (*abbas*), n. 1; Joannes Andreae, lib. I, tit. [40] *h.t.,* c. 2 (*abbas*), n. 2.

[52] Dossetti (*La Violenza nel Matrimonio,* p. 266) does not include *dolus* in his listing which he designates as an exhaustive one. Nevertheless, Hostiensis (*supra,* p. 33, note 19), Joannes Andreae (*supra,* p. 34, note 23) and the *glossa ordinaria* to the Gregorian Decretals (*supra,* p. 35, note 33), in commenting upon the case of *dolus* reported in c. 1, X, *de eo qui duxit in matrimonium quam polluit per adulterium,* IV, 7, permitted the use of coercion in this case.

[53] *Summa,* ad c. 22, C. XXII, q. 4.

[54] Lib. IV, tit. [1] *de sponsalibus et matrimoniis,* c. 17 (*requisivit*), n. 1.

ther refinement and to distinctions that would give them a more scientific application, it must be conceded that, even in this form, they admitted the interpretation of an abstract validity that was not necessarily circumscribed by a mere listing of concrete cases.

In searching for a theory on the justice and injustice of coercion, the decretalists naturally turned to the Roman Law. If it served as a help, it ultimately served also as a hindrance.[55]

Damasus (1210-1215) wrote as follows:

> In summa nota, quod si aliquis incidit in metum ex culpa sua, non excusatur . . . si tamen vim inferendam legitimo modo sibi timeat; si vero vim iniuriosam timeret, licet ex culpa sua incidisset in metum, excusaretur. . . .[56]

This important development in the canonical jurisprudence of coercion may be presented as follows:

- *Metus*
  - *ex culpa sua*
    - *vis timetur inferenda legitimo modo*: *non excusat*
    - *vis timetur iniuriosa seu inferenda modo non legitimo*: . . . *excusat*
  - *non ex culpa sua*: . . . . *excusat*

Goffredus de Trano (1241-1243), in evident dependence upon Damasus, made the same distinctions and applied them to marriage:

> Sed quod dixi metum non excusare in quem quis incidit sua culpa, recipit contrarium inf. *de spons.* c. *Veniens* [c. 15, X, *de sponsalibus et matrimoniis,* IV, 1]. Ad quod respondeo metus ex culpa meticulosi pro-

[55] An example of the confusion caused by recourse to the Roman Law on this point is seen in Panormitanus, lib. IV, tit. [1] *de sponsalibus et matrimoniis,* c. 15 (*veniens*), n. 8: "et ideo . . . iuste poterat cominari mortem, et ideo talis metus, ut a iure approbatus habet excusare, ut in 1, *si mulier* [D. (4, 2) 21] . . . ," *et passim in toto capitulo.* It seems quite evident that the conclusion should have been negative instead of positive in this case.

[56] Ad c. 1, Comp. III, *de his, quae vi metusve causa fiunt,* I, 23—*apud* Kuttner, *Kanonistische Schuldlehre,* p. 313.

> veniens non excusat, si sit legitimus et a iure sumat initium; si autem iniuriosus id est iniuriam timens excusat.[57]

The outline of the doctrine of Goffredus is the same as that of Damasus. Goffredus went one step further and applied the distinctions to marriage. Then he hesitated about the application and remarked that marriage possibly enjoys a special prerogative, so that whether the fear was threatened in a legitimate or in an illegitimate way, the invalidity of the marriage would always result.[58]

The *glossa ordinaria* to the Decretals indicated its familiarity with the new distinction, but did not apply it to marriage.[59]

Hostiensis appealed to Goffredus, used the new distinction, applied it to marriage, and then hesitated about whether or not marriage enjoyed a special prerogative in this regard.[60] In his hesitation Hostiensis stated elsewhere:

> Excipiuntur tamen casus in quibus, etsi quis in metum culpa sua inciderit, subvenitur. Primo in matrimonio. . . .[61]

The same application and the same hesitancy were evident in the work of Joannes Andreae.[62]

Finally there appeared two authors who proposed the doctrine without hesitation—Antonius de Butrio (circa 1390)[63] and

---

[57] *Summa*, lib. I, *de his, quae vi metusve causa fiunt*, n. 2—*apud* Dossetti, *La Violenza nel Matrimonio*, p. 268. Dossetti, however, makes no note of the apparent dependence of Goffredus upon Damasus.

[58] "Vel praerogativa matrimonii, de quo ibi tractatur, hoc habet ut metus quamvis legitimus efficaciam matrimonii impediat."—*Loc. cit.*

[59] Ad c. 4, X, *de his, quae vi metusve causa fiunt*, I, 40, s.v. *causa*.

[60] ". . . tunc metus ex culpa proveniens non excusat, si sit legitimus, et a iure sumatur, ratione interesse, sin autem sit iniuriosus, tunc excusat, secundum Goffredum. . . . Vel dicas speciale esse in matrimonio."—Lib. IV, tit. [1] *de sponsalibus et matrimoniis*, c. 15 (*veniens*), nn. 5-6.

[61] Lib. I, tit. [40] *de his, quae vi metusve causa fiunt*, c. 2 (*abbas*), nn. 10-11.

[62] Lib. IV, tit. [1] *de sponsalibus et matrimoniis*, c. 15 (*veniens*), n. 8.

[63] Lib. IV, tit. [1] *h.t.*, c. 15 (*veniens*), n. 7—*apud* Dossetti, *La Violenza nel Matrimonio*, p. 269.

Franciscus Zabarella (ante 1391)[64] proposed the distinction made by Goffredus and applied it to marriage without any mention of marriage as enjoying a special prerogative:

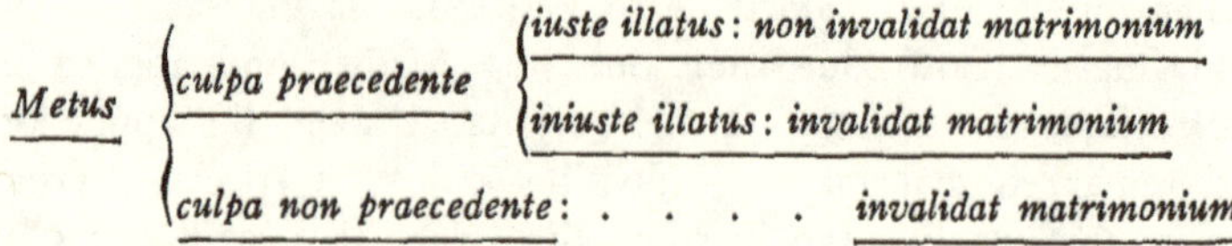

The problem was not yet settled, however, and some were to return to the old indecision before a definitive solution was reached.[65] Furthermore, until clear definitions of *metus iuste illatus* and *metus iniuste illatus* had been formulated and accepted, it remained a matter of doubt whether or not this distinction could be applied only to the specific cases frequently discussed by the decretalists: *dolus, seductio, stuprum, sponsalia.*

The contribution of Dominicus Soto (1553-1557) in this regard will be taken up below in Chapter VI.

§ 5. *The Courts and the Justice of Coercion*

The *glossa ordinaria* to the Gregorian Decretals has a note concerning injustice in the courts. This is recorded here for possible future reference.

It was observed that sometimes fear of the judge could have the juridical effect of invalidating an act or of giving place to the remedy of the pretor: *in pluribus aliis casibus excusat metus . . . quandoque metus iudicis* 2, q. 1, *in primis* [c. 7, C. VII, q. 1] *vel alicuius potentis.* In further explanation of this phrase, the *glossa* added that, though normally the judge was not spoken of as inflicting *fear,* still it was possible that the judge also should commit an injustice.[66]

[64] Lib. IV, tit. [1] *h.t.,* c. 15 (*veniens*), n. 1—*apud* Dossetti, *op. cit., loc. cit.*

[65] E.g., Panormitanus, lib. IV, tit. [1] *h.t.,* c. 15 (*veniens*), *per totum,* esp. n. 8b: "Secundo solvitur per Abbatem et Goffredum quod speciale est in matrimonio in praerogativam ipsius; et haec solutio multum mihi placet. . . ."

[66] Ad c. 6, X, *de his, quae vi metusve causa fiunt,* I, 40, s.v. *metum mortis*: ". . . iudex vero alicui non dicitur inferre metum . . . sed iniuriam facere potest. . . ."

The sense of this entire passage seemed to be the following: if proper recourse was had to a judge for legal redress, there was a presumption that no injustice would be done, and consequently any fear that might arise because of the anticipated action of the judge would be a vain fear. Any act performed under the influence of such fear would ordinarily be valid and no recourse could be had for restitution. However, it remained possible for a judge to injure the rights of others, and if he did so then legal redress was not denied.

ARTICLE III. THE SOURCE OF INVALIDITY

The question to be examined here is the following: did the canonical science of the period from Gratian to the Council of Trent consider the invalidating effects of coercion in marriage as arising from the natural law or as arising merely from the positive law?

On the one hand, during this period, as during all subsequent periods, the principle was universally accepted in canon law that *consent makes marriage.*[67]

Since it was universally admitted that consent is of the very nature and essence of marriage (*in fieri*), there is no room for any discussion regarding the source of the invalidating effects of absolute violence, for the simple reason that when absolute violence existed there was *no consent* on the part of the victim. Had the question been proposed in these terms, any author of the period would have immediately responded that absolute violence draws its invalidating effects from the natural law.

On the other hand, all admitted that slight fear or mere trivial coercion did not affect the validity of marriage. For this reason, slight fear, too, is eliminated from the discussion.[68]

Consequently, the question is limited to a discussion of the source of the invalidating effects of grave fear (*vis conditionalis* or *metus cadens in virum constantem*).

---

[67] Cf. the comment of authors upon c. 14, X, *de sponsalibus et matrimoniis,* IV, 1, where the following statement is made: "matrimonium autem assensu solo contrahitur—ubi de ipso quaeritur, plena debet libertate gaudere."

[68] *Supra,* p. 29, note 6.

This grave fear had the effect of reducing the spontaneity of the act of the will whereby the contracting parties transferred matrimonial rights and assumed matrimonial obligations.

The question is: did this reduction of spontaneity deprive the act of the will of the effect of producing matrimonial rights and obligations

1. in virtue of the natural law, prior to the intervention of a human legislator? or

2. in virtue only of the intervention of a human legislator, who intervened to declare that such an act of consent, though of itself capable of producing the marriage bond, was nevertheless deprived of producing that effect?

A more philosophical discussion of the problem may more properly be reserved to a later chapter.

It is almost immediately evident that the reply of an author to these questions reflected a necessary relation to his opinion concerning the degree of coercion which the Church could validly and licitly use to bring a person to marriage, for example, under the circumstances of a previous contract or of a previous delict. If an author was not clear regarding the degree of coercion admissible under such circumstances, it appears impossible to conclude definitely where he placed the source of the invalidating effects of grave coercion.

Only in rare instances, in this particular period from Gratian to the Council of Trent, did authors explicitly propose the question of the source of the invalidating effects of coercion. When they did propose the question, it remains to determine the degree of coercion which they had in mind. When the question was not proposed, one can at most determine in a general way which solution to the question proved most consistent with their principles and their other conclusions in the matter of matrimonial coercion. Attention here will be directed rather to the over-all picture of the period than to an exhaustive consideration of the opinions of individual authors.

Saint Raymond of Pennafort (1175-1275) seemed to have a ready answer. He stated that the "impediment of violence or fear," from its very nature, and without any action on the part of the Church, precludes matrimonial consent.[69] Saint Raymond, however, quite evidently treated only of absolute violence, for he declared that the marriage was valid if any consent whatsoever remained in spite of the coercive measures used.[70] It is seen, therefore, that he did not propose a solution to the present question. Furthermore, since Saint Raymond admitted the validity of marriage in the face of any fear compatible with some degree of voluntary action, it seems that a positive law origin of the invalidating effects of *grave fear,* when and if invalidity ever resulted from such fear, was more consistent with his doctrine.

The statement was frequently made during this period that matrimonial consent must enjoy *complete freedom* for its validity. Completeness of the freedom of consent was stressed as an essential condition for the validity of marriage.[71] This seems to constitute a strong indication that the authors who made this statement were of the opinion that grave fear draws its invalidating effects from the natural law. Such a position could logically

---

[69] "Circa impedimentum violentiae, seu metus, notandum, quod ex sui natura, etiam sine constitutione Ecclesiae, matrimonialem consensum excludit: nam ubi metus, vel coactio intercedit, non potest consensus locum habere; per consequens nec matrimonium, quod solo consensu contrahitur. Causa XXVII, q. 2, c. Sufficiat; extra, de sponsalibus, c. Cum locum [c. 14, X, *de sponsalibus et matrimoniis,* IV, 1]."—*Summa,* lib. IV, tit. II.

[70] "Quid, si praecesserit coactio, et metus qui caderet in constantem virum, sed tamen sic compulsus factus est volens; numquid est matrimonium? Resp. Credo quod sic. . . ." "Sed si consensit, quamvis per metum quantumcumque, matrimonium est. . . ."—*Loc. cit.*

[71] *Glossa ordinaria* ad c. 22, C, XXII, q. 4, s.v. *matrimonium*: "Videtur . . . quod coactio conditionalis non impediat matrimonium: sicut nec impedit alia sacramenta. . . . Sed contra, matrimonia debent esse libera, et . . . animus debet gaudere plena libertate." *Glossa ordinaria* ad c. 2, X, *de eo qui duxit in matrimonium quam polluit per adulterium,* IV, 7, *casus*: "Nota quod matrimonium per vim contractum non valet: quia libera debent esse matrimonia." Panormitanus, lib. IV, tit [1] *de sponsalibus et matrimoniis,* c. 6 (*de muliere*), n. 2: ". . . in matrimonio non habet locum illa regula: coacta voluntas, voluntas est . . . quia in matrimonio requiritur de substantia liber consensus, ut in c. *cum locum* [c. 14, X, *h.t.,* IV, 1], et c. *gemma* inf. e. [c. 29, X, *h.t.,* IV, 1] unde consensus coactus est bene consensus, sed non liber; et sic deficit qualitas libertatis, quae est de substantia consensus matrimonialis. . . ."

be maintained as long as a given author never permitted the Church to use grave coercive measures under any circumstances. This the *glossa ordinaria* to the Decree of Gratian seemed to do when it interpreted the phrase *matrimonium sit firmun et stabile* (c. 22, C. XXII, q. 4, s.v. *matrimonium*) as a mere exhortation to marry, instead of interpreting it as permitting the use of grave coercive measures in view of the previous delict of the party concerned.[72]

In attempting to evaluate the statement which required *complete* freedom of matrimonial consent, it must be observed that, whereas the most natural explanation of this principle is that grave coercion draws its invalidating effects from the natural law, it must also be admitted as theoretically possible that the *completeness* of matrimonial freedom was postulated simply by the positive law. This latter explanation seems to explain more readily the frequent insistence that complete freedom was a requisite condition for the avoidance of the unhappy effects that generally follow upon marriages which are the result of coercion.[73] When the statement was made that the Pope did not permit coercion in marriage because of the evil effects consequent upon it, there seemed to be the implication that the marriage would have been valid as far as the natural law is concerned, but that it was prohibited and invalidated by the positive law. In this way the door was left open for the possibility of admitting the use of coercive measures in exceptional cases, such as the case of previous contract under oath.

Another argument for the natural law origin of the invalidating effects of grave fear is found in the occasional insistence that coerced marriage is invalid *ipso iure* because of grave fear, whereas most other acts are valid from the beginning and sub-

[72] "Videtur ex loco isto quod coactio conditionalis non impediat matrimonium: . . . Quod autem dicitur hic matrimonium sit . . . istud sit non ponitur praeceptive, sed hortative. . . ."—Ad c. 22, C. XXII, q. 4, s.v. *matrimonium.*

[73] *Glossa ordinaria* ad c. 2, X, *de sponsalibus et matrimoniis,* IV, 1, s.v. *praeterea, casus*: "Respondet Papa, quod matrimonium illud fieri non permittitur, ne deterius quid contingat, nisi iuramentum intervenisset." Cf. also *glossa ordinaria* ad c. 14, *h.t.,* IV, 1, s.v. *provenire.*

ject only to a later rescission.[74] A ready explanation of this phenomenon could be found in the fact that, if such was the case, grave coercion invalidated marriage in virtue of the natural law, at least in the internal forum. On the other hand, it is entirely possible that the legislator, by mere positive designation, determined by law that marriage was invalidated, both in the internal and in the external forums, by grave coercion, so that in consequence no subsequent act of rescinding the marriage was required. Panormitanus could easily have intended this explanation when he wrote: *et ideo iura induxerunt, ut matrimonium sit ipso iure nullum.*[75]

The position which supported the purely positive law origin of this phenomenon was corroborated by the fact that not only marriage, but also the promise of a dowry, the transfer of ecclesiastical property and other transactions were also listed by the authors as being invalid (*mero iure*) from the beginning and not merely subject to a later rescission.[76] As there seemed to be nothing in the very nature of the promise of a dowry which would have placed it in a special category of things which are invalid from the beginning, such a promise of dowry must have enjoyed this prerogative simply in virtue of the positive law. Consequently the mere existence of such a prerogative did not imply any conclusive argument that marriage entered into under grave coercion was invalid in virtue of the natural law.

The strongest argument for the natural law theory presented by the canonical science of this period is found in an explanation of *the reason* why marriage entered into under grave coercion is invalid from the beginning. The reason assigned was that the *three benefits* (*tria bona*) of marriage were precluded in a coerced marriage, and consequently such a marriage had to be regarded as invalid from the beginning:

> Sed est pulchrum videre rationem, quare regulariter teneant quae fiunt per metum, et non sic in matrimonio

[74] Hostiensis, lib. I, tit. [40] *de his, quae vi metusve causa fiunt,* c. 2 (*abbas*), nn. 3-5; *Panormitanus,* lib. IV, tit. [1] *de sponsalibus et matrimoniis,* c. 14 (*cum locum*), n. 6 b.

[75] Lib. IV, tit. [1], *de sponsalibus et matrimoniis,* c. 14 (*cum locum*), n. 8.

[76] Hostiensis, lib. I, tit. [40] *de his, quae vi metusve causa fiunt,* c. 2 (*abbas*), nn. 10-11 c; Panormitanus, lib. I, tit. [40] *h.t.,* c. 2 (*abbas*), nn. 8-20.

> . . . quod in matrimonio reperiuntur tria bona, fides, proles et sacramentum . . . quae omnia metus intercedens habet excludere . . . et matrimonium est sacramentum quia significat unionem inter Christum et Ecclesiam. . . .[77]

In this passage Panormitanus produced a substantial argument: marriage has three essential effects; all three effects are precluded by (grave) fear; therefore grave fear invalidates in virtue of the natural law. However, Panormitanus did not draw this conclusion. To the contrary, he seemed to detract from it by adding immediately: *et ideo iura induxerunt, ut matrimonium sit ipso iure nullum.*[78]

Attention is now directed to several special cases as mentioned in the canonical science of this period, from which cases one could argue definitely in favor of the opinion that grave fear draws its invalidating effects purely from the positive law.

1. It was admitted that deceit (*dolus*) does not invalidate marriage. And yet the element of deceit by misleading the intellect could reduce the relationship of the act of the will towards its object, the marriage bond, just as notably as coercion could reduce the spontaneity of the act of the will. As a matter of fact, Panormitanus even envisaged the case in which deceit would completely destroy the freedom of the will, and only in this extreme case did he admit that *dolus* invalidated marriage.[79] If, therefore, deceit and coercion had an equally drastic effect upon the freedom of the will, and the one did not invalidate marriage, while the other did, then neither derived its invalidating

[77] Panormitanus, lib. IV, tit. [1] *de sponsalibus et matrimoniis,* c. 14 (*cum locum*), n. 7.

[78] *Ibidem,* n. 8.

[79] *Glossa ordinaria* ad c. 5, C. XX, q. 3, s.v. *cogantur*: ". . . contractum matrimonii non rescindit dolus. . . . Et est mirum quod in spiritualibus contractus dolo initus tenet, sed contractus metu initus non tenet, cum secundum leges penitus contrarium fit, nam secundum leges contractus dolo initus nullus est, sed contractus metu initus tenet, licet rescindatur per actionem quod metus causa. . . ." Panormitanus, lib. I, tit. [40] *de his, quae vi metusve causa fiunt,* c. 6 (*cum dilectus*), n. 13: "Et nota glossa singulariter in alio, in eo scilicet quod dicit tenere matrimonium, licet dolus dederit causam contractui. . . . Quod ego limitarem, nisi talis et tantus esset dolus, quod habuisset tollere consensum. . . ."

effects from the natural law, and thus the difference of effect was explained by the intervention of the positive law in one case and the failure of the positive law to intervene in the other.

2. It was frequently admitted that under the decretal law, in certain urgent cases, a father could give his minor child in marriage contrary to the will of the child. This expression can be interpreted only as meaning that grave coercive measures were permitted in these exceptional cases. If, however, grave coercion invalidated marriage in virtue of the natural law, marriage could never have been permitted under such circumstances. If, on the other hand, grave coercion invalidated marriage only in virtue of the positive law, the legislator could, for a sufficient cause, permit the use of such measures in exceptional cases.[80]

3. It has been seen above that a number of authors of this period permitted the use of grave coercive measures to bring about a marriage after the contract of espousals had been made or after certain delicts had been committed.[81]

This being the case, these authors must have been of the opinion that the invalidating effects of coercion derived from the positive law, since the natural law does not admit of exceptions, based as it is upon the very essences of things.

It could be objected that the Church could define the conditions under which the natural law was operative. That point must be conceded. However, this does not mean that any human power, by positive enactment, could supply that which was necessary in an act to make it effective in the ontological order. If the reduction of the freedom of consent which was produced in the will by grave fear affected the act of the will in such

---

[80] *Glossa ordinaria* ad c. 2, X, *de desponsatione impuberum,* IV, 2, s.v. *ubi non est, casus*: "Ubi non est consensus . . . districtius inhibemus, ne aliqui . . . coniungantur: Nisi forte aliqua urgentissima necessitate interveniente: utpote pro bono pacis talis coniunctio toleretur. . . . Nota, quod pro bono pacis reformando toleratur matrimonium quod alias fieri interdiceretur." Joannes Andreae, lib. IV, tit. [2] *h.t.,* c. 1 (*tua fraternitas*), n. 1: "Filium hoc ratificare decet." *Ibidem,* n. 4: ". . . sed ipsum de iure non potest adstringere, si nullo modo consentiat. . . ." Panormitanus, Lib. IV, tit. [2] *h.t.,* c. 1 (*tua fraternitas*), n. 3: "ex urgenti necessitate vel pro bono pacis potest quandoque recedi a dispositione legali, seu canonica. . . ."

[81] *Supra,* pp. 36-38, notes 40-50.

a way as to make it incapable, in virtue of the natural law, of producing the effect of the marriage bond, this deficiency could never be supplied by any human positive law even in exceptional cases. The objection as stated above had wide application in regard to the lawfulness of acts, but its application was quite limited as regards the validity of acts.

CHAPTER V

Saint Thomas Aquinas (1225-1274)

ARTICLE I. CONCEPTS, DISTINCTIONS, USE OF TERMS

In his consideration of voluntary and involuntary acts in general, Saint Thomas enunciated certain general principles which later he applied to marriage.

He proposed the question: can violence be done to the will? He answered by saying that it is impossible to do violence to the proper and specific act of the volitional faculty which is *to will,* but that violence can be done to those acts which are commanded by the will if they are put into effect through the agency of the external powers and faculties.[1]

He then raised the question whether actions which are the result of fear are strictly involuntary actions. He answered that acts which are caused by fear are the result of the action of the will directed towards them, not for their own sake, but in order to avoid some evil which is feared. Since, however, an act may be voluntary not only by being willed as an end in itself, but also by being willed as a means to some other end, that which is done through fear is voluntary.[2] Only hypothetically are actions involuntary, if performed through fear, in the sense, namely, that they would not be voluntary if certain conditions did not exist.[3] Saint Thomas described the voluntariness of actions performed through fear by saying: *quod per metum fit, simpliciter voluntarium est, secundum quid autem involuntarium.*[4]

---

[1] S. Thomas Aquinatis *Summa Theologica* (6 toms., Taurini: Marietti, 1932), I-II, q. 6, a. 4, *conclusio.*

[2] *Ibidem,* a. 6, *ad primum.*

[3] *Ibidem, ad tertium.*

[4] *Ibidem, conclusio.*

Saint Thomas accepted the Roman Law definitions of *vis* (*maioris rei impetus, qui repelli non potest*),[5] and of *metus* (*instantis vel futuri periculi causa mentis trepidatio*).[6]

He identified *vis* with what he called *involuntarium simpliciter*, namely coercion, the product of which derives totally from a source outside the victim, and which results in a purely mechanical response on the part of the victim.[7]

He then identified *metus* with what he called *voluntarium simpliciter, sed involuntarium secundum quid*.[8]

Finally, in his treatment of coercion in marriage, Saint Thomas ruled out the discussion of *vis* in the sense of *involuntarium simpliciter*, and limited the discussion of coercion in marriage to that *vis* which he identified with *metus* and which produces a *voluntarium simpliciter sed involuntarium secundum quid*:

> Sed nunc agitur de consensu interiori, in quem non cadit coactio, *seu* vis, quae a metu distinguitur. Et ideo, quantum ad propositum pertinet, idem est coactio quod metus.[9]

And thus, by identifying as fear (*metus*) that which the decretalists preferred to call conditional violence (*vis conditionalis*), and by eliminating absolute violence from the discussion of coercion in marriage, Saint Thomas followed the same approach which was almost universally, if not universally, adopted by the decretalists.[10]

---

[5] *Summa Theologica, Supp.* III, q. 47, a. 1, *tertio.*

[6] *Ibidem, in corpore.*

[7] *Summa Theologica,* I-II, q. 6, a. 5, *in corpore;* I-II, q. 6, a. 6, *in corpore;* I-II, q. 6, a. 6, *ad primum.*

[8] *Summa Theologica,* I-II, q. 6, a. 6, *in corpore* and I-II, q. 6, a. 6, *ad primum.*

[9] *Summa Theologica, Supp.* III, q. 47, a. 1, *in corpore.* The Marietti edition renders the foregoing as *in quem non cadit coactio sed vis . . . ,* which is evidently a mistake. The reading given above has been taken from the Leonine Edition: *Opera Omnia* (15 toms., Romae: ex Typographia Polyglotta, 1882—), Tom. XII (1906), *Summa, Suppl.* III, q. 47, a. 1, *in corpore;* cf. also *Sent.,* IV, d. 29, q. 1, a. 1.

[10] Cf. *supra,* pp. 29-30.

ARTICLE II. THE INJUSTICE OF MATRIMONIAL COERCION AND THE OBLIGATION TO MARRY AS ARISING EX DELICTO AND EX CONTRACTU

Saint Thomas did not give any consideration to the injustice of coercion in marriage.

Concerning the obligations incurred by a man who seduced a virgin still living under the authority of her parents, Saint Thomas quoted *Deut.* 22, 16:

> Si seduxerit quis virginem nondum desponsatam dormieritque cum ea, dotabit eam, et habebit uxorem. Si autem pater virginis dare noluerit, reddet pecuniam juxta modum dotis quam virgines accipere consueverunt.

and *Deut.* 22, 28:

> Si invenerit vir puellam virginem, quae non habet sponsum, et apprehendens concubuerit cum illa, et res ad judicium venerit, dabit qui dormivit cum ea, patri puellae quinquaginta siclos argenti, et habebit eam uxorem: et quia humiliavit illam, non poterit dimittere eam cunctis diebus vitae suae. . . .[11]

From these texts he concluded that seduction involved a double injury: against the virgin on the one hand, and against her father on the other. Therefore the seducer was bound to make satisfaction to both.[12]

Saint Thomas made no further comment upon the Old Testament texts which he quoted.

With regard to espousals, the doctrine of Saint Thomas may be summarized as follows: some obligation was certainly engendered by espousals; even in the instance of a simple promise to marry, the Church imposed a penance upon those who broke the promise; if the espousals had been confirmed by oath, some approved of the use of coercion in order to effect the marriage, others disapproved of the use of coercion. Saint Thomas seemed to imply that if coercion was used in this latter case, the marriage was valid.[13]

---

[11] *Summa Theologica,* II-II, q. 154, a. 6, *ad tertium.*

[12] *Loc. cit.*

[13] *Summa Theologica, Suppl.* III, q. 43, a. 1, *ad tertium.*

ARTICLE III. THE SOURCE OF INVALIDITY

A fundamental principle in Saint Thomas' concept of law was that all human law, in order to have binding force, had to derive from the natural law. This did not mean, however, that all law drew its cogency immediately from the natural law.[14] Laws derive from the natural law in two ways: first, by deduction, in a manner similar to that in which conclusions of the speculative order are drawn from first principles which are immediately self-evident; secondly, by specification, as, for example, when a particular punishment is attached to the commission of a specific crime.[15]

In the strict sense of the word, the natural law consists in first principles which are the first rule and measure of all human acts:

> Quaedam sunt leges quae ipsi rationi sunt inditae, quae sunt prima mensura et regula omnium humanorum actuum . . . et hae leges ius naturale dicuntur.[16]

These first principles of the natural law are expressed in judgments which are the work of man's reason, but they are acquired naturally, without recourse to a discursive process.[17]

On the other hand, those rules of conduct which are drawn from these first principles after the manner of conclusions of the speculative order from self-evident first principles were assigned by Saint Thomas to the *ius gentium,* while the *specifications* of the natural law were assigned to the *ius civile.*[18]

The *ius gentium* was conceived as being, in a certain sense, the natural law proper to man as a rational creature.[19]

The precepts of the natural law, taken both in its strictest sense, and also in the broader sense of the *ius gentium,* had their cogency in terms of the relationship of man and his actions to the end and

---

[14] *Summa Theologica,* I-II, q. 95, a. 2, *conclusio.*

[15] *Ibidem, in corpore.*

[16] Sancti Thomae *Opera Omnia* (34 vols., Parisiis: Vivés, 1871-1880), Vol. IX (1873), *Commentum in Quattuor Libros Sententiarum Magistri Petri Lombardi,* in III, d. 37, q. 1, a. 3, *in corpore.*

[17] *Summa Theologica,* I-II, q. 91, a. 2, *in corpore.*

[18] *Summa Theologica,* I-II, q. 95, a. 4, *in corpore.*

[19] *Ibidem, ad primum.*

purpose of man and his actions. Strictly understood, the natural law commanded only those things which are necessary to the attainment of man's final end: *praeceptum legis naturae non est nisi de eo quod est necessarium ad salutem.*[20]

With regard to negative precepts, the natural law forbade those things which make impossible the attainment of the principal end of a being. Such actions were prohibited by the very first principles of the natural law. On the other hand, actions which were opposed only to the secondary end of a being, or were opposed to the primary end only in the sense that they rendered its attainment more difficult or less likely, were prohibited not by the first principles of the natural law, but by its secondary principles. These secondary principles were those which were drawn from the first principles after the manner of conclusions.[21]

Now, Saint Thomas taught that these secondary precepts of the natural law have a strict binding force only in virtue of the restatement they receive from the divine or human *positive law*:

> . . . illa quae sunt . . . quasi ex primis principiis legis naturae derivata non habent vim coactivam per modum praecepti absolute, nisi postquam lege divina et humana sancita sunt. . . .[22]

In this connection Saint Thomas set forth the primary end of marriage as the procreation and education of children. The secondary end was the mutual assistance which man and wife render to each other in the difficulties of life.[23]

The question could then have been asked: did grave fear absolutely preclude the primary end of marriage which is the procreation and the education of children? Or did it simply render this difficult and less likely, while opposing the secondary end of mar-

[20] *Sent.*, IV, d. 15, q. 3, a. 1, sol. 5, *ad secundum.*

[21] *Sent.*, IV, d. 33, q. 1, a. 1, *solutio.*

[22] *Sent.*, IV, d. 33, q. 1, a. 1, *ad secundum;* Odon Lottin, *Le Droit Natural chez Saint Thomas d'Aquin et ses Predecesseurs* (2. ed., Bruges: Charles Beyaert, 1931), p. 77. This does not contradict the statement: *Sed ea quae sunt primi modi . . . habent aliquid vigoris ex lege naturali. . . .—Summa Theologica,* I-II, q. 95, a. 2, *in corpore.*

[23] *Sent.*, IV, q. 33, q. 1, a. 1, *solutio.*

riage which is the mutual assistance of the consorts? Saint Thomas seems not to have discussed this question explicitly. In the abstract, however, according to the principles of Saint Thomas, when it is considered that marriage which is the result of grave fear is simply voluntary and only hypothetically involuntary, and that according to his rational nature a higher sense of duty will impel man to overcome his repugnance in that to which he has given his consent, then it appears quite evident that grave fear does not preclude the procreation and education of children, though it does render more difficult the mutual aid of the consorts.

That this conclusion is in harmony with the teaching of Saint Thomas is clearly illustrated by way of comparison with an example which he did use explicitly. Polyandry, he stated, is absolutely opposed to the first end of marriage, while polygyny does not make the first end of marriage impossible but only creates great difficulties in regard to the secondary end of marriage. Polyandry, therefore, according to Saint Thomas, was forbidden by the natural law, while polygyny was simply supremely undesirable.[24]

Now, certainly, grave fear is no more opposed to the ends of marriage than is polygyny. It must be concluded, therefore, that the whole tenor of Saint Thomas' teaching indicated that the use of grave fear to effect marriage was highly undesirable, but that, if such fear was to invalidate marriage, this determination had to derive from the positive law.

Against this conclusion it may be objected that Saint Thomas insisted that complete freedom is required in matrimonial consent.[25] The objection is well taken, but this does not mean that Saint Thomas taught that complete freedom is required *by the natural law.* The requirement of a complete freedom could just as easily be the result of positive intervention. And, if it is further objected that Saint Thomas based his plea for the necessity of complete freedom upon the fact that marriage is indissoluble, it may be replied that Saint Thomas also consigned indissolubility to the

---

[24] *Sent.*, IV, d. 33, q. 1, a. 1, *solutio;* Lottin, *op. cit.*, pp. 75-76.

[25] *Summa Theologica, Suppl.*, III, q. 47, a. 3, *secundo* and *ad secundum.*

secondary principles of the natural law, which, therefore, derived their strict binding power only in virtue of positive determination.[26]

If attention is now directed to the passage in which Saint Thomas actually discussed coercion in marriage, it will be seen that he placed as his reason why grave fear invalidates marriage the fact that all other contracts entered into under grave fear may subsequently be rescinded by proper authority, while marriage, once validly contracted, cannot be rescinded. Therefore a coerced marriage was invalid from the beginning:

> Metus autem qui cadit in constantem virum, perpetuitatem contractus tollit, quia potest peti restitutio in integrum. Et ideo haec coactio metus quae cadit in constantem virum tollit matrimonium et non alia. . . .[27]

In order properly to evaluate this passage, one must recall that contracts which were later rescinded because of grave fear were *valid until the act by which they were rescinded had taken place.* Consequently they were not invalid in virtue of the natural law. If, therefore, a given contract (marriage) was invalid from the beginning, this followed, not in virtue of the natural law, but in virtue of the positive intervention of the proper authority.[28]

In this sense the words of Saint Thomas, *"judicat Ecclesia consensum illum non esse sufficientem,"* admit the spontaneous interpretation that the invalidating effects of grave fear in marriage derive from the positive law of the Church:

> Unde Ecclesia praesumit eum consensisse, sed judicat consensum illum extortum non esse sufficientem ad faciendum matrimonium.[29]

Therefore, the conclusion of Dominicus Soto seems to be well drawn:

> Quaestionem hanc D. Thomas non tractat. Neque vero satis constat in quam partem propenderit. Licet ratio

[26] *Summa Theologica, Suppl.,* III, q. 67, a. 2, *in corpore* and *ad tertium.*

[27] *Summa Theologica, Suppl.* III, q. 47, a. 3, *in corpore.*

[28] Those who subscribe to the natural law theory will say that contracts made under grave fear are invalid from the beginning in the internal forum, and bind only in the external forum until rescinded.

[29] *Loc. cit.*

> eius, quae vitio impressorum multis in locis corrupta est, videatur ad secundam opinionem Ricardi [favoring a positive law origin of the invalidating effects of grave fear in marriage] inclinare.[80]

Authors who cite Saint Thomas as favoring a natural law origin of the invalidating effects of grave fear in marriage seem to do so without having weighed thoroughly the whole teaching of Saint Thomas which has a bearing on the point.[81]

---

[80] *Commentariorum in Quartum Sententiarum Tomus Secundus* (Venetiis, 1584), d. 29, q. 1, a. 3.

[81] Cf. Gasparri, *De Matrimonio* (ed. nova, 1932), II, n. 840, in note.

CHAPTER VI

Dominicus Soto (1494-1560)[1]

ARTICLE I. TERMINOLOGY AND DISTINCTIONS

Dominicus Soto recognized the accepted fact that actions which are the result of grave fear are, nevertheless, the product of an act of consent of the will.[2]

Having distinguished between force which completely opposes the use of the will and produces a merely passive, mechanical reaction in the victim (*vis physica*), and force which does not destroy the will of the victim (*vis conditionata*), he pointed out that this *vis conditionata* is applicable only in the case of men and animals and that it always operates through fear.[3] He then identified conditional violence and fear.[4] Finally, he eliminated absolute violence from the discussion of coercion.[5]

Having thus eliminated absolute violence from the discussion, he also eliminated slight fear (*metus levis*), and he limited his entire study of coercion to a consideration of grave fear, which according to the accepted terminology of the times he also called *just fear* (*metus iustus*), not in reference to the virtue of justice,

---

[1] A special chapter is devoted to Dominicus Soto because he was the first author ever to bring together in a unified way all the various problems related to the injustice of coercion in marriage. For this reason his work marks the turning point in the development of the canonical jurisprudence on the injustice of coercion in marriage. A clear outline of his work on this point will serve as a valuable norm of reference.

[2] *Commentariorum in Quartum Sententiarum Tomus Secundus* (Venetiis, 1584), dist. 29, q. 1, a. 1: "Et quamvis primum principium motus: nempe, timor, extrinsecus incutiatur, consensus tamen ad motum ab intrinseco appetitu elicitur."

[3] "Violentia seu vis secundi generis, scilicet conditionata in sola voluntate et brutorum appetitu reperiri potest, eademque nonnisi per metum."—*Loc. cit.*

[4] ". . . vis hoc secundo modo et metus convertuntur."—*Loc. cit.*

[5] "Usurpatur ergo hic vis humano more pro ea, quae homini fit, quae idem est quod metus."—*Loc. cit.*

but in reference to the law (*ius*) which postulated a grave fear for the invalidation of marriage.[6]

The division of coercion made by Soto is the same as that reached by the canonists from Gratian to Trent, and by Saint Thomas.[7]

ARTICLE II. THE SOURCE OF INVALIDITY

Immediately after making these distinctions, Soto discussed the question of the source of the invalidating effects of grave fear, namely whether invalidity arises from the natural or merely from the positive law. He used this discussion as a preface to his treatment of the injustice of coercion, which will be taken up in the following article.

He first disposed of two opinions which were so poorly founded that they are not even discussed today. According to the first of these, marriage, if entered into under grave fear, was considered valid from the beginning, but subject to rescission later through the action of the proper authority. According to the second, marriage entered into under grave fear was deemed valid as far as the divine law was concerned, but the Church treated the marriage as invalid on the *presumption* that the person did not give consent.[8]

Soto then turned his attention to an examination of the two major opinions on the origin of the invalidating effects of coercion in marriage.

§ 1. *Opinion of Those Who Ascribed the Invalidating Effects of Coercion in Marriage to the Natural Law*

Soto designated Duns Scotus (*Sent.* IV, d. 29, a. 2) as the foremost exponent of the opinion which ascribed the invalidating ef-

---

[6] *Op. cit.,* dist. 29, q. 1, a. 2: ". . . si verbera et carceres et bonorum iactura non sunt adeo gravia, tunc metus non est iustus, sed levis"; *ibidem,* a. 3: "consensus coactus per metum cadentem in constantem virum, non est ad matrimonium perficiendum validus. . . . Metus levis non obstat quominus consensus sit validus."

[7] *Supra,* p. 52, note 10.

[8] *Op. cit.,* dist. 29, q. 1, a. 3.

fects of grave coercion in marriage to the natural law.[9] Of the reasons proposed in defense of this opinion, the following are the soundest:

1. Of its very nature the matrimonial contract demands the greatest freedom because of its permanency and because of the education of the offspring.[10]
2. Consent which is the result of coercion invalidates all other contracts in virtue of the natural law.[11]
3. If grave fear invalidated marriage only in virtue of ecclesiastical law, coerced marriages between infidels would be valid, even if these parties later became Catholics, since the Church has no power over infidels.[12]

To these arguments Soto offered the following refutation:

Ad 1. Consent which is the result of coercion is nevertheless a real consent to enter this particular marriage, which is sufficient.[13]

Ad 2. In virtue of the natural law other contracts which are the result of grave fear are *not* invalid from the beginning; rather, they are valid from the beginning, though they may be rescinded later through the intervention of the proper authority. Since once a marriage is valid it cannot be rescinded, the Church establishes that marriage is invalid from the beginning if entered into under grave fear.[14]

---

[9] *Loc. cit.*

[10] "Contractus matrimonii natura sua exigit, ut sit liberrimus tum propter perpetuam cohabitationem . . . tum propter educationem prolium. . . . "—*Loc. cit.*

[11] "Consensus iusto coactus omnes alios contractus iure naturali enervat. . . ."—*Loc. cit.*

[12] "Si solo iure ecclesiastico consensus coactus infirmaretur . . . si inter infideles tale matrimonium contraheretur, esset validum, etiam si ad ecclesiam post transmigrarent: quia ecclesia erga infideles nihil potest disponere. . . ."—*Loc. cit.*

[13] ". . . respondetur, consensum coactum . . . esse simpliciter voluntarium in particulari. . . ."—*Loc. cit.*

[14] ". . . neque alii contractus . . . per metum celebrati sunt ipso iure nulli, sed debent in irritum revocari. . . . Et hoc facit quod nobis, quia secundum merum ius naturae etiam matrimonium deberet tenere; at quia rescindi nequit, statutum per ecclesiam est, ut non sit validum."—*Loc. cit.*

Ad 3. Though the Church has no authority over infidels, the State does have such authority, and the marriages of infidels which are the result of grave fear are invalid in virtue of the Law of Nations and of the Civil Law.[15]

§ 2. *Opinion of Those Who Ascribed the Invalidating Effects of Coercion in Marriage to the Positive Law*

The opinion which assigns a positive law origin to the invalidating effects of grave coercion in marriage was attributed by Soto to many authors, among whom he names Petrus Paludanus (circa 1280-1342). Soto stated that, though Saint Thomas did not treat the question, his entire manner of reasoning seemed to favor this position.[16]

Among the arguments proposed in favor of this opinion, which Soto himself embraced, the following points were stressed:

1. Slight fear does not invalidate marriage according to the natural law. Yet, grave fear is specifically the same as slight fear and differs only according to degree. Furthermore, the loss of money and of good name are considered as giving rise to only a slight fear and as not invalidating marriage. Therefore slight fear can scarcely be distinguished from grave fear except in the judgment of skilled men (*prudentum*). Consequently, if slight fear does not invalidate marriage, while grave fear does invalidate it, this difference of effect must be ascribed purely to the positive law.
2. To marry a wife whom one does not want is a lesser evil when compared to death (or other grave matters): therefore nature does not forbid a man to redeem his life by choosing to enter marriage.[17]

---

[15] ". . . neque inter infideles huiusmodi consensus tenet: quoniam licet ecclesia erga illos nihil disponere valeat, nihilominus, ius gentium et civile vim habuit invalidandi . . . qua est civilis contractus."—*Loc. cit.*

[16] "Quaestionem hanc D. Thomas non tractat. Neque vero satis constat in quam partem propenderit. Licet ratio eius, quae vitio impressorum multis in locis corrupta est, videatur ad secundam opinionem Ricardi inclinare."—*Loc. cit.*

[17] *Loc. cit.*

ARTICLE III. THE INJUSTICE OF MATRIMONIAL COERCION

Dominicus Soto introduced his study of the injustice of coercion in marriage by first dividing grave fear into fear of intrinsic origin (conscience, health, the powers of nature) and into fear of extrinsic origin. Only fear of extrinsic origin could invalidate marriage. But not all fear of extrinsic origin invalidated marriage, for the justice of the fear had also to be considered.[18]

As an illustration of his point that not all fear of extrinsic origin invalidated marriage, Soto indicated a practical case. In some provinces, where theft was a capital crime, thieves were granted their lives if they entered marriage with public women, and such marriages were considered valid. This case, Soto noted, was provided for in the distinction made by Sylvester Prierias (1456-1523), who distinguished between just fear and unjust fear. Just fear did not invalidate marriage; unjust fear did invalidate marriage.[19]

Soto is not entirely satisfied with this distinction for, as he pointed out, it was possible for fear to be substantially just and still to invalidate marriage, as in the case in which a thief is caught in his crime and the private person who catches him threatens to turn him over to the officers of the law unless the thief marries his daughter. Soto considered such fear substantially just, and yet the resultant marriage he regarded as invalid. A further distinction needed to be made.[20]

---

[18] *Op. cit.,* dist. 29, q. 1, a. 3. It is worthy of note that the manner in which Soto divided and subdivided fear is almost identical with that of canon 1087, § 1: *Invalidum quoque est matrimonium initum ob vim vel metum ab extrinseco et iniuste incussum. . . .* This point is of notable significance.

[19] Soto, *op. cit., loc. cit.*: ". . . iuxta morem quarundarum provinciarum si fur publicam meretricem uxorem optaverit, donatur vita, matrimonium tenet, si conditionem acceptet. Et ideo Sylvester verbo Metus, § 6, aliter distinguit: scilicet, quod si metus sit iustus, matrimonium non vitiatur, si vero sit iniustus, tunc vitiatur." It should be noted, however, that Sylvester did not draw the distinction as clearly as Soto seems to indicate. Cf. Sylvester Prierias, *Summae Sylvestrinae Quae Summa Summarum merito Nuncupantur* (s. XVI in.) (2 vols. Venetiis, 1601), s.v. *Metus,* n. 6.

[20] "Sed re vera neque ista distinctio tuta est: quoniam potest esse metus iustus, qui tamen matrimonium vitiet, ut si qui furem in crimine deprehendit, comminetur ei se eum delaturum, nisi filiam suam uxorem duxerit, re vera

For this reason Soto insisted that with regards to grave fear of extrinsic origin a further distinction was called for between fear inflicted for the specific purpose of causing the marriage and fear inflicted for some other purpose. If the purpose of the infliction of the fear was not the enforced contracting of marriage but the victim of the fear spontaneously chose the contracting of marriage as a means of liberating himself from the fear, then such a marriage was to be regarded as valid. If, on the other hand, the particular purpose for which the fear was inflicted looked precisely to a compelling of the victim to contract marriage, Soto initially maintained that such a fear always invalidated the marriage. Yet, a few paragraphs later he modified this statement by proposing that even a fear which was inflicted with the specific purpose of causing the marriage did not have an invalidating effect if provision for this was made in the law. He pointed out, however, that if such an enforced marriage was to be regarded as valid the inflicted fear had to derive from someone in authority (*magistratus*), and in a manner provided for in the law.[21]

On the other hand, according to Soto, if the fear was inflicted without the intention of causing marriage, such fear did not invalidate marriage, no matter whether it was justly or unjustly inflicted.[22]

---

metus iure incutitur, et tamen matrimonium non tenet. Suffragatur enim ei edictum. . . ."—Soto, *Commentariorum in Quartum Sententiarum Tomus Secundus,* dist. 29, q. 1, a. 3.

[21] "Regula ergo generalis et tuta est, quod quoties metus ad hoc peculiariter incutitur, ut matrimonium contrahatur, ille, si est cadens in constantem virum, vitiat matrimonium sive iuste sive iniuria fuerit oblatus. . . . Pariter si pater invenit, quem cum filia sua deprehendit, cominetur accusare nisi eam duxerit matrimonium non tenet, quia metum infert, licet, iuste possit eum accusare. . . . Si autem ipse, quo metum evadat, conditionem illam sponte eligat, matrimonium tenet. Eadem ratione tenet matrimonium, si metu et ad illum finem incusso contrahatur quando metus ille est lege propositus, ut si sit lex, quod qui virginem violaverit, eum ducat, ut cap. 1, de adult. [c. 1, X, *de adulteriis et stupro,* V, 16] tunc quamvis iudex, etiam metu corporis compellat eum, ille consensus solidus est et firmus. Et ita intelligendum est verbum 1. *Continet* § *Sed vim* ff., quod metus causa [D (4, 2) 3], scilicet, quod vis, quam magistratus recte intulit iure licito non vitiat contractum."—*Loc. cit.*

[22] "Rursus quamvis inferatur ab hominibus extrinsece non illo fine, ut matrimonium contrahatur, sed alio, matrimonium tenet, etiam si iniuste inferatur."—*Loc. cit.*

This entire doctrine may be summarized as follows:

1. Metus gravis, ab intrinseco incussus, non invalidat matrimonium—
2. Metus gravis, ab extrinseco incussus, sed non praecise ad matrimonium ita ut metum passus sponte accipit matrimonium ut evadat metum, non invalidat matrimonium—
3. Metus gravis, ab extrinseco incussus praecise ad matrimonium, si metus est a lege propositus et magistratus recte eum intulit, non invalidat matrimonium—
4. Metus gravis, ab extrinseco incussus praecise ad matrimonium, etiamsi metus iure offeri potest, si tamen metus non est a lege propositus, invalidat matrimonium—
5. Metus gravis, ab extrinseco incussus praecise ad matrimonium, etiamsi metus a lege sit propositus, si tamen non recte infertur a quocumque, invalidat matrimonium—
6. Metus gravis, ab extrinseco incussus praecise ad matrimonium, si iniuria seu iniuste incutitur, invalidat matrimonium.

Thus, in the writings of Dominicus Soto, a theologian, there finally was offered a synthesis in which all the various elements of force and fear were brought together in an organic pattern that transcended a mere commentary upon concrete cases. In arriving at his synthesis, Soto had drawn upon Roman Law, upon Gratian and the Decretals, and he had used freely the work of Saint Thomas and that of the decretists and decretalists who had preceded him. His synthesis was of prime importance. Substantially it is now reflected in the structure of canon 1087, § 1, in the Code of Canon Law. One big difference is to be noted between the outline of Soto and the structure of canon 1087: Soto introduced the elements *"praecise ad matrimonium vel non,"* which in the present law are not similarly differentiated.

The Council of Trent abstracted from all treatment of the question of the injustice of coercion in marriage.

CHAPTER VII

Canonical Science from the Council of Trent to the Code of Canon Law

ARTICLE I. TERMINOLOGY

Having specifically stated, or at least clearly presumed, the distinction between *absolute force*, which propels its victim without any voluntary co-operation whatsoever on the part of the victim, and *conditional force*, which, on the part of the victim, results in a voluntary action that would not have been performed if the force had not spurred the victim to action, the authors of the period from the Council of Trent to the Code of Canon Law then took one of three positions:

1. Some stated in explicit terms that only conditional force called for consideration in the canonical treatment of coercion in marriage. This attitude was taken, for example, by Gonzalez-Tellez (died *post* 1673),[1] Ferraris (died ca. 1763),[2] Saint Alphonsus (1696-1787)[3] and De Becker (1857-1936).[4]

2. The second group agreed with the first group at least by way of implication. In discussing coercion in marriage, they actually treated only conditional force. Many of these authors also added the note that *conditional force* was to be identified with *fear* for all practical purposes. This was the procedure of the vast majority of the authors from the Council of Trent to the Code of

[1] Emmanuel Gonzalez-Tellez, *Commentaria Perpetua in Singulos Textus Quinque Librorum Decretalium Gregorii IX* (5 toms., Lugduni, 1576), lib. I, tit. 40, cap. 1, n. 12 (hereafter cited *Commentaria Perpetua*).

[2] Lucius Ferraris, *Prompta Bibliotheca Canonica, Iuridica, Moralis, Theologica, nec non Ascetica, Polemica, Rubricistica, Historica* (9 toms., Romae, 1885-1899), s.v. *Matrimonium*, art. V, n. 118 (hereafter cited *Bibliotheca*).

[3] S. Alphonsus M. de Ligorio, *Theologia Moralis* (4 toms., ed. L. Gaudé, Romae: Typis Polyglottis Vaticanis, 1905-1912), lib. VI, n. 1046.

[4] Julius De Becker, *De Sponsalibus et Matrimonio Praelectiones Canonicae* (2. ed., Lovanii, 1903), p. 61.

Canon Law. Rebello (1547-1608),[5] Sanchez (1550-1610),[6] Laymann (1574-1635),[7] Barbosa (1589-1649),[8] De Lugo (1583-1660),[9] Fagnanus (1598-1678),[10] Pirhing (1606-1679),[11] Reiffenstuel (1642-1703)[12] and Schmalzgrueber (1663-1735)[13] may be cited as representative of this predominant group.

3. Shortly before the publication of the Code of Canon Law a few authors gave a brief but explicit treatment to *absolute force* within the context of their treatment of coercion in marriage. This position was taken by Wernz (1842-1914)[14] and Gasparri (1852-1934).[15]

Both Wernz and Gasparri pointed out that while *vis* and *metus* are really correlatives, in the sense that *force* is the cause

---

[5] Fernandus Rebello, *De Obligationibus Iustitiae, Religionis, et Caritatis* (Lugduni, 1608), lib. III, q. XI, sect. 1, n. 1 (hereafter cited *De Obligationibus Iustitiae*).

[6] Thomas Sanchez, *De Sancto Matrimonii Sacramento* (3 toms., Antverpiae, 1626), lib. IV, disp. I, nn. 1, 3, 9.

[7] Paulus Laymann, *Theologia Moralis* (Venetiis, 1630), lib. V, tract. X, pars I, cap. 1, n. 1.

[8] Augustinus Barbosa, *Collectanea in Ius Pontificium* (6 toms., Lugduni, 1656), lib. IV, tit, I, cap. 15, n. 4.

[9] Joannes de Lugo, *Opera Omnia* (4 toms. in 2 vols., Venetiis, 1718), Vol. II. *de iustitia et iure,* disp. XXII, sect. VII, nn. 110-113 (hereafter cited *De Iustitia et Iure*).

[10] Prosper Fagnanus, *Commentaria in Quinque Libros Decretalium* (4 vols., Venetiis, 1696), lib. I, *de his quae vi metusve causa fiunt,* cap. 5, n. 17 (hereafter cited *Commentaria*).

[11] Ernricus Pirhing, *Jus Canonicum in V Libros Decretalium* (4 toms., Dilingae, 1722), lib. I, tit. 40, n. 1; *ibidem, ante* n. 7; lib. IV, tit. 1, n. 98 (hereafter cited *Jus Canonicum*).

[12] Anacletus Reiffenstuel, *Jus Canonicum Universum* (6 toms., Romae, 1831-1834), lib. I, tit. 40, nn. 11-15.

[13] Franciscus Schmalzgrueber, *Jus Ecclesiasticum Universum* (5 toms. in 12, Romae, 1843-1845), lib. IV, tit. 1, n. 384.

[14] Franciscus X. Wernz, *Ius Decretalium* (6 toms., Romae, Tom. I, 2. ed., 1905; Tom. II, 1899; Tom. III, 1901; Tom. IV, 1904; Tom. V, 1914; Tom. VI, 1913); Tom. IV, nn. 260 and 261, I.

[15] Petrus Gasparri, *Tractatus Canonicus de Matrimonio* (2 vols., 3. ed., Parisiis, 1904), II, n. 926 (hereafter cited *De Matrimonio*). Throughout this chapter the 1904 edition of this work will be cited unless indication be given to the contrary.

of *fear,* nevertheless the terms were generally interchanged in actual application and identified in their meaning.[16]

These concepts are clarified considerably if one recalls that absolute force does not produce fear. Absolute force produces only a mechanical reaction. Consequently *absolute force* and *fear* are not correlatives and therefore the terms *force* and *fear* may be interchanged and identified in their meaning only when conditional force is being considered. From this it follows that the authors of this period generally did not consider absolute force within the context of their treatment of coercion in marriage.

ARTICLE II. SUMMARY STATEMENTS CONCERNING THE LAW ON COERCION IN MARRIAGE

Prior to any discussion of individual points of canonical jurisprudence as they were treated in this period, it will be helpful to review and compare some of the brief statements in which the authors and Roman tribunals summarized their teaching on coercion in marriage. These statements are of particular interest because they were the forerunners of canon 1087 of the Code of Canon Law.

REBELLO: "Haec tamen regula statuenda est . . . quoties metus ab extrinseco incutitur eo fine peculiariter, ut in matrimonium consentias, quantumvis iustam causam timendi praebueris per culpam, matrimonium esse irritum si metus cadit in virum constantem; alioqui esse validum."[17]

It is to be noted that Rebello placed the emphasis upon the intention of the person causing the fear. If this intention was to produce matrimonial consent, the marriage was invalid, the question of the justice or the injustice of the fear was not considered.

SANCHEZ: "Solus enim metus iniuste illatus ad extorquendum matrimonium illud dirimit . . . a quocumque inferatur. . . ."[18]

The fact that, in this passage, Sanchez was discussing only grave fear appears from the wording of the *dubium* treated in

[16] *Operibus citatis, locis citatis.*

[17] *De Obligationibus Iustitiae,* pars II, lib. II, q. XI, sect. 2, n. 12.

[18] *De Sancto Matrimonii Sacramento,* lib. IV, disp. XII, n. 8.

disp. XII: "An metus cadens in virum constantem, iniuste incussus, irritet matrimonium?" Sanchez clearly specified that the justice and the injustice of the fear were points of essential consideration. This doctrine was to be universally accepted. Furthermore, he used the adverbial form *iniuste incussus,* thus stressing the manner of infliction rather than the substantive justice or injustice of the fear produced. From the summary statements of other authors of the period quoted immediately below it will be seen that the vast majority followed Sanchez in this.

LAYMANN: "Matrimonium contractum ex gravi, et ad id iniuste incusso metu, Ecclesiastico iure irritum est."[19]

BARBOSA: "Adverte quod licet Matrimonium nullum fit in utroque foro per metum cadentem in constantem virum ad eum finem iniuste incussum . . . tamen illud irritum non reddit metus quando iuste incutitur. . . ."[20]

CONZALEZ-TELLEZ: ". . . vera est assertio . . . metum gravem iniuste illatum a causa extrinseca, animo extorquendi consensum ad matrimonium, illud ipso iure nullum reddere ex iuribus. . . ."[21]

DE LUGO: "Quare si metus [gravis] iuste infertur . . . valebit contractus [matrimonii]; si vero iniuste . . . vitiabitur . . . [nec] requiritur, quod metus incutiatur directe ad contractum, sed sufficit si iniuste inferatur. . . ."[22]

Rebello had stressed the intention of the person causing the fear to the neglect of any consideration of the justice or the injustice of the fear. Le Lugo took a position directly opposed to this: he considered the justice or the injustice with which the fear was inflicted to be a matter of essential consideration, and ruled out any necessity of considering the intention in the mind of the person who brought fear to bear upon the victim. This attitude of De Lugo was a major turning point in the history of canonical jurisprudence on coercion in marriage as will be seen in subsequent articles.

PIRHING: ". . . hoc [matrimonium] per metum cadentem

[19] *Theologia Moralis,* lib. V, tract. X, pars I, cap. 1, n. 1.
[20] *Collectanea in Ius Pontificium,* lib. IV, tit. I, cap. 15, n. 4.
[21] *Commentaria Perpetua,* lib. IV, tit. 1, cap. 15, n. 4.
[22] *De Iustitia et Iure,* disp. XXII, sect. VII, n. 180.

in constantem virum injuste incussum ad extorquendum matrimonialem consensum est ipso iure Ecclesiastico nullum in utroque foro. . . .[23]

SCHMALZGRUEBER: "Quare dicendum, quod solus ille metus invalidet matrimonium, qui gravis est, et a causa libera iniuste incussus . . . etsi metu coactus vere consenserit in matrimonium. . . .[24]

FERRARIS: "Metus gravis iniuste incussus dirimit matrimonium. . . ."[25]

D'ANNIBALE (1815-1892): "[Metus dirimit matrimonium quando] 1. incussus fuerit ad matrimonium extorquendum; 2. fuerit iniustus, quoad substantiam inquam; et 3. gravis, seu absolute, seu relative; licet tantum reverentialis fuerit."[26]

It is worthy of note that D'Annibale became an authority *par excellence* in the matter of matrimonial coercion. In the Rota decisions published after the year 1909 he was quoted in almost every case of force and fear in marriage.[27]

It has been noted above (p. 69) that the authors from the Council of Trent to the Code of Canon Law generally used the adverbial form *iniuste incussus* in discussing the injustice of matrimonial coercion. In this way they had clearly emphasized the manner in which the fear was inflicted. D'Annibale, on the other hand, used the expression *metus iniustus* and made a clear distinction between fear which was substantially unjust and fear which was unjust only in the manner in which it was inflicted. The distinction and the controversy consequent upon it will be discussed in a later article dealing with the injustice of fear.

---

[23] *Jus Canonicum,* lib. I, tit. 40, n. 23.

[24] *Jus Ecclesiasticum Universum,* lib. IV, tit. 40, n. 392.

[25] *Bibliotheca,* s.v. *Matrimonium,* art. V, n. 123. Elsewhere Ferraris postulated that the fear be inflicted for the purpose of effecting marriage.—*Op. cit.,* s.v. *metus,* n. 24 with n. 18.

[26] Iosephus Cardinalis D'Annibale, *Summula Theologiae Moralis* (4 vols., 5. ed., Romae: 1908-1909), III, n. 445.

[27] Cf. *Sacrae Romanae Rotae Decisiones seu Sententiae . . . quae prodierunt ab anno 1909* (Romae: *Typis Polyglottis Vaticanis,* 1912—), *passim* (hereafter cited *S.R.R. Dec.*).

GASPARRI: "Igitur matrimonium certo irritat metus gravis, naturalis, ex causa libera, injustus quoad substantiam, ac directus ad extorquendum consensum matrimonialem: et haec est regula canonica certissima et ab omnibus admissa in hac materia."[28]

THE SACRED CONGREGATION OF THE COUNCIL: "At ista plena securitas frustra in themate requiritur, quandoquidem 1. in ipsum (i.e. the victim of coercion) gravis ceciderit timor sicuti in constantem quemcumque virum; 2. ab extrinseco fuerit incussus; 3. et quidem iniuste ad extorquendum consensum in matrimonium."[29]

THE ROTA: "Vis autem conditionalis, seu metus, quum a causa externa et libera sit inducta, sitque gravis, iniusta et directe incussa, etiamsi ex parte contrahentis adfuerit assensus in matrimonium, tamen hoc nullum reddit scilicet est impedimentum dirimens. . . ."[30]

With the foregoing summary statements quoted by way of general preview, the following articles will be devoted to a detailed study of those points of canonical jurisprudence which are the special subject of this dissertation.

ARTICLE III. RELATIONSHIP BETWEEN THE INTENTION OF THE PERSON WHO CAUSES FEAR IN THE VICTIM, AND THE MARRIAGE WHICH IS THE RESULT OF SUCH FEAR: *Metus Directe Incussus vs. Metus Indirecte Incussus*

Dominicus Soto, in his treatment of coercion in marriage, had given consideration to the intention of the person who gave rise to the fear in the mind of the victim, who, as the result of fear, entered marriage. According to Soto, fear invalidated marriage only if it was inflicted with the purpose of bringing a marriage about.[31] In the period after Soto, fear which was inflicted for

[28] *De Matrimonio,* II, n. 953.

[29] S.C.C., *Calven. et Theanen., Matrimonii,* 18 dec. 1869—*Thesaurus Resolutionum Sacrae Congregationis Concilii* (167 vols., Urbini et Romae: 1718-1908), CXXVIII, 621-622 (hereafter cited S.C.C. *Thesaurus*).

[30] S.R.R., *Vicariatus Apostolici Taikon* (*Corea*), *Nullitatis Matrimonii,* 16 ian. 1913, coram R.P.D. Frederico Cattani Amadori, Dec. V, n. 2—*S.R.R. Dec.,* V (1913), 54.

[31] Cf. *supra,* p. 64, notes 21 and 22.

the specific purpose of causing marriage came to be known as *metus directe incussus,* while fear which was inflicted for some other purpose but which nevertheless caused a marriage to take place came to be known as *metus indirecte incussus.* In this connection the intention of the person who caused the fear in the mind of the victim became the topic of important consideration in the development of a canonical jurisprudence on coercion in marriage.

An examination of the summary statements of the authors quoted in the preceding article shows that Rebello, Sanchez, Laymann, Barbosa, Gonzalez-Tellez, Pirhing, Ferraris, D'Annibale, and Gasparri held that only *metus directe incussus* invalidated marriage. This was certainly the more common opinion. In a careful study of this particular point Wyszynski lists also the following authors of the period from the Council of Trent to the Code of Canon Law as having held that only *metus directe incussus* invalidated marriage: Reiffenstuel (1642-1703), the Salmanticenses (1665-1724), Kugler (1654-1727), München (1794-1881), Schulte (1827-1914), Kutschker (1810-1881), Scherer (1845-1918), Feiji (1820-1894), Santi (1830-1885), De Angelis (1824-1881), Heiner (1849-1919), Laurentius (1861-1927), Leitner (1862-1929), Gury (1801-1866), A. Ballerini (1805-1881), Lehmkuhl (1834-1918) and De Smet (1868-1927).[32] This listing shows in an imposing way the historical continuity of this opinion.

The reasons adduced by the authors who maintained this theory can easily be reduced to the following:

1. If the fear was not inflicted for the purpose of causing marriage, then the victim himself was the cause of the marriage: no one required marriage of him; it was precisely he who chose marriage as a means of escape.[33]

2. The involuntary element present in such consent was not intended by the person inflicting the fear. This involuntary element was merely used by the inflicting agent as an *occasion* for obtaining the celebration of a given marriage.[34]

---

[32] M. Wyszynski, "Utrum Metus Indirecte Incussus Dirimere Possit Matrimonium," *Jus Pontificium,* XII (1932), 125-126.

[33] Sanchez, *De Sancto Matrimonii Sacramento,* lib. IV, disp. XII, n. 3.

[34] *Loc. cit.*

The authors who subscribed to this theory used this particular aspect of their doctrine on coercion in marriage as their chief criterion in the solution of cases.

On the other hand the theory which held that fear could invalidate marriage even when it was *indirecte incussus* was not without formidable support. Joannes De Lugo was the father of this opinion.[35] Schmalzgrueber became De Lugo's most powerful ally.[36] Among others, Wyszynski cites the following as having held this opinion: Wiestner (1640-1709), Ploch (whose work *De Matrimonio Vi ac Metu Contracto* appeared in 1853), Phillips (1804-1872), Grandclaude (1826-1900) and Palmieri (1829-1909).[37]

The arguments in support of this view may be summarized as follows:

1. C. 14, X, *de sponsalibus et matrimonio,* IV, 1, is general in its tenor and makes no distinction between *metus directe* and *metus indirecte incussus.*[38]

2. If the fear is grave and unjust, it affects the will of the victim in just as serious a manner and with equal injury to his rights and integrity when it is indirectly as when it is directly inflicted.[39]

3. Even if fear is inflicted for some other purpose at the beginning, nevertheless, once the question of marriage as a means of escape is injected into the issue, the victim will suffer the injury which he fears *unless he enters the marriage.* Thus a fear indirectly inflicted from the beginning becomes a fear directly inflicted when the question of marriage has actually been proposed.[40]

The authors who defended this position generally had recourse to the element of the justice or the injustice of the fear as their chief criterion in working out the solutions to cases.

The jurisprudence of the Roman Tribunals on this particular

---

[35] *De Iustitia et Iure,* disp. XXII, sect. VII, nn. 176-180.

[36] *Jus Ecclesiasticum Universum,* lib. IV, tit. 40, n. 392.

[37] "Art. cit.," *Jus Pontificium,* XII (1932), 125.

[38] Cf. *supra,* p. 17, note 5.

[39] De Lugo, *De Iustitia et Iure,* disp. XXII, sect. VII, nn. 176-177.

[40] *Ibidem,* n. 180.

point makes an interesting study. In the majority of cases the Sacred Congregation of the Council and the Sacred Roman Rota ruled clearly and definitely that only *metus directe incussus* invalidated marriage.[41] However, a few years before the publication of the Code of Canon Law the decisions of the Rota began to take cognizance of the opinion which held that *metus indirecte incussus* could also invalidate marriage. Thus we read in one decision:

> . . . impedimentum metus, irritat matrimonium si metus sit gravis, iniustus, incussus directe ad extorquendum consensum; quam postremam conditionem non omnes Doctores aeque admittunt (Card. D'Annib., pars II, n. 304).[42]

Another phase of the development of the canonical jurisprudence on this point is seen in the statement made by the Rota in adjudicating a marriage contracted under the pre-Code law, though the sentence was passed after the promulgation of the Code of Canon Law. In this instance the Rota quoted the opinion held by Reiffenstuel and others, according to which in cases of doubt as to whether the fear was directly or only indirectly inflicted it was to be presumed that it was directly inflicted.[43]

---

[41] E.g., S.C.C., *Calven et Theanen., Matrimonii,* 18 dec. 1869—S.C.C., *Thesaurus,* CXXVIII, 621-622; S.R.R., *Varsavien. seu Lublinen, Nullitatis Matrimonii,* 21 iul. 1910, coram R.P.D. Gulielmo Sebastianelli, Dec. XXVIII, n. 2—*S.R.R. Dec.,* II (1910), 289; S.R.R., *Vicariatus Apostolici Taikon (Corea), Nullitatis Matrimonii,* 16 ian. 1913, coram R.P.D. Frederico Cattani Amadori, Dec. V, n. 2—*S.R.R. Dec.,* V (1913), 54; S.R.R., *Parisien., Nullitatis Matrimonii,* 13 mart. 1911, coram R.P.D. Seraphino Many, Dec. XII, n. 2—*S.R.R. Dec.,* III (1911), 115; S.R.R., *Osnabrugen., Nullitatis Matrimonii,* 11 ian. 1912, coram R.P.D. Francisco Heiner, Dec. III, n. 4—*S.R.R. Dec.,* IV (1912), 22; S.R.R. *Vicariatus Apostolici Novae Pomeraniae, Nullitatis Matrimonii,* 30 apr. 1913, coram R.P.D. Seraphino Many, Dec. XXV, n. 2—*S.R.R. Dec.,* V (1913), 285.

[42] S.R.R., *Nullitatis Matrimonii,* 27 aug. 1912, coram R.mo P.D. Michaele Lega, Decano, Dec. XXXVIII, n. 5—*S.R.R. Dec.,* IV (1912), 441; S.R.R., *Nullitatis Matrimonii,* 29 nov. 1913, coram R.P.D. Ioanne Prior, Dec. L, n. 4 —*S.R.R. Dec.,* V (1913), 613.

[43] S.R.R., *Nullitatis Matrimonii,* 2 iul. 1918, coram R.P.D. Petro Rossetti, Dec. VIII, n. 15—*S.R.R. Dec.,* X (1918), 67.

The final stage of the evolution of the doctrine of the Rota on this point is seen when, in adjudicating a marriage which took place on July 5, 1910, the Rota declared that it makes no difference whether the fear be directly or indirectly inflicted: "nihilque refert, quod metus directe an indirecte influat in matrimonii consensum."[44] It is interesting to note that, in this decision, the opinion which had been the minority opinion before the publication of the Code of Canon Law was endorsed by the Rota as having been the correct interpretation of the pre-Code law. In taking this position the Rota was clearly influenced by the wording of canon 1087 which substituted the phrase *a quo ut quis se liberet, eligere cogatur matrimonium* for the old opinion which required that the fear be *directe incussus.* The words of the decision are of sufficient interest to be quoted fully:

> . . . a quo ut quis se liberet, cogatur eligere matrimonium, quod cum sit quaedam servitus perpetua, postulat in elegente maiorem ac perfectam libertatem, per ss. canones iure meritoque requisitam in nupturientibus . . . utpote veram et propriam electionem non agat, cum matrimonium existimet unicum esse modum ad grave damnum evadendum; nihilque refert, quod metus directe an indirecte influat in matrimonii consensum.[45]

However, this extreme position was exceptional in the decisions of the Rota, and the majority of the decisions affecting marriages contracted before the Code but adjudicated after the Code continued to interpret the pre-Code law as having required *metus directe incussus* in order to invalidate marriage.[46]

---

[44] S.R.R., *Nullitatis Matrimonii,* 9 ian. 1922, coram R.P.D. Iosepho Florczak, Dec. I, n. 3—*S.R.R. Dec.,* XIV (1922), 2-3.

[45] *Loc. cit.*

[46] E.g., S.R.R., *Nullitatis Matrimonii,* 7 mart. 1922, coram R.P.D. Francisco Solieri, Dec. VI, n. 2—*S.R.R. Dec.,* XIV (1922), 51; S.R.R., *Nullitatis Matrimonii,* 7 aug. 1922, coram R.P.D. Maximo Massimi, Dec. XXVIII, n. 2—*S.R.R. Dec.,* XIV (1922), 259; S.R.R., *Varsavien., Nullitatis Matrimonii,* 10 aug. 1923, coram R.P.D. Andrea Jullien, Dec XXVIII, n. 2—*S.R.R. Dec.,* XV (1923), 238.

ARTICLE IV. THE JUSTICE AND THE INJUSTICE OF FEAR

§ 1. *The Problem; Manner of Treatment*

When one reads the authors who wrote from the Council of Trent to the Code of Canon Law it becomes evident that the question of the justice and the injustice of the fear influencing the marriage was closely linked to the question of the intention of the agent inflicting the fear. In this article the writer will seek to furnish a distinct treatment of the former question without, however, losing sight of its relationship to the latter.

It would be difficult to point to an instance in Canon Law in which greater confusion existed among canonists in formulating concepts and in applying these concepts to practical cases. This was not due to the brevity with which the subject of the justice and the injustice of matrimonial coercion was treated, at least not after the time of Sanchez. Quite to the contrary, most of the authors of this period treated the subject with great diffusiveness.

In a generous majority fashion the subject was handled by means of the presentation of cases. From these the underlying idea or principle can generally be extracted. Rather than narrate numerous cases which vary so little from author to author as to invite the notion of a repetition, an effort will be made in this article to isolate the principles involved and to present them in the form of simple statements.

The subject will be treated in four paragraphs:

1. The four distinctive opinions, or schools of thought, presenting the whole subject of the justice and injustice of the fear influencing the marriage will be summarized. Here the four schools of thought are distinguished from one another not in terms of their treatment of concrete cases, but rather in terms of the abstract position which they assigned to the element of the justice and the injustice of the fear as a determining factor in the effect which coercion had upon the validity of the marriage in question.

2. The genesis of the distinction between fear *iniustus quoad substantiam* and *iniustus quoad modum tantum* will be discussed.

Examples of the two types of injustice will be cited. The dispute concerning the application of this distinction will be briefly outlined.

3. Typical examples of coercion which the authors considered to be instances of *just fear* will be reviewed. Invalidating effects were not attributed to the infliction of fear in these instances.

4. Typical examples of coercion which the authors agreed upon as being instances of *unjust fear* which invalidated marriage will be reviewed.

§ 2. *Distinctive Opinions on the Justice and the Injustice of Fear in Marriage*

1. The first distinctive opinion was that of the *glossa ordinaria* to the *Decree* of Gratian and of the *glossa ordinaria* to the Decretals of Gregory IX.[47] According to this opinion, grave fear always invalidated marriage whether it was justly or unjustly inflicted. This theory continued to receive at least some nominal support in this period. However, soon after the Council of Trent this position began to be abandoned.[48]

2. The second distinctive opinion was that of Dominicus Soto.[49] According to this theory:

a. Justly inflicted fear did not invalidate marriage.

b. Fear was justly inflicted for the purpose of causing marriage only when the law specifically provided for its use, as in the cases of broken espousals and seduction.

c. Any other fear inflicted for the purpose of causing marriage was unjustly inflicted and invalidated the marriage.

d. Even the fear for the use of which the law made provision was unjustly inflicted if it was inflicted in a manner other than that which was required by law. Fear inflicted in an illegal manner invalidated the marriage.

---

[47] Cf. *supra,* p. 35, notes 31-34.

[48] Rebello (*De Obligationibus Iustitiae,* pars II, lib. II, q. XI, sect. 2, n. 12) at first subscribed to this opinion, but later abandoned it in practical application and conformed to the opinion of Dominicus Soto as outlined in § 2, n. 2 of this article.—*Ibidem,* n. 13.

[49] Cf. *supra,* pp. 63-64, notes 18-22.

This opinion continued to exert considerable influence after the Council of Trent.[50]

3. The third opinion was that of Sanchez. It was a rather radical modification of the opinion of Dominicus Soto and received wide support, so much so that the opinion of Sanchez became the *opinio communior* if not the *opinio communis* of the period. According to this theory:

a. There was no need of a specific provision in the law before the inflicted fear could be a just fear.

b. Fear justly inflicted did not invalidate the marriage; fear unjustly inflicted invalidated the marriage. However, this rule had to be taken in conjunction with the consideration of the intention (direct or indirect) with which the fear was inflicted.

c. If the fear was inflicted for some purpose other than marriage, it did not invalidate the marriage whether it was justly or unjustly inflicted.

d. If the fear was inflicted for the specific purpose of causing marriage, it did not invalidate the marriage if it was justly inflicted; it did invalidate the marriage if it was unjustly inflicted.[51]

4. The fourth opinion was that of Joannes De Lugo. In its distinctive elements it was a minority opinion prior to the publication of the Code of Canon Law. Nevertheless it was this opinion that was adopted by the Code.

De Lugo simplified the position of Sanchez. The intention of the agent who inflicted the fear was ruled out as a point of essential consideration and the element of the justice or injustice of the fear was made autonomous. A *justly inflicted fear did not invalidate* the marriage regardless of whether or not pro-

---

[50] Cf. e.g., Laymann, *Theologia Moralis,* lib. V, tract. X, pars I, cap. 1, n. 3.

[51] Sanchez, *De Sancto Matrimonii Sacramento,* lib. IV, disp. XIII, n. 4, where it is to be noted that Sanchez, in his examples, consistently reduced justly inflicted fear to *metus ab intrinseco;* Barbosa, *Collectanea in Ius Pontificium,* lib. IV, tit. I, cap. 28, n. 2; Gonzalez-Tellez, *Commentaria Perpetua,* lib. IV, tit. I, cap. 15, n. 4; Pirhing, *Jus Canonicum,* lib. I, tit. 40, n. 23; Reiffenstuel, *Jus Canonicum Universum,* lib. I, tit. 40, n. 28; Ferraris, *Bibliotheca,* s.v. *Matrimonium,* art. V, nn. 123-127; S. Alphonsus, *Theologia Moralis,* lib. VI, nn. 1049-1051; Wernz, *Ius Decretalium,* tom. IV, n. 265; Gasparri, *De Matrimonio,* II, n. 953.

vision for its use was made in the law; an *unjustly inflicted fear always invalidated* the marriage.[52]

§ 3. *The Distinction Between "Metus Iniustus Quoad Substantiam" and "Metus Iniustus Quoad Modum Tantum"*

It has been seen in the previous chapter that the element of injustice was formally and explicitly introduced into the canonical treatment of coercion only in the thirteenth century.[53] An examination of the summary statements of the authors of the period after the Council of Trent illustrates clearly that even after the Council of Trent the only distinction made in dealing with the justice and injustice of coercion in marriage was the distinction between *metus iuste illatus* and *metus iniuste illatus.*[54] Eventually, however, the authors, in their efforts to find nicer refinements of doctrine, worked out a still further distinction between *metus iniustus quoad substantiam* and *metus iniustus quoad modum.*[55]

Fear was considered unjust *quoad substantiam*: a. when it was caused by threats of punishment for a crime that had not been committed;[56] b. when it was caused by threats of punishment for a crime that had been committed, but the particular punishment which was threatened was not merited by the particular crime which had ben committed.[57]

Fear was considered unjust *quoad modum*: a. when it was

---

[52] De Lugo, *De Iustitia et Iure,* disp. XXII, sect. VII, nn. 176-177. This opinion did not rule out the possibility that the infliction of the fear for the specific purpose of causing the marriage could in certain instances constitute an injustice in itself.

[53] Cf. *supra,* p. 40, note 56.

[54] Cf. *supra,* pp. 68-71, notes 17-30.

[55] Cf., e.g., D'Annibale, *Summula Theologiae Moralis,* III, n. 445; Gasparri, *De Matrimonio,* II, n. 948 and n. 953.

[56] Gasparri, *De Matrimonio,* II, n. 948; S.R.R., *Nullitatis Matrimonii,* 4 iun. 1927, coram R.P.D. Iulio Grazioli, Dec. XXV, nn. 3-4—*S.R.R. Dec.,* XIX (1927), 201-202.

[57] D'Annibale, *Summula Theologiae Moralis,* III, n. 445; Gasparri, *De Matrimonio,* II, n. 948; S.R.R., *Nullitatis Matrimonii,* 28 ian. 1918, coram R.mo P.D. Gulielmo Sebastianelli, Decano, Dec. II, n. 10—*S.R.R. Dec.,* X (1918), 18.

caused by threats of an evil or punishment which was due to the victim, but not from the person who made the threats, for example, threats by a judge who did not have proper jurisdiction;[58] b. when it was caused by threats of an evil or punishment which was due to the victim from the person who made the threats, which threats, however, were made in an improper manner as when a judge disregarded the proper process of law, or when parents exceeded moderate persuasion in urging their children to marry.[59]

In the history of the application of this distinction a definite process of evolution can be traced. Sanchez (1550-1610) had not explicitly made the distinction. However, in solving a certain case he had concluded that the marriage was valid, though it had been brought about by the infliction of a fear which later authors called unjust *quoad substantiam*. The case was one in which a judge in passing sentence upon an innocent person had acted in accordance with the charges and proofs made in court.[60] De Lugo agreed with Sanchez in this conclusion.[61] Prior to the time that Sanchez expressed this opinion, however, Veracruz (*circa* 1560) had discussed the same case and had concluded that the marriage was invalid. In effect, his conclusion was that a marriage which was caused by a fear which was unjust *quoad substantiam* was invalid.[62] After the time of De Lugo, the opinion of Veracruz prevailed, and none of the later authors even seemed

---

[58] D'Annibale, *Summula Theologiae Moralis,* III, n. 445; Gasparri, *De* Matrimonio, II, n. 948; S.R.R., *Nullitatis Matrimonii,* 28 ian. 1918, coram R.mo P.D. Gulielmo Sebastianelli, Decano, Dec. II, n. 10—*S.R.R. Dec.,* X (1918), 18; S.R.R., *Rottenburgen., Nullitatis Matrimonii,* 13 aug. 1924, coram R.P.D. Francisco Parrillo, Dec. XL, n. 4—*S.R.R. Dec.,* XVI (1924), 369-370.

[59] D'Annibale, *Summula Theologiae Moralis,* I, n. 138; Gasparri, *De Matrimonio,* II, n. 948; S.R.R., *Nullitatis Matrimonii,* 9 ian. 1922, coram R.P.D. Iosepho Florczak, Dec. I, n. 19—*S.R.R. Dec.,* XIV (1922), 11; S.R.R., *Rottenburgen, Nullitatis Matrimonii,* 13 aug. 1924, coram R.P.D. Francisco Parrillo, Dec. XL, n. 4—*S.R.R. Dec.,* XVI (1924), 369-370.

[60] *De Sancto Matrimonii Sacramento,* lib. IV, disp. XII, n. 18; *ibidem,* disp. XIII, n. 8.

[61] *De Iustitia et Iure,* disp. XXII, sect. VII, n. 163.

[62] *Apud* Sanchez, *op. cit., loc. cit.*

to call it into question.[63] Thus, before the Code of Canon Law was published it was universally admitted that fear, unjust *quoad substantiam,* invalidated marriage.[64]

With regard to fear that was unjust *quoad modum tantum* there was some authority before the Code for the opinion that it also invalidated marriage.[65] Nevertheless, grave authors cast some doubt upon this or even denied it explicitly, and, therefore, before the publication of the Code of Canon Law, a marriage could not be declared invalid when the fear that brought it about was unjust only in the manner of its infliction.[66]

This dispute was to be settled in consequence of the doctrine expressed in canon 1087 of the Code of Canon Law. As a result, after the publication of the Code, certain Rota decisions which settled the cases of marriages contracted *before* the Code ruled that marriage was invalidated by fear which was unjust *quoad modum tantum.*[67]

§ 4. *Fear Which Was Considered Just*

The purpose of this paragraph is to review the chief typical

---

[63] Schmalzgrueber, *Ius Ecclesiasticum Universum* lib. IV, tit. 1, n. 400; Sanctus Alphonsus, *Theologia Moralis,* lib. VI, n. 1052; Gasparri, *De Matrimonio,* II, n. 950.

[64] D'Annibale, *Summula Theologiae Moralis,* III, n. 445; S.R.R., *Tarvisina, Nullitatis Matrimonii,* 11 mart. 1912, coram R.P.D. Frederico Cattani, Dec. XI, n. 2—*S.R.R. Dec.,* IV (1912), 125-126; S.R.R. *Nullitatis Matrimonii,* 6 iun. 1918, coram R.P.D. Petro Rossetti, Dec. VIII, n. 4—*S.R.R. Dec.,* X (1918), 43.

[65] De Lugo, *De Iustitia et Iure,* disp. XXII, sect. VII, n. 151; Schmalzgrueber, *Ius Ecclesiasticum Universum,* lib. I, tit. 1, n. 390; Wernz, *Ius Decretalium,* tom. IV, n. 265; S.C.C., *Calven. et Theanen., Matrimonii,* 18 dec. 1869—S.C.C., *Thesaurus,* CXXVIII, 614; S.R.R. *Nullitatis Matrimonii,* 28 ian. 1918, coram R.mo P.D. Gulielmo Sebastianelli, Decano, Dec. II, n. 6—*S.R.R. Dec.,* X (1918), 15; S.R.R., *Nullitatis Matrimonii,* 8 iun. 1918, coram R.P.D. Petro Rossetti, Dec. VIII, n. 3—*S.R.R. Dec.,* X (1918), 60. Cf. also the doctrine of Soto, *supra,* p. 65.

[66] D'Annibale, *Summula Theologiae Moralis,* III, n. 445; Gasparri, *De Matrimonio,* II, n. 950; S.R.R., *Nullitatis Matrimonii,* 9 iul. 1911, coram R.P.D. Ioanne Prior, Dec. XXII, n. 5—*S.R.R. Dec.,* III (1911), 239.

[67] Cf., e.g., S.R.R. *Nullitatis Matrimonii,* 4 iun. 1927, coram R.P.D. Iulio Grazioli, Dec. XXV, nn. 3-4—*S.R.R. Dec.,* XIX (1927), 201-202.

examples of what the authors of the period considered as *just* fear.

1. Fear could justly be inflicted upon a person who gave cause to having the fear inflicted upon him, as long as the fear was inflicted by a person vested with the authority to do so and provided that it was inflicted in a legitimate manner.[68] The Sacred Congregation of the Council expressed this principle in the following manner:

> Neque quidquam officit illud iuris canonici effatum, quod *coacta voluntas est voluntas*. Hoc enim effatum locum quidem habet quando legitimus iudex procedit ad coactionem ex iusta ac probata causa; quo in casu factum iudicis censeri potest factum partis iudiciali coactioni causam dantis.[69]

2. One could justly threaten to accuse a person to the proper authority in instances in which a crime had certainly been committed.[70]

3. Parents could justly bring *moderate* pressure to bear upon their children in order to induce them to enter a certain marriage. Parents acted within the limits of their rights and responsibilities as long as *due moderation* was exercised.[71] This principle, however, was not universally admitted without further qualification. Some, for example, insisted that the parents committed

[68] Schmalzgrueber, *Jus Ecclesiasticum Universum,* lib. I, tit. 40, n. 2.

[69] S.C.C., *Calven. et Theanen., Matrimonii,* 18 dec. 1869—S.C.C., *Thesaurus,* CXXVIII, 614; cf. also S.R.R., *Nullitatis Matrimonii,* 15 ian. 1923, coram R.P.D. Iulio Grazioli, Dec. I, n. 3—*S.R.R. Dec.,* XV (1923), 4.

[70] Sanchez, *De Sancto Matrimonii Sacramento,* lib. IV, disp. XIII, n. 4; Laymann, *Theologia Moralis,* lib. V, tract. X, cap. 1, n. 3; De Lugo, *De Iustitia et Iure,* disp. XXII, sect. VII, nn. 112, 153 fine, 156; Pirhing, *Jus Canonicum,* lib. I, tit. 40, n. 40; *op. cit.,* lib. IV, tit. 1, n. 104; Schmalzgrueber, *Jus Ecclesiasticum Universum,* lib. I, tit. 40, n. 8; *op. cit.,* lib. IV, tit. I, nn. 389, 391; Sanctus Alphonsus, *Theologia Moralis,* lib. VI, n. 1049; Gasparri, *De Matrimonio,* II, n. 949.

[71] Sanchez, *De Sancto Matrimonii Sacramento,* lib. IV, disp. XXII, n. 5; S.R.R., *Nullitatis Matrimonii,* 11 apr. 1922, coram R.mo P.D. Ioanne Prior, Decano, Dec. XI, n. 2—*S.R.R. Dec.,* XIV (1922), 93-94; S.R.R., *Nullitatis Matrimonii,* 18 oct. 1922, coram R.P.D. Petro Rossetti, Dec. XXXV, n. 9—*S.R.R. Dec.,* XIV (1922), 325.

an injustice if their moderate coercion was directed towards marriage with a *certain person;*[72] others taught that the parents acted unjustly in using moderate coercion unless they were prompted by a cause of utmost gravity.[73]

4. One could justly refuse to assist a person in need, if one was not bound by some title of justice to assist such a person.[74] However, in a very interesting sentence, the Rota pointed out that this principle was subject to further scrutiny. In this sentence the Rota discussed the case of a certain Gabriela, whose grandmother had threatened to cut off the subsidy she granted to Gabriela unless the latter entered a certain marriage. The marriage was contracted in 1906. The court of first instance found the marriage invalid in 1920. On November 26, 1921, the court of second instance reversed this decision with this comment: "Gabrielae avia, iure non tenebatur subsidia parti praebere: unde iniuste agere non videbatur, comminando huiusmodi subsidiorum, usque tunc praestitorum, cessationem." On August 13, 1924, the Rota reversed the decision of the court of second instance, and held that the action of the grandmother was unjust. The substance of the Rota's comment was that, whereas the grandmother may not have acted unjustly in cutting off the subsidy, she did act unjustly in demanding marriage as the condition upon which the subsidy would be continued:

> . . . tum illum iniuste agere dicimus, qui per metum gravem exigit id ad quod ius non habet, tum illum qui, licet ius habeat exigendi rem, mediis tamen iniustis utitur." ". . . licet (avia) minas exsequi potuisset, non poterat tamen per haec media exigere, quod nullo iure ipsi competebat, nempe matrimonium." ". . . nefas ei

[72] Cf., e.g., S.R.R., *Varsavien. seu Lublinen, Nullitatis Matrimonii,* 21 iul. 1910, coram R.P.D. Gulielmo Sebastianelli, Dec. XXVIII, n. 8—*S.R.R. Dec.,* II (1910), 293.

[73] Cf., e.g., S.R.R., *Nullitatis Matrimonii,* 24 iun. 1912, coram R.P.D. Francisco Heiner, Dec. XXV, n. 13—*S.R.R. Dec.,* IV (1912), 305.

[74] Sanchez, *De Sancto Matrimonii Sacramento,* lib. IV, disp. XIII, n. 4; De Lugo, *De Iustitia et Iure,* disp. XXII, sect. VII, n. 183; Schmalzgrueber, *Jus Ecclesiasticum Universum,* lib. IV, tit. 1, n. 403; Sanctus Alphonsus, *Theologia Moralis,* lib. VI, n. 1053; Wernz, *Ius Decretalium,* tom. IV, n. 265.

erat et iustitiae leges, prout neptis libertatem, violabat, quando illis mediis abutebatur ad exigendum, quod nullo iure ipsi competebat, matrimonium.[75]

5. A judge could justly threaten excommunication in order to cause a person to enter marriage after a contract of espousals. Authors differed only in the degree of caution and prudence which they enjoined upon the judge in such cases.[76]

6. Under certain circumstances, a judge could justly force a seducer to marry the girl he had seduced. This principle was of particular importance, and, since the jurisprudence on the point is extremely complicated it will be treated in a special article, Article V of this chapter.

§ 5. *Fear Which Was Considered Unjust*

Once it was established under which conditions fear could justly be inflicted, the injustice of the fear inflicted in a particular case could be deduced by logical conclusion. Nevertheless, it is helpful to examine the statements made *ex professo* by the authors and by the Roman tribunals relative to the fear which they considered unjust. These statements will frequently have to be read in conjunction with their remarks on the distinction between fear unjust *quoad substantiam* and fear unjust *quoad modum* if one is to determine the particular type of injustice which they considered to be verified in a given case.[77] In other instances they specified the type of injustice in the text of their remarks.

---

[75] S.R.R., *Rottenburgen., Nullitatis Matrimonii,* 13 aug. 1924, coram R.P.D. Francisco Parrillo, Dec. XL, n. 4—*S.R.R. Dec.,* XVI (1924), 369.

[76] Sanchez, *De Sancto Matrimonii Sacramento,* lib. IV, disp. XIII, n. 4; Barbosa, *Collectanea in Ius Pontificium,* lib. IV, tit. I, cap. 17, n. 2; Gonzalez-Tellez, *Commentaria Perpetua,* lib. IV, tit. I, cap. 15, n. 4; De Lugo, *De Iustitia et Iure,* disp. XXII, sect. VII, n. 159; Pirhing, *Jus Canonicum,* lib. IV, tit. 1, n. 104; Reiffenstuel, *Jus Canonicum Universum,* lib. I, tit. 40, n. 28; Schmalzgrueber, *Jus Ecclesiasticum Universum,* lib. IV, tit. 40, n. 391; Gasparri, *De Matrimonio,* II, n. 949; S.R.R., *Nullitatis Matrimonii,* 6 iun. 1925, Coram R.P.D. Francisco Morano, Dec. XXVIII, n. 4—*S.R.R. Dec.,* XVII (1925), 220.

[77] Cf. *supra,* pp. 79-80, notes 56-59.

The authors of this period considered the following to be instances of unjust coercion:

1. It was unjust for a private person to threaten to inflict punishment for a crime or a delict, since only a person in public authority had this right.[78]

2. It was unjust for a judge who did not possess proper jurisdiction to threaten a person with punishment, even though the person had been guilty of a crime which deserved such punishment.[79]

3. The fear was unjust if it was caused through a penalty imposed by a judge upon an innocent person, even though the judge possessed proper jurisdiction and acted according to due process of law.[80] This was considered a case of injustice *quoad substantiam.*

4. The fear was unjust if it was caused through the imposition of a penalty upon a person guilty of a crime or a delict by a judge who possessed jurisdiction but who either did not observe the due process of law or imposed a penalty that was not merited by the crime which had been committed.[81] If an undue penalty was imposed it was considered an injustice *quoad substantiam;* if the due process of law was not observed it was considered an injustice *quoad modum.*

5. The fear was unjust if it was caused through the imposition of a penalty upon a guilty person, but contrary to the charges and proofs as brought out in the trial before a court.[82]

---

[78] Barbosa, *Collectanea in Ius Pontificium,* lib. IV, tit. I, cap. 15, n. 4; Gonzalez-Tellez, *Commentaria Perpetua,* lib. IV, tit. I, cap. 15, n. 4; De Lugo, *De Iustitia et Iure,* disp. XXII, sect. VII, n. 156; Pirhing, *Jus Canonicum,* lib. I, tit. 40, n. 40; *op. cit.,* lib. IV, tit. 1, nn. 100, 102; Schmalzgrueber, *Jus Ecclesiasticum Universum,* lib. I, tit. 40, n. 2; *op. cit.,* lib. IV, tit. 1, nn. 391, 393, 400; Sanctus Alphonsus, *Theologia Moralis,* lib. VI, n. 1049.

[79] S.C.C. *Calven. et Theanen., Matrimonii,* 18 dec. 1869—S.C.C., *Thesaurus,* CXXVIII, 614; S.R.R., *Nullitatis Matrimonii,* 28 ian. 1918, coram R.mo P.D. Gulielmo Sebastianelli, Decano, Dec. II, n. 10—*S.R.R. Dec.,* X (1918), 18.

[80] Cf. references quoted *supra,* p. 79, note 56, and S.R.R., *Nullitatis Matrimonii,* 28 ian. 1918, coram R.mo P.D. Gulielmo Sebastianelli, Decano, Dec. II, n. 10—*S.R.R. Dec.,* X (1918), 18.

[81] Cf. *supra,* p. 79, note 57.

[82] Sanchez, *De Sancto Matrimonii Sacramento,* lib. IV, disp. XXII, sect.

6. It was unjust for a person to refuse to render assistance to another person in need if the one who refused was under obligation in justice to render such assistance.[83]

7. It was unjust for parents to use anything more than mildly coercive measures to cause their children to enter marriage.[84]

8. It was unjust to inflict fear upon another for the specific purpose of causing that person to marry under any circumstances in which the person inflicting the fear did not have the specific right to demand marriage from the victim of the fear.[85]

9. It was unjust for a judge to force a seducer to marry the woman whom he had seduced unless the judge acted within the framework of certain defined moral and canonical principles. As these principles involve difficulties and yet are of the utmost importance they will be treated in a special article, Article V of this chapter.

ARTICLE V. THE JUSTICE AND THE INJUSTICE OF FORCE AND FEAR IN CASES OF SEDUCTION

§ 1. *The Problem*

As a matter of historical fact, many of the cases of force and fear in marriage are caused, or at least occasioned, in conse-

VII, n. 163. This may be taken as the common opinion, since the authors called into question another aspect of the teaching of Sanchez on this point, while passing over the present aspect in silence.

[83] Schmalzgrueber, *Jus Ecclesiasticum Universum,* lib. IV, tit. 1, nn. 393, 400; Sanctus Alphonsus, *Theologia Moralis,* lib. VI, n. 1053; Gasparri, *De Matrimonio,* II, n. 953.

[84] S.R.R., *Varsavien. seu Lublinen., Nullitatis Matrimonii,* 21 iul. 1910, coram R.P.D. Gulielmo Sebastianelli, Dec. XXVIII, n. 8—*S.R.R. Dec.*, II (1910), 293; S.R.R., *Tarvisina, Nullitatis Matrimonii,* 11 mart. 1912, coram R.P.D. Frederico Cattani, Dec. XI, n. 2—*S.R.R. Dec.,* IV (1912), 125-126; S.R.R., *Nullitatis Matrimonii,* 24 iun. 1912, coram R.P.D. Francisco Heiner, Dec. XXV, n. 13—*S.R.R. Dec.,* IV (1912), 305; S.R.R., *Nullitatis Matrimonii,* die 2 iul. 1918, coram R.P.D. Petro Rossetti, Dec. VIII, n. 19—*S.R.R. Dec.,* X (1918), 70; S.R.R., *Nullitatis Matrimonii,* 9 ian. 1922, coram R.P.D. Iosepho Florczak, Dec. I, n. 19—*S.R.R. Dec.,* XIV (1922), 11.

[85] S.R.R., *Rottenburgen., Nullitatis Matrimonii,* 13 aug. 1924, coram R.P.D. Francisco Parrillo, Dec. XL, n. 4—*S.R.R. Dec.,* XVI (1924), 369-370.

quence of seduction or of some similar crime. It is not surprising then to find the authors and the decisions of the Roman Tribunals from the Council of Trent to the Code of Canon Law treating this subject in some detail.

The fundamental idea in this treatment signalized the fact that seduction (*stuprum* and *seductio*) was considered to be a sin which was specifically different from *fornicatio simplex,* involving, as it did, an injury (*iniuria*) to the rights of the woman. This injury did not consist specifically in the destruction of physical virginity, but rather in the lessening of the woman's reputation and of her normal chances of entering a marriage compatible with her station. This fundamental idea dominated the thought of the authors in their treatment of the entire subject: the justice and the injustice of the fear brought to bear upon an alleged seducer was determined very largely in terms of the injury (*iniuria*) done to the woman. Around this central consideration the authors worked out an elaborate jurisprudence for determining the obligation of the seducer and the justice and injustice of bringing pressure to bear upon him to fulfill this obligation.

§ 2. *Terms*

1. *Stuprum* in the strictest sense of the word was the depriving of a virgin of her corporal virginity by the use of force.[86]

2. *Stuprum* in the strict sense of the word was the depriving of a virgin of her corporal virginity by inducing her to consent to the action through the use of fraud or unjustly inflicted fear.[87]

3. On the other hand, if the virgin was induced to consent to the loss of her corporal virginity by the use of flatteries, insistencies and importunate entreaties, the authors disputed whether or not the specific note of *stuprum* was verified. Pirhing held that *stuprum* was not committed in such cases, though he ad-

---

[86] Pirhing, *Jus Canonicum,* lib. V, tit. 16, n. 37; Ferraris, *Bibliotheca,* s.v. *stuprator, stuprum,* nn. 1-3, cf. *supra,* p. 24, note 43.

[87] Pirhing, *Jus Canonicum, loc. cit.;* Schmalzgrueber, *Jus Ecclesiasticum Universum,* lib. V, tit. 16, n. 16.

mitted the probability of the opposite opinion.[88] Saint Alphonsus held the same opinion, but excepted cases in which the flatteries and insistencies were practically equivalent to the use of force.[89] Reiffenstuel[90] and Schmalzgrueber[91] held that the culprit had no special and peculiar obligation towards the seduced in such cases, as far as conscience was concerned and prior to the passing of an adverse sentence by a court.

4. If the woman who was violated was not a virgin, but was generally and publicly thought to be a virgin, Reiffenstuel held that the man who violated her was responsible to the same extent as if *stuprum* had been committed (against a virgin).[92] Pirhing[93] and Schmalzgrueber,[94] on the other hand, held that the culprit was bound to make only such satisfaction as prudence dictated, and that he was not held to the consequences of the crime of *stuprum*.

5. All other cases of illicit sexual relations with unmarried women were classified as simple fornication. In such cases the man was bound to the consequences of *stuprum* only if he revealed the sin and thus injured the character of the woman.[95]

These concepts were used by the authors in conjunction with the principles explained below in determining the justice and the injustice of fear that was brought to bear upon the seducer in cases of seduction.

§ 3. *Presumptions*

Normally two presumptions militated in favor of the woman involved in a case of alleged seduction: 1. it was presumed that

[88] *Jus Canonicum,* lib. V, tit. 16, n. 50.

[89] *Theologia Moralis,* lib. III, n. 640.

[90] *Jus Canonicum Universum,* lib. V, tit. 1, nn. 71-76.

[91] *Jus Ecclesiasticum Universum,* lib. V, tit. 16, n. 38.

[92] *Jus Canonicum Universum,* lib. IV, tit. 1, n. 79.

[93] *Jus Canonicum,* lib. V, tit. 16, n. 48.

[94] *Jus Ecclesiasticum Universum,* lib. V, tit. 16, n. 37.

[95] Pirhing, *Jus Canonicum,* lib. V, tit. 16, n. 48; Reiffenstuel, *Jus Canonicum Universum,* lib. IV, tit. 1, n. 78; Schmalzgrueber, *Jus Ecclesiasticum Universum,* lib. V, tit. 16, n. 37; Sanctus Alphonsus, *Theologia Moralis,* lib. III, n. 641.

she was a virgin, and, if her virginal integrity became violated, 2. it was presumed that she was seduced.

These presumptions, however, were voidable through stronger presumptions to the contrary, for example, through the fact of the woman's abject morals and through the normal signs of a corrupt and dissolute life. Furthermore, the presumptions which a woman normally enjoyed were operative against a *specific* man only when this man admitted that he had had relations with the woman, or when the woman proved that such relations had occurred.[96] Consequently, in most of the trials it remained for the woman to prove that the man had actually indulged in such relations with her. Ordinary presumptions did not suffice for establishing this fact. Thus, though the man was frequently seen with the woman, even in remote and obscure places, such an association did not suffice as proof that he had actually seduced her, unless he had continued such an association after due warning had been given.[97]

Finally, Saint Alphonsus noted that, though the law established the presumption that a woman was a virgin, or that she was seduced, if in fact she was not a virgin, or if she was not seduced, then the man had no obligation in conscience: "leges enim quae fundantur in falsa facti praesumptione non obligant in conscientia."[98]

§ 4. *Circumstances in Which the Man Had No Obligation Either to Marry the Woman or to Endow Her*

Under certain circumstances the penalties proper to *stuprum* did not attach to illicit relations with a woman, though there may have been some obligation to pay limited damages. If in such circumstances pressure was brought to bear upon a man in

[96] Barbosa, *Collectanea in Ius Pontificium,* lib. V, tit. 16, cap. 1, n. 5; Reiffenstuel, *Jus Canonicum Universum,* lib. V, tit. 16, n. 46, and lib. IV, tit. 1, n. 84; Pirhing, *Jus Canonicum,* lib. V, tit. 16, nn. 61-62; Schmalzgrueber, *Jus Ecclesiasticum Universum,* lib. V, tit. 16, nn. 50-52.

[97] Pirhing, *op. cit., loc. cit.;* Schmalzgrueber, *op. cit.,* lib. V, tit. 16, n. 54; Pirhing (*loc. cit.*) reported a number of authors as carrying the idea to this extreme: "etiamsi . . . in eodem lecto simul . . . deprehensi sunt, praesertim si induti. . . ."

[98] *Theologia Moralis,* lib. III, n. 641.

order to cause him to marry the woman or to endow her, the fear arising from such pressure was unjust *quoad substantiam.*[99]

The following may be cited as instances in which, according to the jurisprudence of the period, there was no obligation on the part of the man either to marry or to endow the woman:

1. In cases of simple fornication, even though the woman was a virgin.[100] Thus, if a man had relations with a woman without promising to marry her, without the use of force, fraud or unjustly inflicted fear, he certainly had no obligation either to marry or to endow her.[101]

2. In cases of merely attempted seduction, for the penalties attached only to a completed criminal act.[102]

3. In cases in which the woman was of a common or disreputable life, or when she was a vagrant who did not observe the normal rules of modesty.[103]

4. In cases in which the seducer's marriage with the seduced woman would furnish probable occasion for scandal or other serious and detrimental effects. This did not mean, however, that he was not bound to pay appropriate damages. It did mean, however, that if he was unable to pay damages he could not be forced to marry the woman as otherwise might be the case.[104]

---

[99] Cf. *supra*, p. 79, notes 56 and 57; p. 81, note 64.

[100] Cf. *supra*, p. 88, note 95.

[101] Barbosa, *Collectanea in Ius Pontificium*, lib. V, tit. 16, cap. 1, n. 2; Reiffenstuel, *Jus Canonicum Universum*, lib. V, tit. 16, n. 46; Schmalzgrueber, *Jus Ecclesiasticum Universum*, lib. V, tit. 16, n. 19; Sanctus Alphonsus, *Theologia Moralis*, lib. III, n. 640. For a disputed case cf. *supra*, pp. 87-88, notes 88-91.

[102] Barbosa, *op. cit.*, lib. V, tit. 16, cap. 1, n. 6. Schmalzgrueber, *op. cit.*, lib. V, tit. 16, n. 17; *et alii passim.*

[103] Barbosa, *op. cit.*, *loc. cit.*; Fagnanus, *Commentaria*, lib. V, *de adulteriis et stupro*, cap. 2, nn. 1-2; Schmalzgrueber, *Jus Ecclesiasticum Universum*, lib. V, tit. 16, n. 17; S.C.C., *Calven. et Theanen.*, *Matrimonii*, 18 dec. 1869—S.C.C., *Thesaurus*, CXXVIII, 624-625; S.C.C., *Melvitana*, *Sponsalium*, 8 maii 1886—S.C.C., *Thesaurus*, CXLV, 352 and 354.

[104] Pirhing, *Jus Canonicum*, lib. V, tit. 16, n. 60 (59); Reiffenstuel, *Jus Canonicum Universum*, lib. IV, tit. 1, n. 131; Sanctus Alphonsus, *Theologia Moralis*, lib. III, n. 640; S.R.R., *Nullitatis Matrimonii*, 28 ian. 1918, coram R.mo P.D. Gulielmo Sebastianelli, Decano, Dec. II, nn. 10-11—*S.R.R. Dec.*, X (1918), 17.

5. In cases in which the seducer had not given any promise of marriage to a woman of much lower station than himself. It was demanded that he make restitution in some other way, for no one was to be obliged to fulfill an obligation with the effect of disproportionate harm to himself.[105]

6. In cases in which the seduced woman absolved the seducer of all responsibility.[106]

7. In cases in which after the commission of *stuprum,* even when attended with the promise of marriage, there arose some diriment impediment, or there intervened some circumstance which normally was considered a sufficient cause for a canonical separation.[107]

8. In cases of *stuprum* committed with a woman seduced as a virgin and attended with a false promise of marriage, the seducer was not obliged to marry the woman: a. if the woman could easily have detected the fraud, and, b. if the woman falsely claimed the status of a virgin for the time prior to the seduction.[108]

9. In cases in which *stuprum* in its strictest sense had been committed, as long as this fact remained secret, so that the vio-

---

[105] Pirhing, *op. cit.,* lib. V, tit. 16, n. 46; Reiffenstuel, *op. cit.,* lib. IV, tit. 1, n. 113; Schmalzgrueber, *op. cit.,* lib. V, tit. 16, n. 30; Ferraris, *Bibliotheca,* s.v. *stuprator, stuprum,* n. 10; Sanctus Alphonsus, *Theologia Moralis,* lib. III, n. 640; S.R.R., *Nullitatis Matrimonii,* 4 iun. 1927, coram R.P.D. Iulio Grazioli, Dec. XXV, nn. 3-4—*S.R.R. Dec.,* XIX (1927), 201-202. Saint Alphonsus (*loc. cit.*) considered as free from the obligation of contracting marriage also those who, under these circumstances, had been guilty of seduction upon a false promise of marriage.

[106] Pirhing, *op. cit.,* lib. V, tit. 16, n. 52; Schmalzgrueber, *op. cit.,* lib. V, tit. 16, n. 35; *et alii passim.*

[107] Pirhing, *op. cit.,* lib. V, tit. 16, n. 52; Schmalzgrueber, *op. cit.,* lib. V, tit. 16, n. 35.

[108] Pirhing, *op. cit.,* lib. V, tit. 16, n. 58; Reiffenstuel, *Jus Canonicum Universum,* lib. IV, tit. 1, n. 128; Sanctus Alphonsus, *op. cit.,* lib. III, n. 640. Saint Alphonsus (*loc. cit.*) included the case in which the woman did not claim to be a virgin, but the man mistakenly thought that she was. Pirhing (*ibidem,* n. 60 [59]) and Reiffenstuel (*loc. cit.*) had presented the same doctrine which Saint Alphonsus later proposed, but they added the specific note that the man was still bound to pay all appropriate damages. They also felt that the seducer was bound to marry the woman if her reputation had suffered to such an extent that she lacked opportunity of entering marriage with a man of her own station in life.

lated virgin was not impeded from marrying a man of her own station. In such cases the seducer (at least in conscience and prior to a condemnatory sentence) was not bound to the rendering of any satisfaction.[109]

The Rota, in adjudicating a marriage which took place (before the Code) on April 16, 1913, expressed this principle in the following terms:

> Ubi illud animadvertendum restitutionis obligationem ex revelatione stupri oriri, ideoque non urgere, quamdiu stuprum latet; quod si innotuerit, inquirendum esse cuius culpa id factum sit. Nam, uti tradit idem E. mus D'Annibale, (*Summula Theologiae Moralis,* III, 45) "si mulieris, sibi imputet, licet vi superata fuerit, nisi illud prodiderit in iudicio iniuriae persequendae causa; sin viri, is damnum sarciet, licet mulier copiam sui fecerit; si neutrius, cum commiscuit, rem sui periculi fecit vir, si oppressit invitam; mulier, si haec copiam sui fecit; atque ideo in priori casu restitutio competit, in posteriori cessat."[110]

§ 5. *Circumstances in Which the Seducer Was Entitled to the Alternative Either of Marrying or of Endowing the Seduced Woman*

The Decretals of Gregory IX had provided literally that a seducer was bound to endow *and* to marry the virgin whom he had seduced: stuprans virginem tenetur eam dotare et ducere in uxorem. . . .[111] However, by force of universal custom this double obligation was supplanted with the alternative obligation either of *marrying or of endowing* the seduced virgin.[112]

---

[109] Schmalzgrueber, *op. cit.,* lib. V, tit. 16, n. 35; Sanctus Alphonsus, *op. cit.,* lib. III, n. 640.

[110] S.R.R., *Nullitatis Matrimonii,* 4 iun. 1927, coram R.P.D. Iulio Grazioli, Dec. XXV, nn. 3-4—*S.R.R. Dec.,* XIX (1927), 201-202.

[111] C. 1, X, *de adulteriis et stupro,* V, 16. Cf. *supra,* p. 00.

[112] Cf., e.g., S.C.C., *Calven. et Theanen., Matrimonii,* 18 dec. 1869—S.C.C., *Thesaurus,* CXXVIII, 624-625; S.C.C., *Melevitana, Sponsalium,* 8 maii 1886—S.C.C., *Thesaurus,* CXLV, 352, 354; S.R.R., *Nullitatis Matrimonii,* 9 iul. 1911, coram R.P.D. Ioanne Prior, Dec. XXII, n. 3—*S.R.R. Dec.,* III (1911), 238, where reference is made to this universal custom and opinion.

Thus, in the generality of cases a seducer could justly be coerced by threats of punishment only to the alternative either of marrying or of endowing the virgin whom he had seduced.[113] This general rule could become subject to modification through the intervention of unusual circumstances which had the effect of freeing the seducer from both obligations,[114] or, on the other hand of obliging him to marry the seduced virgin without the benefit of the alternative.[115] Aside from cases affected by these unusual circumstances, any coercion brought to bear upon a seducer to the neglect of offering him the alternative either of marrying or of endowing the seduced virgin was unjust *quoad substantiam.*[116]

§ 6. *Circumstances in Which the Seducer Was Obliged to Marry the Woman Without Benefit of Alternative*

The jurisprudence of the period from the Council of Trent to the Code of Canon Law specified that there were certain cases in which a seducer was not entitled to the alternative of endowing the seduced virgin. Such cases were generally those in which the injury (*iniuria*) done to the woman could adequately be repaired only in consequence of marriage. Four cases were generally cited as exemplifying this principle:

1. Cases in which the seducer made a sincere promise to a virgin that he would marry her on the condition that she consent to the loss of her corporal virginity prior to the marriage.[117]

---

[113] The justice of the coercion could, however, be perverted either *quoad substantiam* or *quoad modum* through a violation of the rules expressed *supra*, pp. 84-86, notes 77-85.

[114] Cf. *supra*, pp. 89-92, notes 99-110.

[115] Cf. *infra*, pp. 93-95, notes 117-124.

[116] Barbosa, *Collectanea in Ius Pontificium*, lib. V, tit. 16, cap. 1, n. 7; Ferraris, *Bibliotheca*, s.v. *stuprator, stuprum*, n. 6; S.C.C., *Calven. et Theanen., Matrimonii*, 18 dec. 1869—S.C.C., *Thesaurus*, CXXVIII, 624-625; S.R.R., *Nullitatis Matrimonii*, 28 ian. 1918, coram R.mo P.D. Gulielmo Sebastianelli, Decano, Dec. II, n. 10—*S.R.R. Dec.*, X (1918), 18; S.R.R., *Nullitatis Matrimonii*, 4 iun. 1927, coram R.P.D. Iulio Grazioli, Dec. XXV, nn. 3-4—*S.R.R. Dec.*, XIX (1927), 201-202.

[117] Pirhing, *Jus Canonicum*, lib. V, tit. 16, n. 52; Reiffenstuel, *Jus Canonicum Universum*, lib. IV, tit. 1, nn. 67, 125; Schmalzgrueber, *Jus Ecclesiasticum Universum*, lib. V, tit. 16, n. 30; Ferraris, *Bibliotheca*, s.v. *stuprator*,

2. In general, the authors maintained the same strict opinion in cases in which the seducer's promise to marry was insincere. In instances of an insincere promise to marry, however, they absolved the culprit from the obligation to marry the seduced woman: a. if the seduced woman could easily have detected the falseness of the promise to marry her, or, b. if the seduced woman was also guilty of fraud before the seduction by claiming to be a virgin, when in fact she had previously lost her corporal virginity.[118]

Schmalzgrueber was inclined to mitigate this somewhat. He taught that the seducer, at least in conscience and prior to a sentence passed in court, was held only to make satisfactory reparation when he had made an insincere promise of marriage.[119]

When the seducer made a false promise of marriage in view of mistakenly thinking that the woman was a virgin, though she had not in fact asserted that she was, Pirhing[120] and Reiffenstuel[121] held that the seducer was bound only to damages, except in instances in which the woman suffered such a loss of reputation as to make marriage with a person of her station an impossibility. In this latter case the seducer was bound to marry her.

3. Cases of seduction in which the seducer did not make any promise of marriage, but also was unable to make restitution by way of endowment.[122]

4. Cases of seduction in which the seducer was brought before a secular judge who, acting *within the provisions of the secular law*

---

stuprum, n. 11; Sanctus Alphonsus, *Theologia Moralis,* lib. III, n. 640; S.R.R., *Nullitatis Matrimonii,* 9 iul. 1911, coram R.P.D. Ioanne Prior, Dec. XXII, n. 4—*S.R.R. Dec.,* III (1911), 238-239; S.R.R., *Nullitatis Matrimonii,* 28 ian. 1918, coram R.mo P.D. Gulielmo Sebastianelli, Decano, Dec. II, n. 10—*S.R.R. Dec.,* X (1918), 17.

[118] Pirhing, *Jus Canonicum,* lib. V, tit. 16, n. 58; Reiffenstuel, *Jus Canonicum Universum,* lib. IV, tit. 1, n. 128; Sanctus Alphonsus, *Theologia Moralis,* lib. III, n. 640.

[119] *Jus Ecclesiasticum Universum,* lib. V, tit. 16, n. 30. Cf. also Reiffenstuel, *op. cit.,* lib. V, tit. 16, n. 26.

[120] *Op. cit.,* lib. II, tit. 16, n. 60 (59).

[121] *Op. cit.,* lib. IV, tit. 1, n. 115.

[122] Ferraris, *Bibliotheca,* s.v. *stuprator, stuprum,* n. 9; S.R.R., *Nullitatis Matrimonii,* 9 iul. 1911, coram R.P.D. Ioanne Prior, Dec. XXII, n. 7—*S.R.R. Dec.,* III (1911), 240-241; S.R.R., *Nullitatis Matrimonii,* 4 iun. 1927, coram R.P.D. Iulio Grazioli, Dec. XXV, nn. 3-4—*S.R.R. Dec.,* XIX (1927), 201-202.

to which he was subject, bound the seducer simply to marry the seduced woman or to go to prison.[123]

It must be kept constantly in mind, however, that all of these cases were subject to the limitations explained above.[124]

In a matter so complicated it is not surprising to find that no single author covered every aspect of the problem. Differences of opinion also made the solution of actual cases a very difficult responsibility. It is not surprising, therefore, to find Saint Alphonsus recommending that individual bishops declare invalid all promises of marriage when they were made with the condition that the woman consent to premarital relations. The text is of sufficient importance to be quoted verbatim:

> Hic obiter adnotare juvat cum Continuatore Tournely, valde utile fore, ad . . . flagitia vitanda, quod promissiones matrimonii ad obtinendam deflorationem, etiam forte juramento firmatae, invalidae declarentur ab episcopis. . . .[125]

ARTICLE VI. THE SOURCE OF THE INVALIDATING EFFECTS OF FEAR

The question of whether the invalidating effects of conditional force or of grave fear derive, antecedently to any positive legislation, from the natural law, or merely from the positive law, continued in dispute throughout this period. There was a slight trend, however, in favor of the positive law theory.

Rebello,[126] Gonzalez-Tellez,[127] Reiffenstuel,[128] Ferraris[129] and

---

[123] D'Annibale, *Summula Theologiae Moralis,* III, n. 445; Gasparri, *De Matrimonio,* II, n. 949; S.R.R., *Nullitatis Matrimonii,* 9 iul. 1911, coram R.P.D. Ioanne Prior, Dec. XXII, n. 5—*S.R.R. Dec.,* III (1911), 239-240.

[124] Cf. *supra,* p. 85, notes 78-82; pp. 90-91, notes 102-109.

[125] *Theologia Moralis,* lib. III, n. 641. The Code of Canon Law seems to have done precisely this in canon 1017. This point will be considered in the commentary upon canon 1087. Here it will be sufficient to note that, if the Code has removed the right to judicial action for marriage in cases of seduction in which there has been a specific promise of marriage, *a fortiori* the right to such action has also been removed in cases of seduction in which there has been no promise of marriage.

[126] *De Obligationibus Iustitiae,* lib. II, q. XI, sect. 1, n. 8.

[127] *Commentaria Perpetua,* lib. IV, tit. 1, cap. 15, n. 5.

[128] *Jus Canonicum Universum,* lib. I, tit. 40, n. 53.

[129] *Bibliotheca,* s.v. *Matrimonium,* art. V, n. 123.

Wernz[130] preferred the natural law theory, while Sanchez,[131] Laymann,[132] Barbosa,[133] De Lugo,[134] Pirhing,[135] Schmalzgrueber[136] and Gasparri[137] supported the positive law theory.

The principal arguments for either theory can be summarized as follows:

NATURAL LAW THEORY: The Decretal Law on coercion is cast in the form of a mere declaration of nullity and not in the form of an invalidating law. The invalidating effects of coercion are therefore presumed to have existed prior to the declaration reported in the law.

Whatever is the result of violence is not permanent, whereas marriage is permanent of its very nature.

Violence is opposed to the primary end of marriage, which is the procreation of children, and to the secondary end of marriage, which is the mutual assistance of husband and wife.

Every transfer of dominion must be completely free.

The natural law is opposed to the injury (*iniuria*) of others. This injury exists in conditional violence and grave fear.

If conditional violence or grave fear did not invalidate marriage in virtue of the natural law, then the marriages of infidels contracted under such conditions would be valid.

POSITIVE LAW THEORY: Just fear and fear from within weaken the act of the will just as much as unjust fear and fear from an extrinsic agent, yet just fear and fear from within do not invalidate marriage. Consequently neither just nor unjust fear, neither fear from within nor fear from without, invalidates marriage in virtue of the natural law, for, if it did, the invalidity would necessarily result in all cases.

Nothing is more opposed to the freedom of consent than deceit, fraud and error. Yet deceit, fraud and error (except *error per-*

---

130 *Ius Decretalium,* tom. IV, n. 265, in note.

131 *De Sancto Matrimonii Sacramento,* lib. IV, disp. XIV, n. 1.

132 *Theologia Moralis,* lib. V, tract. X, pars I, cap. 1, n. 1.

133 *Collectanea in Ius Pontificium,* lib. IV, tit. 1, cap. 28, n. 3.

134 *De Iustitia et Iure,* disp. XXII, sect. VII, nn. 115-120.

135 *Jus Canonicum,* lib. I, tit. 40, n. 23.

136 *Jus Ecclesiasticum Universum,* lib. IV, tit. 1, nn. 406-407.

137 *De Matrimonii,* II, n. 935.

sonae and *error conditionis*) do not invalidate marriage. If deceit, fraud and error do not invalidate marriage in virtue of the natural law, then neither does conditional force or grave fear.

That which is the result of absolute force is not permanent, as indeed the natural law theory contends, but it does not follow that everything which is the result of conditional force or of grave fear is likewise not permanent. In actions which are placed under conditional force or grave fear the victim makes a true act of the will (*voluntarium simpliciter, involuntarium secundum quid*) by which he transfers rights and assumes the obligations native to the contract which he enters.

Conditional force or grave fear is no more opposed to the primary end of marriage than is deceit, fraud or error. Furthermore, since only unjustly inflicted fear invalidates marriage, the victim of a just fear, in realizing that his rights are not violated by the infliction of the fear, is apt to be strengthened and comforted in mind and will in order to carry out the obligations inherent in the contract of marriage.

There is no transfer of dominion in the face of absolute force, but dominion is transferred in the face of conditional force or grave fear, though the victim of the fear has the right to demand the *restitutio in integrum.*

It is true that the natural law is opposed to the injury of others. On this basis the natural law provides the authority for the human legislator to declare invalid such marriages as are the result of conditional force or grave fear. It does not follow, however, that marriages which are the result of conditional force or grave fear are invalid in virtue of the natural law. It may be conceded that such marriages are *illicit* in virtue of the natural law, which is quite a different thing.

As to the argument of the natural law theory based upon the lack of the usual form of a positive legal enactment in the Decretals, it must be observed that the legislator could have given such a law in oral form, or the positive legislation in the matter could have been the result of custom. In the case of disparity of cult there was no law in the form of positive legislation in the Decretals, and yet all admit that the invalidating effects of this impediment derive only from the positive law.

As to the marriages of infidels, it simply follows that they are subject to the laws of the secular jurisdiction. If the secular jurisdiction to which they are subject has enacted laws invalidating marriages entered into under conditions of conditional force or grave fear, such marriages are invalid. If the secular jurisdiction has not enacted any such laws, then the marriages of infidels entered into under circumstances of conditional force or grave fear are valid.

PART TWO

Canonical Commentary

CHAPTER VIII

Commentary on Canon 1087: the Iniuste Incussus and Other Special Points

Article I. The Right to Matrimonial Liberty and the *Ratio Canonica* of Canon 1087

By his very nature man is free. He has been given the capacity of self-determination by the Creator. Certain limitations are placed upon his personal freedom by the law of God, both natural and positive; certain limitations can also justly be put upon him by the human law of the Church and of the State. With the exception of these restrictions, man has the inherent right to determine his own activity. "Personae privatae sunt, qua tales, in sua mutua relatione aequaliter inviolabiles. . . ."[1] This is true in a special way in the matter of marriage which, according to Saint Thomas, is, in a certain sense, a perpetual servitude, *quaedam servitus perpetua.*[2] Man, therefore, is free to marry.[3] He is also free not to marry, and, if he does wish to marry, to marry the person of his choice. Canon 1087 of the Code of Canon Law was designed to protect these two latter aspects of matrimonial liberty.

An examination of the history of the Canon Law on force and fear in marriage shows clearly that the chief aim of the Church in ruling against matrimonial coercion has always been to protect the full freedom of matrimonial consent.[4] The Church also wished to preclude the unhappy effects which were usually consequent

---

[1] Arthurus Vermeersch, *Theologia Moralis, Principia, Responsa, Consilia* (3. ed., 4 vols., Romae: Pont. Università Gregoriana, Vol. I, 1933; Vol. II, 1937; Vol. III, after 1935; Vol. IV, 1933), II, n. 548 (hereafter cited *Theologia Moralis*).

[2] *Summa Theologica, Supp.* III, q. 47, a. 1.

[3] Canon 1035. "Omnes possunt matrimonium contrahere, qui iure non prohibentur."

[4] Cf. *supra:* Gratian, p. 9, note 1; the Decretals, p. 16, note 3; Saint Thomas, p. 57, note 29; Rebello, p. 68, note 17.

upon marriages which were the result of coercion.[5] Implicit in these two purposes was the desire of the legislator to protect the contracting parties from the injustice usually inherent in coercion to marry. After the time of Sanchez, the authors began to emphasize this point.[6] Gasparri takes all three of these motives into consideration and correctly summarizes the *ratio canonica* of canon 1087: *quia minuit consensum . . . infelices exitus . . . timendi sunt, et iniuria . . . infertur.*[7]

Fedele fails to give the proper emphasis to the motive of protecting matrimonial liberty when he insists that the purpose of the legislator was almost exclusively the suppression of the sin of injustice committed by the person who forces another to marry.[8]

It must be admitted that certain statements of authors and of decisions of the Rota seem to favor the extreme position of Fedele. For example:

> SANGMEISTER: . . . the reason for invalidating such a marriage is the injustice suffered by the innocent party.[9]

> VERMEERSCH-CREUSEN: . . . leges contrahentem ab iniustitia vindicare intendebant; non patitur autem in-

---

[5] Cf. *supra:* Gratian, p. 9, note 2; the Decretals, p. 17, note 5.

[6] Cf. *supra,* pp. 68-71, notes 18-30.

[7] *De Matrimonio* (ed. 1932 which is used exclusively in future references), II, n. 837. Cf. also Matthaeus Conte a Coronata, *De Sacramentis* (3 vols., Taurini-Romae: Domus Editorialis Marietti, Vol. I, 1943; Vol. II, 1945; Vol. III, 1946), III, p. 642, n. 479; A. C. Jemolo, *Il Matrimonio nel Diritto Canonico* (Milano: Casa Editrice Dottor Francesco Vallardi, 1941), p. 228, n. 119; H. Noldin-A. Schmitt, *Summa Theologiae Moralis* (3 vols., Oeniponte-Lipsiae: Sumptibus et Typis Feliciani Rauch, Vol. I, 27. ed., 1940; Vol. II, 27. ed., 1941; Vol. III, 26. ed., 1941), III, n. 633; S.R.R., *Transilvanien., Nullitatis Matrimonii,* 27 mart. 1931, coram R.P.D. Iulio Grazioli, Dec. XIII, n. 4—*S.R.R. Dec.,* XXXIII (1931), 103.

[8] ". . . appare in modo manifesto che la nullità del matrimonio celebrato *ex metu* è da considerare più come una sanzione contro la *iniuria,* l'atto illecito, la nequita, il *peccatum,* del violentatore che non come un mezzo per tutelare la integrità e spontaneità del volere del violentato."—Pio Fedele, *Contributi alla Teoria Canonistica dei Vizi del Consenso Matrimoniale* (Firenze: Casa Editrice del Dottore Carlo Cya, 1940), pp. 57-58 (hereafter cited *Vizi del Consenso Matrimoniale*).

[9] *Force and Fear,* p. 129.

> iustitiam *in contrahendo* qui rem eligit ad quam ab altera parte non cogitur. . . .[10]
>
> MERKELBACH: . . . invalidat . . . quia consensus est fructus iniustitiae. . . .[11]
>
> ROTA: Nonnisi autem ad reparandam hanc iniuriam, cui reparandae attenta matrimonii indissolubilitate nulla alia patebat via, induxit Ecclesia metus impedimentum.[12]

However, one must also keep in mind: 1. that the specific injustice which the Church proposed to suppress was the unwarranted reduction of the liberty of the *contracting party,* and 2. that the law thus favored the *contracting party* rather than proposed punishment for the person using the coercion.[13]

Therefore, while it is true that only *metus iniuste incussus* invalidates marriage, and while it is necessary to grasp the specific nature and importance of the injustice of matrimonial coercion, it does not follow that the chief aim of the Church in legislating against force and fear in marriage was simply that of invoking a sanction *against the coercer.* The point is one that can have an

---

[10] A. Vermeersch-J. Creusen, *Epitome Iuris Canonici* (6. ed., 3 vols., Vol. II, Mechliniae-Romae: H. Dessain, 1940), II, p. 264, n. 376 (hereafter cited *Epitome*).

[11] Benedictus Henricus Merkelbach, *Summa Theologiae Moralis* (3. ed., 3 vols., Parisiis: Typis Desclée de Brouwer et Soc., Vols. I-II, 1938; Vol. III, 1939), III, n. 806 (hereafter cited *Theologia Moralis*).

[12] S.R.R., *Nullitatis Matrimonii,* 6 iul. 1936, coram Exc.mo R.P. Iulio Grazioli, Decano, Dec. XLVIII, n. 4—*S.R.R. Dec.,* XXVIII (1936), 452.

[13] "Hic enim metus futurae indignationis tantus esse potest, ut quamlibet voluntatem passi, iure suo utendi seu iuste resistendi, cohibeat vel opprimat: et in hoc proprie consistit iniustitia, per quam quis dicere cogatur se amare quam odit."—S.R.R., *Romana, Nullitatis Matrimonii,* 11 nov. 1925, coram R.P.D. Ubaldo Mannucci, Dec. LXV, n. 2—*S.R.R. Dec.,* XVII (1925), 363; "Siquidem in favorem metum passi hoc impedimentum induxit Ecclesia ad iniuriam eidem inlatam reparandam et ad damna praecavenda, quae ex invitis solent nuptiis provenire."—S.R.R., *Transilvanien., Nullitatis Matrimonii,* 27 mart. 1931, coram R.P.D. Iulio Grazioli, Dec. XIII, n. 4—*S.R.R. Dec.,* XXIII (1931), 103; "Revera ad iniuriam reparandam ei, cui metus inlatus est, Ecclesia impedimentum induxit vis et metus. . . ."—S.R.R., *Panormitana, Nullitatis Matrimonii,* 11 maii 1931, coram R.P.D. Iulio Grazioli, Dec. XXIII, n. 5—*S.R.R. Dec.,* XXIII (1931), 181.

important bearing upon the interpretation of canon 1087 as will be seen in Article VII of this Chapter.

ARTICLE II. FORCE AND FEAR: CONCEPTS AND DIVISIONS

Canon 1087 reads as follows:

> § 1. *Invalidum quoque est matrimonium initum ob vim vel metum gravem ab extrinseco et iniuste incussum, a quo ut quis se liberet, eligere cogatur matrimonium.*
>
> § 2. *Nullus alius metus, etiamsi det causam contractui, matrimonii nullitatem secumfert.*

Bouscaren-Ellis, as a part of their commentary, translate this canon in the following manner:

> § 1. Likewise invalid is a marriage entered into through force or grave fear unjustly inspired from without, such that in order to escape from it a party is compelled to choose marriage.
>
> § 2. No other fear, even if it furnish the cause for the contract, entails the nullity of marriage.[14]

Since the publication of the Code of Canon Law little has been written about the concepts and divisions of force and fear that had not already been thoroughly discussed for centuries.[15]

The fundamental consideration in both *force* and *fear* is that they are violations of and infringements upon the self-determination of the human being. *Force* necessarily derives from outside its victim; *fear* can derive from outside or from within the victim. However, canon 1087 considers only that fear which derives from a human agent outside the victim.

---

[14] T. Lincoln Bouscaren-Adam C. Ellis, *Canon Law, a Text and Commentary* (2nd printing, Milwaukee: Bruce Publishing Co., 1948), p. 507 (hereafter cited *Commentary*).

[15] Cf. *supra:* Roman Law, pp. 4-5, notes 7-12; canonical science before the Council of Trent, pp. 28-30, notes 1-8; Saint Thomas, pp. 51-52, notes 1-10; Dominicus Soto, pp. 58-59, notes 2-7; canonical science from the Council of Trent to the Code of Canon Law, pp. 65-68, notes 1-16.

In *force* and in *fear* there are three factors to be considered: 1. the *agent* who moves counter to the self-determination of the victim; 2. the *effect* of this action upon the victim, and 3. the *means* used to produce this effect. In both *force* and *fear* the agent, at least as far as Canon Law is concerned, is necessarily a human being.

In *force:* 1. the *effect* is simply the corporal propulsion of the victim. The movement of the agent is not directed towards the influencing of the will of the victim, but only towards his external actions; 2. the *means* used by the agent are physical contact with the victim. If these means are so superior to the strength of the victim that they cannot be resisted, the force is called *physical force* or *absolute force* (*vis physica seu absoluta*). If, on the other hand, the means used by the agent are not of such superior strength as to defy resistance by the victim, the force is called *moral force* or *conditional force* (*vis moralis seu conditionalis seu causativa*). If the means used by the agent are not of such superior strength as to defy resistance, at each given moment of physical contact the will of the victim is faced with the necessity of deciding whether to resist or to cede to violence. Thus, moral or conditional force is invariably linked to *an effect in the will* of the victim. This effect is a certain trepidation of mind, or, rather, of the will, by which the victim naturally recoils from the present evil and from its continuation.

The term *force,* therefore, looks primarily to the *means* used by the agent to produce a result counter to a self determined action by the victim. Only physical or absolute force is *force* in the full and proper sense of the term. Moral or conditional force is called *force* rather by analogy.

In *fear:* 1. the *effect* upon the victim is the primary consideration. This effect is the trepidation of the will of the victim which recoils from the means which an adverse agent thrusts upon it; 2. this *means* is some *harm* or *evil* to be worked upon the victim if he does not make an act of the will which will cause the agent to withdraw the threatened harm or evil. The ultimate *effect* of fear, therefore, is an *act of the will* of the victim which he would not have made except for the impending harm or evil proposed by the agent. Ordinarily, therefore, fear does not destroy the self determination of the victim, but simply reduces its spontaneity.

If, however, the prospects of impending harm or evil are so great as to destroy the self-determination of the victim, the effect becomes a mere physical response, which can be called *fear* only by analogy.

Fear, therefore, can be divided into *conditional fear* (*metus conditionalis*) which is fear in the proper sense of the term, and *absolute fear,* which is called *fear* only by analogy. The *effect* of fear properly so called is a *voluntary act* by the victim which *would not* have been placed except for the fear. This effect, therefore, is called *voluntarium simpliciter sed involuntarium secundum quid.*

Fear has recently been defined by Allers as: "The emotional response to the awareness of a great danger the nature of which is known, even if imperfectly, and which is conceived as imminent and, at the same time, as not absolutely unavoidable."[16]

A comparison of physical or absolute force with absolute fear shows that their ultimate effect is the same: an act which is an *involutarium simpliciter.*

A comparison of fear in the strict sense of the term with moral or conditional force shows the following: in fear the result is an act which is a *voluntarium simpliciter* but an *involuntarium secundum quid;* in conditional force the ultimate effect is the same. Fear differs from conditional force in that fear operates through the medium of a harm or evil which is not physical contact; conditional force operates through the medium of physical contact. By extension the term force is applied to the harm or the evil which is the means of producing the fear. Thus *force* (the harm or evil in fear; the physical contact in conditional force) is the cause of *fear* (the trepidation of the will). In this sense the terms are correlative, that is, they are related to each other as cause and effect. Viewed in consideration of their ultimate effect (a *voluntarium simpliciter* but an *involuntarium secundum quid*) they are identical, and thus the terms *force* and *fear* can be used as synonyms.

[16] Rudolph Allers, "Some Medico-Psychological Remarks on Canons 1068, 1081, and 1087," *The Jurist* (Washington, D. C., 1941—), IV (1944), 351-380 and in particular, 372.

There are no serious disputes among the authors concerning the foregoing definitions and distinctions, though they have expressed themselves with varying degrees of clarity and with minor differences.[17]

Since under one aspect the terms force and fear refer to *cause* and *effect* (which are therefore distinct from each other), and under another aspect to an identical ultimate effect, it is evident that too much emphasis should not be placed upon the mere use of a conjunctive or a disjunctive as the basis of a distinctive interpretation of force-fear terminology. The terms *vis-metus* can be used disjunctively *vis vel metus,* as in canon 1087, and one could argue that the *vel* sets the *metus* off in distinction from *vis physica,* with which it is not synonymous. However, the *vel* could also be used to distinguish *vis* from *metus* as cause is distinguished from effect.

---

[17] Cf., e.g., Stephanus Sipos, *Enchiridion Iuris Canonici* (3. ed., Pécs: ex Typographia "Haladás R.T.," 1936), p. 602 (hereafter cited *Enchiridion*): "Opponitur libertati vis et metus, qui termini sunt correlativi, vis enim est causa metus; quapropter quae de uno dicuntur, valent etiam de altero." *Ibidem,* p. 98: "*Metus* (vel vis moralis) non corpus, sed animum flectit. . . . Repraesentatio periculi, ut illud evitetur, movet voluntatem ad aliquid eligendum, quod alias non elegisset. Metus ergo non excludit (saltem regulariter) deliberationem et voluntatem, sed restringit electionem. Quandoque tamen metus penitus tollit usum rationis et tunc actus pro infectis habendi sunt aeque ac sub influxu vis." Cf. also: Gasparri, *De Matrimonio,* II, n. 832; G. Payen, *De Matrimonio in Missionibus ac Potissimum in Sinis, Tractatus Practicus et Casus* (2. ed., 3 vols., Zi-ka-wei: in Typographia T'ou-sè-wè, 1935-1936), II, n. 1678 (hereafter cited *De Matrimonio*); Felix M. Cappello, *Tractatus Canonico-Moralis de Sacramentis* (5 vols., Augustae Taurinorum-Romae: Domus Editorialis Marietti), Vol. V (5. ed., *De Matrimonio,* 1947), p. 587, n. 605 (hereafter cited *De Sacramentis,* V); Franciscus Xav. Wernz-Petrus Vidal, *Ius Canonicum* (7 vols. in 8, Romae: apud aedes Universitatis Gregorianae), Vol. V (*Ius Matrimoniale,* 3. ed., a Philippo Aguirre recognita, 1946), nn. 495-496 (hereafter cited *Ius Canonicum,* V); Ioannes Chelodi, *Ius Canonicum de Matrimonio* (5. ed., recognita et aucta a Pio Ciprotti, Vicenza: Società Anonima Tipografica Editrice, 1947), p. 142, n. 118 (hereafter cited Chelodi-Ciprotti, *De Matrimonio*); Coronata, *De Sacramentis,* III, pp. 627-630, nn. 466-468; Bouscaren-Ellis, *Commentary,* p. 507; Dossetti, *La Violenza nel Matrimonio,* pp. 86-90; Vermeersch, *Theologia Moralis,* III, n. 735; Noldin-Schmitt, *Summa Theologiae Moralis,* III, n. 633; Merkelbach, *Theologia Moralis,* III, n. 806; Eduardus F. Regatillo, *Ius Sacramentarium* (2 vols., Santander: Sal Terrae, 1945-1946), II, pp. 324-326, nn. 495-496.

Consequently, the argument is not cogent, and some other norm will have to be used to determine the meaning of the term *vis* in canon 1087. This is done in the following article in which the scope of canon 1087 is discussed.

ARTICLE III. THE SCOPE OF CANON 1087

The question is sometimes raised: does canon 1087 embrace *vis absoluta,* or is it limited to a consideration of *vis moralis* and *metus?* Sangmeister is of the opinion that "there seems to be no sound basis for asserting that the case of absolute violence is not contemplated by canon 1087."[18] The majority of authors, however, hold that canon 1087 treats only of *vis moralis,* which in its ultimate effect is identified with *metus.*[19] The entire history of the canonical treatment of force-fear in marriage definitely favors the opinion of the majority.[20] The phraseology *ob vim vel metus* as used in canon 1087 does not contradict this interpretation, since the disjunctive *vel* could well have been used for distinguishing *vis moralis* from *metus* as cause from effect without any denial of their identity as far as the ultimate result is concerned. Consequently, the opinion which holds that canon 1087 treats only of moral or conditional force is the more probable. The dispute has little practical value, however, for, as Coronata observes: "quidquid est de acceptione vocis *vis* in hoc canone, quod dicitur de vi morali valet a fortiori de vi absoluta cui resisti nequit."[21] Any marriage that might be the result of physical force would of course

---

[18] *Force and Fear,* p. 83.

[19] Cf., e.g., Al. De Smet, *Tractatus Theologico-Canonicus de Sponsalibus et Matrimonio* (4. ed., inde a Codice altera, Brugis: Car. Beyaert, 1927), p. 468, n. 543 (hereafter cited *De Sponsalibus et Matrimonio*); Sipos, Enchiridion, p. 602, note 7; Payen, *De Matrimonio,* II, n. 1678; Wernz-Vidal, *Ius Canonicum,* V, n. 496; Chelodi-Ciprotti, *De Matrimonio,* p. 142, n. 118; Jemolo, *Il Matrimonio del Diritto Canonico,* p. 218, n. 115; Vermeersch-Creusen, *Epitome,* II, p. 263, n. 375; Dossetti, *La Violenza nel Matrimonio,* p. 100, n. 29; Noldin-Schmitt, *Summa Theologiae Moralis,* III, n. 633.

[20] Cf. *supra:* canonical science before the Council of Trent, p. 29, note 7; Saint Thomas, p. 52, note 9; Dominicus Soto, p. 58, note 5; canonical science from the Council of Trent to the Code of Canon Law, pp. 66-67, notes 1-15.

[21] *De Sacramentis,* III, p. 628, n. 466.

be invalid in virtue of the natural law as well as in virtue of canon 1081, § 1, and canon 103, § 1.

Gasparri[22] and Coronata[23] make an interesting observation when they observe that if a marriage ceremony were caused by dint of absolute violence, and if the helpless victim, at the proper moment, gave an internal consent to the marriage, the marriage would still be invalid, *quia cum vis physica interveniat, signum externum consensus non manifestat internum consensum.*[24]

The remainder of this dissertation will concern itself solely with conditional force and/or fear.

ARTICLE IV. THE RELATIONSHIP OF CANON 1087 TO THE PRE-CODE LAW

Canon 6 gives the relationship between the Code and the pre-Code law:

> *Codex vigentem huc usque disciplinam plerumque retinet, licet opportunas immutationes afferat. Itaque:*
> 1°. *Leges quaelibet . . . praescriptis huius Codicis oppositae, abrogantur, nisi de particularibus legibus aliud expresse caveatur;*
> 2°. *Canones qui ius vetus ex integro referunt, ex veteris iuris auctoritate, atque ideo ex receptis apud probatos auctores interpretationibus, sunt aestimandi;*
> 3°. *Canones qui ex parte tantum cum veteri iure congruunt, qua congruunt, ex iure antiquo aestimandi sunt; qua discrepant, sunt ex sua ipsorum sententia diiudicandi;*
> 4°. *In dubio num aliquod canonum praescriptum cum veteri iure discrepet, a veteri iure non est recedendum;*
> . . . etc.

That the Code changed certain laws which had a direct *bearing* upon the law on force-fear in marriage is beyond dispute. Before the Code coercion could be used for effecting a marriage if one

[22] *De Matrimonio,* II, n. 832.
[23] *De Sacramentis,* III, pp. 627-628, n. 466.
[24] Coronata, *op. cit., loc. cit.*

of the parties wished to break the contract of espousals.[25] Instead of this ruling the Code substituted canon 1017, § 3:

> *At ex matrimonii promissione, licet valida sit nec ulla iusta causa ab eadem implenda excuset, non datur actio ad petendam matrimonii celebrationem; datur tamen ad reparationem damnorum, si qua debeatur.*

Before the Code, the law specifically provided for coercive measures in instances of the crime of seduction.[26] For this ruling the Code substituted canon 2357, § 1:

> *Laici legitime damnati ob delicta contra sextum cum minoribus infra aetatem sexdecim annorum commissa, vel ob stuprum . . . ipso facto infames sunt, praeter alias poenas quas Ordinarius infligendas iudicaverit.*

Concerning the law on force-fear itself, canon 1087, far from being a mere restatement of the Decretal Law,[27] is rather a summary of the points treated in the pre-Code jurisprudence.[28] The question, therefore, of the relationship of canon 1087 to the pre-Code discipline is rather a question of the relationship of the canon to the pre-Code jurisprudence.

In the pre-Code jurisprudence there were points of perfect agreement, especially in matters concerning the gravity and the extrinsic origin of the fear in question. However, there were also points of disagreement.

1. The majority opinion seemed to be that a *metus iniustus quoad modum tantum* invalidated marriage;[29] however, a strong minority opinion cast serious doubt upon this and held that only a *metus iniustus quoad substantiam* invalidated marriage.[30]

---

[25] Cf. *supra:* the Decretals, p. 22, note 36; canonical science before the Council of Trent, pp. 36-38, notes 40-50; canonical science from the Council of Trent to the Code of Canon Law, p. 84, note 76.

[26] Cf. *supra:* the Decretals, pp. 24-25, notes 44-45; canonical science before the Council of Trent, pp. 31-36; canonical science from the Council of Trent to the Code of Canon Law, pp. 86-95, notes 86-125.

[27] Cf. *supra,* p. 17, note 5.

[28] Cf. the summary statements of authors, *supra,* pp. 68-71, notes 17-30.

[29] Cf. *supra,* p. 81, note 65.

[30] Cf. *supra,* p. 81, note 66.

2. The majority opinion taught that only the fear which was inflicted for the specific purpose of causing a marriage (*metus directe incussus; metus consultus*) invalidated the marriage;[31] a strong minority held that fear inflicted for some other purpose (*indirecte incussus*) could also invalidate marriage.[32]

The question concerning these two disputes, therefore, will be: with which side does canon 1087 agree? There is also the possibility that the canon follows a middle course or makes some altogether new departure.

Before examining particular points one may with interest note the general comparisons which the Rota has made between canon 1087 and the pre-Code law.

1. In adjudicating marriages which were contracted under the Code, the Rota has frequently remarked that the new law simply confirms the old: *praecedens ecclesiastica disciplina confirmatur.*[33]

2. At other times the statement is made that no substantial change has been made in the law: "Metus doctrinam namque quod attinet, novum ius substantialiter non innovavit."[34]

3. A statement difficult to understand in the light of the unformulated status of the pre-Code law is that the Code repeats the old law almost in the same words: *eisdem fere verbis refert.*[35]

4. A statement which seems to be much more precise observes that canon 1087 has introduced certain refinements into the law: *canon 1087 leviter expoliavit* (*anteriorem disciplinam*).[36]

5. Finally, the Rota recognized the possibility of the introduc-

---

[31] Cf. *supra*, pp. 71-72, notes 31-34.

[32] Cf. *supra*, p. 73, notes 35-40.

[33] S.R.R., *Katovicen., Nullitatus Matrimonii*, 3 maii 1930, coram R.P.D Francisco Morano, Dec. XXI, n. 2—*S.R.R. Dec.*, XXII (1930), 253. Cf. also, e.g., S.R.R., *Placentina, Nullitatis Matrimonii*, 28 iun. 1935, coram R.P.D. Andrea Jullien, Dec. XLV, n. 2—*S.R.R. Dec.*, XXVII (1935), 379; S.R.R., *Nullitatis Matrimonii*, 7 apr. 1937, coram R.P.D. Henrico Caiazzo, Dec. XXIV, n. 2—*S.R.R. Dec.*, XXIX (1937), 264.

[34] S.R.R., *Romana, Nullitatis Matrimonii*, 13 dec. 1935, coram R.P.D. Iulio Grazioli, Dec. LXXVIII, n. 2—*S.R.R. Dec.*, XXVII (1935), 655.

[35] S.R.R., *Romana, Nullitatis Matrimonii*, 15 mart. 1933, coram R.P.D. Stansilao Janasik, Dec. XVIII, n. 2—*S.R.R. Dec.*, XXV (1933), 143.

[36] S.R.R., *Romana, Nullitatis Matrimonii*, 9 nov. 1936, coram R.P.D. Alberto Canestri, Dec. LXIX, n. 2—*S.R.R. Dec.*, XXVIII (1936), 659.

tion of more notable changes by canon 1087 when, in adjudicating marriages which had been contracted prior to the date on which the Code went into effect, it noted that these were to be judged under the terms of the pre-Code law. "Cum matrimonium impugnatum anno 1910 celebratum fuerit, recurrendum est ad Ius Decretalium."[37]

From this it appears that the Rota decisions are not in complete harmony regarding the extent to which canon 1087 reflects the earlier law. This emphasizes the fact that for the interpreting of the canon particular attention must be paid to the wording *of the canon itself*. Canon 18 gives the rule of interpretation which must be applied in this most important aspect of the study of any canon:

> *Leges ecclesiasticae intelligendae sunt secundum propriam verborum significationem in textu et contextu consideratum: quae si dubia et obscura manserit, ad locos Codicis parallelos, si qui sint, ad legis finem ac circumstantias et ad mentem legislatoris est recurrendum.*

ARTICLE V. METUS INIUSTE INCUSSUS

§ 1. *Under the Law of the Code "Metus Iniustus Quoad Modum Tantum" Suffices to Invalidate Marriage*

In the summary statements of authors from the Council of Trent to the Code of Canon Law it has been seen that some authors did not consider injustice as an essential element of invalidating fear; most of them, in reference to the injustice that was postulated in fear in order that it invalidate marriage, used simply the phrase *iniuste incussus;* the later authors drew a distinction between *metus iniustus quoad modum* and *metus iniustus quoad substantiam* and began to insist that only the latter invalidated marriage.[38] These statements can be taken as typical of the pre-Code jurisprudence both as to content and as to the relative number of authors who took one of the three positions. From this it follows that the argument which contends that the phrase

---

[37] S.R.R., *Nullitatis Matrimonii,* 4 aug. 1932, coram R.P.D. Arcturo Wynen, Dec. XLII, n. 2—*S.R.R. Dec.,* XXIV (1932), 402, *et alibi passim.*

[38] Cf. *supra,* pp. 68-71, notes 17-30.

iniuste incussus in canon 1087 means *metus iniustus quoad modum* because it changes the pre-Code usage of the adjectival form *metus iniustus* into the adverbial form *iniuste incussus* rests on a weak historical basis.[39] The argument is good under the provisions of canon 18 when it considers the *propriam verborum significationem;* it is weak when it considers the words as a change from the pre-Code usage, unless the pre-Code usage be restricted to the period shortly before the publication of the Code.

The early commentators on the Code of Canon Law by and large admitted that the phrase *iniuste incussus* included fear which was unjust in the manner of its infliction as well as fear which was unjust in substance. Some, however, dissented. Sangmeister, writing in 1932, though he himself held the majority opinion, was forced to the conclusion: "It is evident, of course, that until a decisive interpretation of the Holy See clears away the doubt, no marriage can be declared null and void on the grounds of fear unjustly inflicted *quoad modum*."[40] In spite of Sangmeister's conclusion, it is certain that, given the first argument *ex propria verborum significatione,* the doubt can be removed for all practical purposes short of a decision by the Holy See if it is evident that the authors have come to an agreement and if their conclusions are confirmed by the practice of the Roman Tribunals.

Since 1932 the authors seem to have reached an agreement which is practically unanimous. While Payen in the 1935 edition of his work,[41] and Vermeersch-Creusen as late as 1940[42] simply stated that a marriage is *probabilius irritum* in consequence of fear which is unjust only in the manner of its infliction, the vast majority of authors no longer show any real hesitancy. Among others, the following authors hold that marriage is invalidated by *metus iniustus quoad modum tantum*: De Smet,[43] Sipos,[44]

[39] Cf. Sangmeister, *Force and Fear,* p. 123.

[40] *Force and Fear,* p. 125 and pp. 121-124.

[41] *De Matrimonio,* II, n. 1685.

[42] *Epitome,* II, p. 264, n. 376.

[43] *De Sponsalibus et Matrimonio,* p. 472, n. 538, note 5: *"modus iniustus videtur sufficere"* (in this and in the following notes on this point the authors are quoted directly if they use phraseology which, though only slightly, weakens their position, e.g., *videtur sufficere*).

[44] *Enchiridion,* p. 602, note 11: *"dicendum videtur metum etiam quoad modum tantum iniustum irritare. . . ."*

Cangardel,[45] Wernz-Vidal,[46] Chedlodi-Ciprotti,[47] Coronata,[48] Bouscaren-Ellis,[49] Merkelbach[50] and Regatillo.[51]

A careful examination of all the Rota decisions rendered since 1930 (published 1938) has not revealed any decision that requires *metus iniustus quoad substantiam.* On the other hand the Rota has consistently and explicitly ruled that *metus iniustus quoad modum tantum* is sufficient to invalidate marriage.[52]

With canon 18 as the norm of interpretation, the argument can be summarized as follows:

1. *Secundum propriam verborum significationem* the phrase

---

[45] Louis Cangardel, *Le Consentement des Epoux au Mariage* (Paris: Librairie du Recueil Sirey, 1934), p. 150.

[46] *Ius Canonicum,* V, n. 501, note 24.

[47] *De Matrimonio,* p. 144, n. 118.

[48] *De Sacramentis,* III, p. 635, n. 472: *ex doctrina hodie communiori sufficit. . . .*

[49] *Commentary,* p. 509.

[50] *Theologia Moralis,* III, n. 806.

[51] *Ius Sacramentarium,* II, p. 327, n. 497.

[52] S.R.R., *Nullitatis Matrimonii,* 3 dec. 1930, coram R.P.D., Arcturo Wynen, Dec. LVIII, n. 2—*S.R.R. Dec.,* XXII (1930), 641; S.R.R., *Katovicen., Nullitatis Matrimonii,* 8 aug. 1931, coram R.P.D. Francisco Morano, Dec. XLIV, n. 3—*S.R.R. Dec.,* XXIII (1931), 380; S.R.R., *Romana, Nullitatis Matrimonii,* 9 maii 1933, coram R.P.D. Iulio Grazioli, Dec. XXV, n. 4—*S.R.R. Dec.,* XXV (1933), 298; S.R.R., *Limburgen., Nullitatis Matrimonii,* 7 apr. 1934, coram R.P.D. Francisco Morano, Dec. XIV, n. 2—*S.R.R. Dec.,* XXVI (1934), 145; S.R.R., *Kielcen., Nullitatis Matrimonii,* 28 apr. 1934, coram R.P.D. Francisco Guglielmi, Dec. XXIV, n. 2—*S.R.R. Dec.,* XXVI (1934), 231; S.R.R., *Kielcen., Nullitatis Matrimonii,* 16 iul. 1935, coram R.P.D. Francisco Morano, Dec. LI, n. 2—*S.R.R. Dec.,* XXVII (1935), 434; S.R.R., *Belgraden., Nullitatis Matrimonii,* 2 maii 1936, coram R.P.D. Francisco Guglielmi, Dec. XXXI, n. 2—*S.R.R. Dec.,* XXVIII (1936), 286-287; S.R.R., *Nullitatis Matrimonii,* 24 mart. 1937, coram R.P.D. Andrea Jullien, Dec. XXI, n. 2—*S.R.R. Dec.,* XXIX (1937), 235; S.R.R., *Nullitatis Matrimonii,* 15 iun. 1937, coram R.P.D. Arcturo Wynen, Dec. XLII, n. 2—*S.R.R. Dec.,* XXIX (1937), 411; S.R.R., *Romana, Nullitatis Matrimonii,* 22 dec. 1937, coram R.P.D. Andrea Jullien, Dec. LXXIX, n. 2—*S.R.R. Dec.,* XXIX (1937), 783; S.R.R., *Mediolanen., Nullitatis Matrimonii,* 15 mart. 1939, coram R.P.D. Henrico Caiazzo, Dec. XVIII, n. 4—*S.R.R. Dec.,* XXXI (1939), 149; S.R.R., *Parisien., Nullitatis Matrimonii,* 13 apr. 1939, coram Exc.mo P.D. Iulio Grazioli, Decano, Dec. XXII, n. 2—*S.R.R. Dec.,* XXXI (1939), 193.

iniuste incussus applies to injustice in the manner of the infliction of the fear as well as to the substantial injustice of the fear.

2. *Ex contextu* there is nothing opposed to this interpretation.

3. Though some of the earlier authors may have held that the words remained *dubia et obscura* because of pre-Code doubts about the point, their hesitancy cannot be substantiated by any appeal to parallel places in the Code.[53]

4. The *finis legis* and the *mens legislatoris* were: a. to protect the freedom of matrimonial consent; b. to stave off the unhappy consequences usually attendant upon forced marriages; c. to eliminate injustice. These purposes the lawgiver could fully accomplish only by attaching invalidating effects also to the kind of fear which is unjust simply in the manner in which it is inflicted.[54]

5. There is moral unanimity among current authors that fear invalidates marriage even if it is unjust solely in the manner of its infliction.

6. Since 1930 the Rota has consistently ruled that *metus iniustus quoad modum tantum* invalidates marriage.

CONCLUSION. Diocesan tribunals are completely justified in following the rule that fear invalidates marriage, though the fear be unjust solely in the manner of its infliction. The Rota expresses this rule when it comments that fear *incussus (est) iniuste, si iniustum est malum quo metus iniicitur, sive sit iniustum quoad substantiam, sive sit iniustum quoad modum tantum.*[55]

For purposes of further clarification the nature of injustice *quoad substantiam* and the nature and extension of injustice *quoad modum* are discussed in some detail in § 3 and § 5 of this Article.

§ 2. *Relationship of the Injustice of Fear to the Intention of the Person Who Inflicts It*

It has been seen in the historical synopsis that, after the time of Dominicus Soto, some authors held that fear invalidated mar-

[53] Cf. canons 103, § 2, 1684, 185, 1307, § 3. It should be noted that since marriage is a sacrament *sui generis* (a contract and indissoluble), any use of canons dealing with fear in other matters can scarcely be called *parallel places.*

[54] Cf. *supra,* pp. 101-103, notes 4-13.

[55] S.R.R., Kielcen., *Nullitatis Matrimonii,* 16 iul. 1935, coram R.P.D. Francisco Morano, Dec. LI, n. 2—*S.R.R. Dec.,* XXVII (1935), 434. Cf. also decisions cited in note 52 of this article.

riage only if the person who inflicted the fear did so with the intention of causing the victim to give matrimonial consent (*metus directe incussus seu metus consultus*).[56] Others, following the lead of De Lugo, insisted that fear could invalidate marriage even though it was inflicted for some other purpose.[57] In a subsequent article the devolpment of canonical jurisprudence concerning the intention of the person inflicting the fear will be studied on its own merits. At the moment the following points are important and should be kept constantly in mind.

1. In view of man's inherent right to *matrimonial liberty*[58] a specific and *peculiar* injustice attaches to any fear brought to bear against a person for the formulated purpose of violating this liberty.[59]

2. It remains true, however, that fear can also be *unjustly inflicted* when the person who inflicts it has some intention in mind other than to cause the victim to give matrimonial consent. Whether such fear can invalidate marriage is a point which will be discussed in Article VII of this Chapter where the phrase *a quo ut quis se liberet cogatur eligere matrimonium* is studied.

3. In order to determine the justice or injustice of the *metus directe incusssus* for the purpose of extorting matrimonial consent, it is necessary to consider: a. the victim's obligation *to marry;* b. the agent's right *to demand marriage;* c. the *harm or evil* with which the agent threatens the victim if he does not

---

[56] Cf. *supra*, pp. 71-72, notes 31-32.

[57] Cf. *supra*, p. 73, notes 35-37.

[58] Cf. *supra*, p. 86, note 85; p. 101, notes 1-4.

[59] S.R.R., *Marianopolitana, Nullitatis Matrimonii,* 25 febr. 1933, coram R.P.D. Francisco Morano, Dec. XII, n. 2—*S.R.R. Dec.*, XXV (1933), 97: ". . . si malum hoc intentetur a persona libera eumque in finem ut consensus praestetur, metus qui exinde exoritur est etiam ab extrinseco et iniuste incussus." S.R.R., *Versalien., Nullitatis Matrimonii,* 7 iun. 1934, coram R.P.D. Guillelmo Heard, Dec. XLI, n. 2—*S.R.R. Dec.*, XXVI (1934), 358: "Iniustus est metus non solum quando minitans non habet ius minas exequendi, sed etiam quando sine iniustitia quidem minas exsequi potest, non autem ius habet per illas minas matrimonium exigendi." Vermeersch, *Theologia Moralis,* III, n. 735: ". . . iniustus dicendus est omnis metus ad matrimonium obtinendum incussus. . . ." Whether or not this rule admits of an exception in the case of coercion brought to bear upon a seducer is studied in Article VI of this Chapter.

consent to the marriage; d. the *manner* in which the agent uses or threatens the harm or evil upon the victim.

4. In order to determine the justice or injustice of *metus indirecte incussus,* that is, of fear inflicted for some purpose other than marriage, it is necessary to consider: a. the specific *nature of the victim's obligation to the agent* of the fear; b. the *harm or evil* with which the agent threatens the victim unless he discharges the obligation; c. the *manner* in which the agent uses or threatens the harm or evil upon the victim.

It is on the basis of the considerations mentioned in nn. 3-4 above that the authors have drawn the distinction between *metus iniustus quoad substantiam* and *metus iniustus quoad modum.*

§ 3. *Metus Iniustus Quoad Substantiam*

The following statements of authors give their concept of *metus iniustus quoad substantiam:*

> GASPARRI: Metus est incussus iniuste *quoad ipsam substantiam,* quando pars malum, cuius timore compellitur ad nuptias, omnino non meretur; aliis verbis quando malum est undequaque iniustum.[60]

> PAYEN: Injuste infertur *quoad substantiam,* si est malum indebitum, id est malum quod quis non est promeritus et quo bono sibi debito, sine ullo aut saltem sine stricto jure privatur.[61]

> CORONATA: Iniustus in substantia est si metus vel vis moralis adhibita est in se iniusta et is qui eam infert nullo modo ius habet eam inferendi. . . .[62]

The notion might be explained more adequately as follows: fear is unjust in substance when it is in no way merited by the victim, that is, when the victim has *no obligation* either in conscience or before the law to do that which the agent demands of him, and,

---

[60] *De Matrimonio,* II, n. 854.

[61] *De Matrimonio,* II, n. 1685.

[62] *De Sacramentis,* III, p. 635, n. 472. Cf. also Sangmeister, *Force and Fear,* p. 108; Regatillo, *Ius Sacramentarium,* II, p. 326, n. 496.

therefore, when the agent has *no strict right* either on his own initiative or through the agency of public authority *to demand that which he has demanded* of the victim. It seems, too, that even if the victim had an obligation to the agent, and the agent had the right to demand the fulfillment of the obligation but did so by threatening a *harm or evil* which was out of all proportion to the obligation of the victim and which was not sanctioned by public authority, then the fear thus caused would also be unjust *quoad substantiam.*

The following are given by the authors and decisions as typical examples of *metus iniustus quoad substantiam*:

1. If a penalty is threatened for an offense that has not been committed. The fear in this case is unjust in substance, though all parties act in good faith, and though the threat is made by a competent judge with all the proper formalities of the law.[63]

2. If an offense has been committed or an obligation assumed, and, consequent thereto the agent of the fear has threatened the victim with a particular *harm* or *evil* other than that which *is due* to the particular offense committed or obligation assumed. Thus, for example, a person guilty of a crime is brought into court and the judge could justly threaten the penalty provided in the law *for that crime,* but, instead, he threatens some other penalty. Some authors treat this case as one of a *metus iniustus quoad substantiam;*[64] others treat it as *metus iniustus quoad modum.*[65]

The former opinion seems to be the sounder one for the simple reason that in this case *this penalty* is *in no way due* to this man. Consequently, it is entirely and completely unjust.

3. If a person accuses or threatens to accuse an *innocent man* before public authority, the fear which arises from such an action is certainly unjust *quoad substantiam.*

4. If parents exceed all moderation in their insistencies that their

---

[63] Cf. *supra,* pp. 80-81, notes 60-63; p. 85, note 80; Sangmeister, *Force and Fear,* pp. 109, 111, 116, 120; Wernz-Vidal, *Ius Canonicum,* V, n. 501, note 24.

[64] Sangmeister, *Force and Fear,* p. 116; Bouscaren-Ellis, *Commentary,* p. 509. Cf. *supra,* p. 85, note 81.

[65] Gasparri, *De Matrimonio,* II, n. 858; Vermeersch-Creusen, *Epitome,* II, p. 264, n. 375; Jemolo, *Il Matrimonio nel Diritto Canonico,* p. 224, n. 118.

child enter marriage, especially (but not exclusively) if they insist upon marriage with a particular person. Here injustice is identified with the lack of moderation on the part of the parents. Parents have the right to use moderate persuasion with their children in the matter of marriage. They can explain to them the objective reasons for entering marriage, or even a particular marriage. However, when parents indulge in prolonged indignation, constant unpleasantness, threats or blows, even of a slight nature, especially if often repeated, these things are a *malum undequaque indebitum* to the child and the fear caused by them is *iniustus quoad substantiam.*[66]

Concerning *reverential fear* the Rota has remarked that in line with its peculiar nature (*est per se levis*) *the intention of causing marriage* is always postulated in connection with any resulting invalidity for the marriage: *"Metus* autem *reverentialis qualificatus* ne percipi quidem potest, nisi auctor metus extorquere intendat et extorqueat consensum matrimonialem filii vel subditi."[67] This opinion seems to find the peculiar injustice of reverential fear in the fact that it is *directe incussus.* The point is limited in the text to that type of fear which is not *in se gravis.* However, when one considers that parents have no right to abuse their children even in a way that is not *per se gravis* it is difficult to understand why it is necessary for them to abuse a child *for the purpose of marriage* before their action could be considered unjust. It is true that an abuse for the purpose of extorting matrimonial consent has a *special malice,* but it does not follow from this that abuse administered for some other purpose is just.

---

[66] S.R.R., *Scepusien., Nullitatis Matrimonii,* 4 apr. 1930, coram R.P.D. Iulio Grazioli, Dec. XVIII, n. 5—*S.R.R. Dec.,* XXII (1930), 204-205: "Cum tamen parentibus praesertim ius et officium sit liberos dirigere et . . . consiliis praesto esse, nonnisi si sua auctoritate ipsi abutantur et filios vexent, de iniusto metu accusari iidem possunt." S.R.R., *Mediolanen, Nullitatis Matrimonii,* 25 iun. 1930, coram R.P.D. Andrea Jullien, Dec. XXXII, n. 2—*S.R.R. Dec.,* XXII (1930), 366: ". . . tam natura quam iura vetant parentes ad matrimonium adigere filios per minas, verbera, aut per instantissimas preces vel reprehensiones vehementes, quae vim habeant minarum, seu per quosvis modos importunos atque iniustos." Cf. also, Gasparri, *De Matrimonio,* II, n. 854.

[67] S.R.R., *Lincien., Nullitatis Matrimonii,* 5 dec. 1933, coram R.P.D. Arcturo Wynen, Dec. LXXII, n. 4—*S.R.R. Dec.,* XXV (1933), 610.

§ 4. *Material Injustices Suffices to Invalidate Marriage*

As has been seen in § 3 the authors agree that fear is unjust *quoad substantiam* whenever the *harm or evil* with which a person is threatened is in *no way due* to him. It follows from this that fear can be unjust *quoad substantiam* independently of any moral culpability on the part of the agent inflicting it. This doctrine is found exemplified in the historical example of the innocent man who was found guilty by a competent judge according to due process of law. Though Sanchez considered the marriage which resulted from this fear to have been valid he found small support for his position and for centuries the authors have agreed that this was a case of injustice *quoad substantiam.*[68]

From this it follows that the *injustice* mentioned in canon 1087 points not merely to a formal injustice inflicted by an agent who has acted with moral culpability, but also to a *material injustice* which has emanated without sin from some human agent, but which in the objective order violates the rights of the victim. This conclusion follows also from a consideration of the *ratio canonica* of canon 1087: material injustice reduces the spontaneity of matrimonial consent; marriage which is the result of material injustice is apt to be attended by unhappy consequences; the objective rights of the victim are violated.

§ 5. *Metus Iniustus Quoad Modum*

The following are typical statements of authors concerning the nature of *metus iniustus quoad modum tantum:*

> SANGMEISTER: Fear is unjustly inflicted *quoad modum* if the evil is just but is threatened in an unjust manner, that is, not in compliance with the formalities of the law.[69]

> GASPARRI: . . . si nempe pars malum aliquod reipsa meretur, sed non illud quod timet et quo compellitur ad nuptias; aut malum quod meretur ei comminatur persona

---

[68] Cf. *supra*, pp. 80-81, notes 60-64.

[69] *Force and Fear*, p. 109.

> incompetens; aut illud comminatur persona competens, sed non servato ordine iuris. . . .[70]
>
> PAYEN: Injuste infertur *quoad modum,* si est malum debitum, sed *indebito modo* illatum, adeoque a judice non competente, aut a judice competente contra ordinem juris, v.g. sine probationibus, aut adhuc sine ulla, in poenis moderatione.[71]

Fear is unjust *quoad modum tantum,* therefore, when the victim has an *obligation* to the agent either in conscience or according to canon or secular law, and the agent has the right to threaten him with a *certain harm or evil,* but this *harm or evil* is threatened by a person who has no authority to do so, or by a person who, though he has authority, abuses his authority by having recourse to methods and procedures which are illegitimate. If the victim has an obligation to the agent, and a person with proper authority inflicts or threatens a *harm or evil* other than the specific harm or evil which he is authorized to inflict or threaten, it is disputed among the authors whether this constitutes a *metus iniustus quoad substantiam* or only a *metus iniustus quoad modum* as has been noted above in § 3, and as appears from the words of the authors quoted in this section.

The following are cited by the authors and decisions as typical examples of fear which is unjust *quoad modum tantum:*

1. If an incompetent judge imposes or threatens a penalty even for a crime which has been committed.[72]

2. If a competent judge imposes or threatens a penalty upon a

---

[70] *De Matrimonio,* II, n. 855.

[71] *De Matrimonio,* n. 1685. Cf. also Cappello, *De Sacramentis,* V, p. 590, n. 607; Chelodi-Ciprotti, *De Matrimonio,* p. 143, n. 119; Coronata, *De Sacramentis,* III, p. 635, n. 472; Jemolo, *Il Matrimonio nel Diritto Canonico,* p. 118, n. 224; Vermeersch-Creusen, *Epitome,* II, p. 263, n. 375; Regatillo, *Ius Sacramentarium,* II, p. 326, n. 496.

[72] Sangmeister, *Force and Fear,* p. 109; Gasparri, *De Matrimonio,* II, n. 855; Chelodi-Ciprotti, *De Matrimonio,* p. 141, n. 118; S.R.R., *Nullitatis Matrimonii,* 31 mart. 1933, coram R.P.D. Iulio Grazioli, Dec. XXI, n. 3—*S.R.R. Dec.,* XXV (1933), 166; S.R.R., *Angelorum et S. Didaci, Nullitatis Matrimonii,* 4 ian. 1934, coram R.P.D. Guillelmo Heard, Dec. I, n. 2—*S.R.R. Dec.,* XXVI (1934), 3. Cf. also *supra,* p. 85, note 79.

person who, though he be guilty has not been *proved guilty* according to law.[73]

3. If a competent judge imposes or threatens a penalty upon a person in whose case there is guilt and indeed cogent proof of the guilt, but the *procedures prescribed by the law* have been violated.[74]

The authors do not specify *how serious* the breach of procedural law would have to be before it would constitute such an injustice *quoad modum* as to be sufficient to invalidate the marriage that would result from the coercive measures thus applied. There is no room for doubt that, if the procedural law has been violated in a detail which is required *ad validitatem,* then the marriage is invalid. Furthermore, it seems reasonable that, if the violation of a procedural law was a *conditio sine qua non* for the imposition or the effective threat of penalties then likewise the resulting marriage is to be regarded as invalid, even though the violation did not result in the invalidity of the process as such. Thus if a given jurisdiction did not make *illegal arrest* an invalidating factor in a criminal process, but the *illegal arrest* was a *conditio sine qua non* of the culprit's trial and conviction, it seems that the injustice *quoad modum* in such a case would be sufficient to fulfill the requirements of the phrase *iniuste incussus* of canon 1087.

4. If a private person inflicts or threatens to inflict penalties which are provided in the law.[75]

5. If someone accuses or threatens to accuse some person of some specific crime, whereas the person in question is guilty of *another* crime, then the fear thus caused is certainly unjust at least *quoad modum.* The authors do not seem to discuss the point. However, no one has the right to make a false accusation against another, and to do so is a gross injustice especially when the crime

---

[73] Sangmeister, *Force and Fear,* p. 121; Gasparri, *De Matrimonio,* II, n. 855; Chelodi-Ciprotti, *De Matrimonio,* p. 141, n. 118. Cf. also *supra,* p. 85, note 82.

[74] Sangmeister, *Force and Fear,* p. 116; Coronata, *De Sacramentis,* III, p. 635, n. 472; Bouscaren-Ellis, *Commentary,* p. 509.

[75] S.R.R., *Angelorum et S. Didaci, Nullitatis Matrimonii,* 4 ian. 1934, coram R.P.D. Guillelmo Heard, Dec. I, n. 2—*S.R.R. Dec.,* XXVI (1934), 3. Cf. also *supra,* p. 85, note 78.

with which the person is charged is of a more serious nature than the crime which the person actually committed.

6. If a person accuses another of a crime without observing the normal rules of prudence as demanded by the principles of moral theology.[76] The justice and injustice of threats to accuse are discussed below in Article VI, § 10.

§ 6. *Special Problem Cases*

The following cases involve special difficulties and, therefore, merit special consideration:

1. If a girl has been violated by a man who wishes to marry her, but she refuses to marry him because she intends to associate with him in a sinful way and to retain thus her freedom to marry someone else, the girl's parents are completely justified in threatening to disinherit her or to force her to leave the paternal home.[77] Under these circumstances the father would certainly be justified in saying to the girl: "either marry the man *or* I will disinherit you and exclude you from our home." The girl has no right to live in sin, to disgrace her family, to put her family in the position of affording at least material co-operation in her sinful manner of living. The father's action is justified, therefore, so long as he uses threats which fall short of physical violence or unusual corporal punishment.

2. If a girl finds herself with child, but marriage to the father of the child is repugnant to her, the parents are nevertheless justified in urging the marriage with moderation. But if in these circumstances, the girl is repentant in that she sincerely intends to discontinue the earlier life of sin, the parents have no right to threaten her with exposure or with an elimination of the means of support. The parents do have the right to remove the girl to a distant place where the child can be born without disgrace to the family name, even if this action places the girl in some moderate danger of being exposed. However, the parents have a natural obligation to the girl and accordingly they are bound to offer her

---

[76] Cf. *supra,* note 75, *decisio cit.,* n. 6. p. 6. Cf. also can. 1946 § 2, n. 3.

[77] Coronata, *De Sacramentis,* III, p. 640, n. 478; Jemolo, *Il Matrimonio nel Diritto Canonico,* p. 234, n. 121.

reasonable assistance. If, instead, they threaten the girl with disinheritance or with other abuses, their action is unjust *quoad substantiam* since it exceeds the rights of the parents.[78]

Though the foregoing conclusion appears certain and has the support of considerable authority, still, in a similar case on at least one occasion the Rota took a different view:

> Neque iniuste incussus fuisse metus videtur, nam Vera consentiens in intimam relationem cum Fabio . . . culpa non caruit, et ideo iniustum dici nequit malum quo pater eam compulit ad nubendum viro, a quo mater effecta fuerat, quique . . . ius habebat vitandae infamiae.[79]

In actual practice the solution will depend largely upon concrete circumstances.

3. If a lover or the father of a person threatens suicide unless the person enters marriage, in the abstract it is possible that no injustice be done to the person. In the concrete, however, the scandal that could arise from the suicide, or the depriving of a minor of the support which he or she has a right to expect from his or her parents, could constitute an injustice *quoad substantiam.*[80] It also appears that neither lover nor father has the right to use *such a means* in order to extort matrimonial consent, and on this basis the action constitutes an injustice *quoad modum.*

4. It is certainly unjust for a person (e.g. a doctor or a lawyer) to refuse assistance to one if he has assumed *an obligation* to render service to that person. A marriage that would be caused through fear arising from such threats to refuse assistance would be in-

---

[78] Cf. Jemolo, *Il Matrimonio nel Diritto Canonico,* p. 234, n. 121; S.R.R., *Plocen., Nullitatis Matrimonii,* 14 febr. 1933, coram R.P.D. Arcturo Wynen, Dec. IX, n. 2—*S.R.R. Dec.,* XXV (1933), 72; S.R.R., *Nullitatis Matrimonii,* 13 apr. 1935, coram R.P.D. Arcturo Wynen, Dec. XXVI, n. 3—*S.R.R. Dec.,* XXVII (1935), 229; S.R.R., *Nullitatis Matrimonii,* 15 iun. 1937, coram R.P.D. Arcturo Wynen, Dec. XLII, n. 2—*S.R.R. Dec.,* XXIX (1937), 411-412.

[79] S.R.R., *Romana, Nullitatis Matrimonii,* 29 ian. 1937, coram R.P.D. Ioanne Teodori, Dec. VII, n. 6—*S.R.R. Dec.,* XXIX (1937), 52-53.

[80] Jemolo, *Il Matrimonio in Diritto Canonico,* pp. 221-222, n. 117.

valid if the other conditions of the law concerning gravity, etc., were fulfilled.[81]

5. In instances in which fear is caused by a threat to withdraw aid or sustenance to which the victim of fear has no strict right, the sounder view seems to be that the fear is not *iniuste incussus.*[82] This opinion is held by Cappello,[83] and Wernz-Vidal.[84] However, some authors, prompted perhaps by certain statements of the Rota,[85] have adopted a somewhat more lenient view. For example Coronata explains a case as follows:

> . . . non habendam esse solummodo rationem iuris stricti iuridici ab aliqua lege positiva admissi et recogniti, sed etiam iuris naturalis scilicet prohibetur ne qui in potestate alterius constitutus eidem sine stricta pactione serviens sine salario, cogi possit ad matrimonium ab eo cui servit et in cuius veluti familia vivit vitam familiarem, sub minis eiectionis e domo aut subtractionis alimentorum.[86]

Jemolo explains the injustice inherent in the withdrawal of aid to a person who has been relieved of a condition of abject misery but without any demand in strict justice upon his benefactor:

> . . . the injustice consists in this: that it is not permitted to profit from the granting of a favor, no matter how spontaneous, for the purpose of coercing another in a matter so essential as marriage, namely, by first giving life as a free gift and then taking back the gift thereby exposing the beneficiary to the necessity of relapse into his former miserable condition.[87]

In such cases the justice or injustice of an action will be determined not so much *by the agent's right* to withdraw assistance, as by his *lack of right to use this means to demand marriage.*[88]

---

[81] Cf. *supra,* p. 86, note 83.

[82] Cf. *supra,* p. 83, note 74.

[83] *De Sacramentis,* V, p. 591, n. 607.

[84] *Ius Canonicum,* V, n. 501, note 24.

[85] Cf. the case quoted above, pp. 83-84, note 75.

[86] *De Sacramentis,* III, pp. 639-640, n. 478.

[87] *Il Matrimonio nel Diritto Canonico,* p. 225, n. 118 (translation by the writer).

[88] Cf. *supra,* p. 116, n. 1, notes 58-59.

§ 7. *Coercion in View of Espousals*

Canon 1017 of the Code of Canon Law reads as follows:

> § 1. *Matrimonii promissio sive unilateralis, sive bilateralis, irrita est pro utroque foro, nisi facta fuerit per scripturam subsignatam a partibus et vel a parocho aut loci Ordinario, vel a duobus saltem testibus.*
>
> § 3. *At ex matrimonii promissione, licet valida sit nec ulla iusta causa ab eadem implenda excuset, non datur actio ad petendam matrimonii celebrationem, datur tamen ad reparationem damnorum, si qua debeatur.*

In the first paragraph of this canon *all obligation,* in conscience as well as in the external ecclesiastical forum, is ruled out in every promise to marry that has not been made in the due canonical form. Consequently, no person has a right on his private initiative or by means of recourse to an ecclesiastical court to demand damages or the contracting of marriage in such a case. Fear arising from threats attached to any such demands would be unjust *quoad substantiam.* This problem, however, can be proposed: suppose that the secular laws of a given jurisdiction allow a claim against a person who breaks his promise of contracting marriage. If this were the case it would be difficult to class as unjust any action that the offended party might take under the provisions of such a law. If the law provided for a simple payment of damages in such a case, and the judge were to assign damages under the strict provisions of this law with no intention of extorting matrimonial consent, the action apparently would be just. If, however, the accuser or the judge took action aimed at the extorting of matrimonial consent, then a different problem becomes involved. If the law did not permit an action *ad petendum matrimonium,* the action would be certainly unjust. If the law did permit an action *ad petendum matrimonium,* it is likely that the action and the fear arising from it would be just. However, under modern laws the case is not likely to occur.[89]

The third paragraph of canon 1017 considers the obligation

---

[89] In secular law, *breach of promise* suits generally allow only damages.

attaching to formal, canonical espousals. In this paragraph the canon prescinds from all consideration of the obligation in conscience. In the external, ecclesiastical forum it admits only an action for damages if any have been sustained by the offended party. Consequently any coercion used by a private person on his own authority, as also any action by an ecclesiastical court *ad petendum matrimonium,* would be unjust. Concerning action before a secular judge, the remarks of the preceding paragraph are equally applicable here.

ARTICLE VI. THE SPECIAL QUESTION OF THE JUSTICE AND THE INJUSTICE OF COERCION IN CASES OF SEDUCTION

§ 1. *The Problem*

In the pre-Code jurisprudence it was held that one could assume an actionable obligation to marry as arising *ex delicto.*[90] The delict in question was that of *stuprum* or seduction. From this it followed that the use of force-fear against a seducer could be justified under certain circumstances according to the pre-Code law. The problem to be discussed here is the nature of the obligation to marry as arising *ex delicto* as it prevails under the Code of Canon Law and the consequent justice and injustice of the use of force-fear in such cases.

This raises one of the most difficult problems in the application of canon 1087. Some order and clarity can be brought to the subject through a separate treatment of the seducer's obligations *in conscience,* in the *ecclesiastical external forum,* and in *the secular forum.*

§ 2. *The Concept of "Stuprum"*

The Code does not define *stuprum.* The definitions of the authors agree with the definitions which prevailed before the Code:[91]

---

[90] Cf. *supra,* pp. 87-95, notes 86-125.

[91] Cf. *supra,* 87-89; Sangmeister, *Force and Fear,* p. 110; Vermeersch-Creusen, *Epitome,* III (6. ed., 1946), p. 352, n. 560; Vermeersch, *Theologia Moralis,* II, n. 589; Noldin-Schmitt, *De Sexto Praecepto et de Usu Matrimonii* (31. ed., Oeniponte-Lipsiae: Sumptibus et Typis Feliciani Rauch, 1940), nn. 23-24; Merkelbach, *Theologia Moralis,* II, nn. 383, 1008.

1. In the *strictest sense, stuprum* is the depriving of a *virgin* of her corporal virginity by use of force.

2. In the *strict sense, stuprum* is the depriving of a *virgin* of her corporal virginity by use of *fraud* or *unjust fear.*

3. In a less strict sense, *stuprum* is carnal knowledge of any *woman of good repute* by use of force, fraud or grave fear.

4. In a wide sense, *stuprum* is the depriving of a *virgin* of her corporal virginity, or carnal knowledge of any woman of good repute, by the use of unusual *flatteries, persuasion, insistencies.*

§ 3. *General Obligation of the Seducer "in Foro Conscientiae"*

Stuprum is not only a sin of lust, it is also a sin of injustice. As a sin against justice it places upon the seducer the obligation of making restitution to the woman to the extent that she has unjustly suffered temporal loss.[92]

The temporal loss which the woman sustains consists in the lessening of her normal chances of marriage according to her station and of the support that she would derive from such a marriage. This damage is aggravated in instances in which a child is conceived in the seduction.[93] Substantially, this damage the seducer can repair either by marrying the woman, or by making a financial settlement in her favor which will restore her normal chances of marriage by making marriage to her more attractive in the eyes of persons of her station.[94] In general terms, therefore, the seducer has the obligation in conscience either to marry the woman or to endow her. Special circumstances can modify this obligation even in the *forum* of conscience. Variations in the obligations of the seducer according to varying circumstances will be examined in subsequent paragraphs.

So long as a temporal loss is unjustly sustained by the woman the seducer has an obligation *in conscience* to make restitution.

---

[92] Cf. Vermeersch, *Theologia Moralis,* II, nn. 533-535; 540-542; Noldin-Schmitt, *Summa Theologiae Moralis,* II, nn. 409-411; 429-434; 453-454; Merkelbach, *Theologia Moralis,* II, nn. 237-238; 245; 278-279.

[93] Vermeersch, *Theologia Moralis,* II, n. 589; Merkelbach, *Theologia Moralis,* II, n. 1008.

[94] Vermeersch, *Theologia Moralis,* II, n. 590; Noldin-Schmitt, *Summa Theologiae Moralis,* II, n. 469; Merkelbach, *Theologia Moralis,* II, n. 384.

This is true whether the act of *stuprum* be such in the strictest or only in the wide sense of the term.

Since the seducer's general obligation in conscience is *either* to endow the woman *or* to marry her, the general conclusion is valid: that coercive measures are unjust when taken against a seducer in disregard of his right to this alternative. Possible modifications of this general conclusion will be examined in subsequent paragraphs.

§ 4. *Circumstances in Which the Seducer Has No Obligation in Conscience Either to Endow or to Marry the Woman*

From the principles enunciated in the preceding paragraph it follows that a seducer has *no obligation in conscience* either to marry or to endow the woman in the following circumstances:

1. If the seduction did not *de facto* decrease the woman's normal chances of marriage according to her station. The reason is: if nothing is taken away, nothing need be returned.

2. If the seduction remained entirely secret. The reason is: the woman suffers no loss because of the seduction.

3. If the woman could not or did not wish to marry anyone. The reason is: the woman has repudiated or does not wish to accept that which the seducer is obliged to restore to her.

4. If the woman *de facto* married someone else.

5. If the woman were of a common or disreputable life. The reason is: her chances of marriage were lost through her own conduct and not in consequence of this particular seduction.

6. If the woman consented to the illicit relations apart from the man's use of force, fraud or unusual insistencies. The reason is: *scienti et consentienti non fit iniuria.*

7. If the seducer became known only through the indiscretion of the woman. The reason is: her loss is directly occasioned through her own indiscretion rather than through the seduction.

8. If the woman absolved the man. The reason is: debts between persons can be condoned.[95]

---

[95] Cf., e.g., Vermeersch, *Theologia Moralis,* II, nn. 534-590; Noldin-Schmitt, *Summa Theologiae Moralis,* II, nn. 411, 469; Merkelbach, *Theologia Moralis.* II, nn. 237, 384.

§ 5. *Circumstances in Which, According to Some Authors, the Seducer Has the Obligation in Conscience to Marry the Woman Without Benefit of Alternative*

The question here does not concern the obligations of the seducer as they are modified by the accidental circumstance of his inability to endow the woman. This problem will be examined in § 7 below. The question here deals rather with the problem of circumstances *intrinsic* to the seduction which cause it to place a more specific obligation upon the seducer.

Before the Code the authors generally agreed that, if a man promised to marry a woman and she consented to relations with him on the basis of this promise, the seducer was obliged *to marry the woman* without benefit of the alternative of endowing her. The reasoning which led to this conclusion was that a contract had been made; the woman had fulfilled her part of the contract; the man was bound to fulfill his part; his part of the contract was that he would marry the woman. In this case the woman's *title* to marriage was not the *sin* which had been committed but rather the extrinsic element of the loss which had been sustained under condition that the loss would be redeemed.[96]

After the Code some authors have continued to hold this view, as far as the question of obligation *in conscience* is concerned:

> Qui tamen, per veram aut fictam matrimonii *promissionem* puellam flexit, hanc secundum communissimam sententiam, ducere debebit. Nec obstat nullitas canonica promissionis, cum haec ut instrumentum deceptionis seu fraudis consideretur.[97]

Other authors, however, hold that even in this case the seducer's obligation is only the alternative obligation *either* of marrying *or* of endowing the woman. They base their opinion upon canon 1017 which invalidates in *utroque foro* every promise to contract marriage if the promise is not made according to the solemn canonical form.[98] Though the first opinion enjoys extrinsic probability in

---

[96] Cf. *supra*, pp. 93-95, notes 117-125.

[97] Vermeersch, *Theologia Moralis*, II, n. 590; Merkelbach, *Theologia Moralis*, II, n. 384; Sangmeister, *Force and Fear*, p. 111.

[98] Cf., e.g., Noldin-Schmitt, *Summa Theologiae Moralis*, II, n. 469; Dossetti, *La Violenza nel Matrimonio*, p. 305, note 3.

virtue of the support which it receives, the latter appears more probable, if not also certain, on the basis of intrinsic argumentation. It must be recalled that the discussion here deals only with the seducer's obligation *in conscience* independently of positive legislation and independently of judicial action.

Furthermore, all authors agree that the obligation in conscience of the seducer who has promised marriage can be modified by circumstances. These circumstances are discussed in the following paragraph.

§ 6. *Circumstances in Which Even the Seducer Who Has Promised Marriage Is Not Obliged in Conscience to Marry the Woman*

Even those authors who hold that the seducer who used his promise of contracting marriage as the means of seduction has an obligation in conscience to marry the woman admit that the obligation *to marry* ceases under the following circumstances:

1. If the woman had been guilty of deceit by *falsely* telling her seducer that she was a virgin. Any liability that the man might have towards the woman is canceled by her deceit.[99]

2. If, from the circumstances surrounding the seduction, the woman could easily have known that the seducer would not keep his promise to marry her. In this case the woman is presumed to have been *sciens et volens.*[100]

3. If the woman, after the seduction, has illicit relations with another man. By such an action the woman forfeits her right to expect the man to enable her to marry according to her station.[101]

4. If the marriage would give rise to scandal. It stands to reason that no one can be bound to make restitution in a way which will cause grave spiritual harm to himself or to others.[102]

5. If the circumstances are such that quite evidently the mar-

---

[99] Vermeersch, *Theologia Moralis,* II, n. 590. For the opinions of pre-Code authors cf. *supra,* p. 91, n. 8, note 108.

[100] Vermeersch, *Theologia Moralis,* II, n. 590; Merkelbach, *Theologia Moralis,* II, n. 384. For the opinions of Pre-Code authors cf. *supra,* p. 91, n. 8, note 108.

[101] Merkelbach, *Theologia Moralis,* II, n. 384.

[102] Sangmeister, *Force and Fear,* p. 111; Merkelbach, *Theologia Moralis,* II, n. 384. Cf. *supra,* p. 90, n. 4, note 104.

riage would terminate in failure. If the man were to marry the woman in these circumstances, he would be exposing her to a new and greater danger instead of repairing the one which he had already caused.[108]

§ 7. *The Obligation in Conscience of a Seducer Who Lacks the Means to Endow the Woman*

Ordinarily a man who has seduced a woman, at least if he has done so apart from any promise to marry her, is entitled to the alternative of making restitution either by marrying the woman or by endowing her. However, what of the case in which such a seducer does not have the financial resources to make an endowment?

If the circumstances are such as to relieve him of all obligation, as explained above in § 4, there is of course no problem.

If the woman had forfeited her right to expect marriage, as explained above in § 6, nn. 1-3, the man is still not bound to marry the woman, though his obligation to pay appropriate damages as the opportunity arises will remain. The extent of these damages, if any, will depend upon the concrete circumstances of each case.

If the marriage would give rise to scandal, or the circumstances are such that it is morally certain that the marriage would end in failure, the seducer may not marry the woman even though he is unable to endow her. His obligation to endow her remains and must be fulfilled as the opportunity arises according to the normal rules governing restitution.

In all other cases the man would have the obligation *in conscience* of marrying the woman. The reason is that his obligation is *to marry or to endow;* he is incapable of endowing; therefore he has the obligation of marrying the woman.

Thus far consideration has been given to the obligations of the seducer in so far simply as they bind him in the *forum of conscience.* In § 8 the actionability of these obligations in the ecclesiastical courts and the possible justice and injustice of such action will be briefly examined.

---

[108] Sangmeister, *Force and Fear,* p. 111; Dossetti, *La Violenza nel Matrimonio,* p. 304, n. 105, note 3; Merkelbach, *Theologia Moralis,* II, n. 384; Payen, *De Matrimonio,* II, n. 1685, note 1. Also cf. *supra,* p. 91, n. 5, note 105.

§ 8. *The Justice and the Injustice of Action Against a Seducer in the Ecclesiastical Courts*

The Decretals had ruled:

> Si seduxerit quis virginem nondum desponsatam dormieritque cum ea, dotabit eam, et habebit uxorem;[104]

> . . . aut quam stupravit uxorem habeat, aut . . . si renuendum putaverit, . . . corporaliter castigatus excommunicatusque, in monasterio, in quo agat penitentiam, retrudatur. . . .[105]

Accordingly, before custom changed the law, a seducer had the canonical obligation of marrying the woman whom he had seduced. If he refused, severe penalties were to be inflicted upon him. The threat of the application of these penalties could not be construed as unjust.

However, the history of canonical jurisprudence on this point shows that this law was eventually revised by custom. Before the promulgation of the Code of Canon Law, a seducer had the canonical obligation *either of marrying or of endowing* the woman. The ecclesiastical judge could impose this alternative upon him. If the seducer refused either to marry or to endow the woman he could be punished. So long as the judge offered the seducer the alternative either of marrying or of endowing the woman, the fear that was caused by threats of canonical penalties in the event that the seducer refused to do either did not constitute unjust fear.[106]

At the same time, however, the pre-Code law provided that, if the seducer had promised the woman that he would marry her and she consented to the seduction on this condition, then the canonical obligation of the seducer was that *he had to marry the woman.* The same was true in instances in which the seducer, though entitled to the alternative of endowing the woman, was unable to do so. In these two cases the judge could threaten severe canonical penalties

[104] C. 1, X, *de adulteriis et stupro,* V, 16—*supra,* p. 24, note 44.

[105] C. 2, X, *de adulteriis et stupro,* V, 16—*supra,* p. 24, note 45.

[106] Cf. *supra,* pp. 92-93, notes 111-116.

to be inflicted upon the seducer *unless he married* the woman, and in these cases the coercion was just and the marriage was valid.[107]

Now, the problem is to see whether or not this law has undergone any modification through the legislation of the Code of Canon Law.

Canon 2357, § 1, provides:

> *Laici legitime damnati ob . . . stuprum . . . ipso facto infames sunt, praeter alias poenas quas Ordinarius infligendas iudicaverit.*

Stuprum therefore is a delict; penalties attach to the delict only after the accused has been found guilty either in a secular or in an ecclesiastical court; once the accused is found guilty, *ipso facto* he becomes infamous and, over and above this, the judge can impose other penalties, their severity to be determined by the circumstances of the case.[108]

The delict of *stuprum* gives rise to a contentious action for damages and to a penal action for punishment of the crime and the two actions can be defined by the same judge if the action has been instituted on a criminal basis:

> Canon 2210, § 1. Ex delicto oritur:
>
> 1. *Actio poenalis ad poenam declarandam vel infligendam et ad satisfactionem petendam;*
> 2. *Actio civilis ad reparanda damna, si cui delictum damnum intulerit.*
>
> § 2. *Utraque actio explicatur ad normam can. 1552-1959; et idem iudex in criminali iudicio potest ad instantiam partis laesae civilem actionem ad examen revocare et definire.*

---

[107] Cf. *supra*, pp. 93-94, nn. 1-3, notes 117-122.

[108] According to the axiom *odiosa sunt restringenda* and the provisions of canons 2219, § 1 and § 3, 2228, and 2233, § 1 it seems that the delict of *stuprum* is committed only when the strictest or a strict sense of the term is verified; cf. *supra*, p. 128, nn. 1-3; Vermeersch-Creusen, *Epitome*, III, p. 252, n. 560.

If, therefore, criminal action has been instituted against a seducer, the seduced woman can claim damages and demand restitution before the ecclesiastical judge.[109]

The present problem can be simply stated as follows: can an ecclesiastical judge justly bind a man who has been found guilty of *struprum to marry* the seduced woman under threat of severe penalties, or is he limited to binding the seducer to the alternative *either* of marrying *or* of endowing the woman?[110]

In current jurisprudence some authority can be found for the opinion that the judge is justified *in imposing the obligation to marry* in certain circumstances:

> ROTA: Dantur enim crimina, quorum in poenam et etiam ad damna reparanda quis adigi potest ad matrimonium ineundum.[111]

> ROTA: Qui enim ex propria culpa ad matrimonium aliquod contrahendum a legitima auctoritate seu a Iudice damnatur, nullam patitur iniuriam, dum deliquit, ipse metum intulit.[112]

> CORONATA: . . . erit iustus metus si matrimonium exigatur a iuvene qui virginem cognoverit promittendo ei matrimonium.[113]

Unfortunately, in making such statements the authors and decisions generally do not specify whether they are speaking of the ecclesiastical judge, the secular judge, or both. This is true of the statements quoted above. Their general tenor, however, is such as to leave little doubt that they hold that the ecclesiastical judge can,

---

[109] Since canon 2357, § 1 speaks of *legitime damnati* it follows that though a secular judge had found the man guilty, the offended woman could still have further recourse to the ecclesiastical judge.

[110] It is a question here of threatening the *alias poenas* mentioned in canon 2357, § 1.

[111] S.R.R., *Nullitatis Matrimonii,* 31 mart. 1933, coram R.P.D. Iulio Grazioli, Dec. XXXI, n. 3—*S.R.R. Dec.,* XXV (1933), 165-166.

[112] S.R.R., *Parisien., Nullitatis Matrimonii,* 13 apr. 1939, coram Exc. mo P.D. Iulio Grazioli, Decano, Dec. XXII, n. 2—*S.R.R. Dec.,* XXXI (1939), 193-194.

[113] *De Sacramentis,* III, p. 635, n. 472.

under certain circumstances, even under threat of severe penalties, impose upon the seducer the absolute obligation of marrying the seduced woman. There has been little doctrinal discussion of the point, as far as this writer can ascertain, since the promulgation of the Code of Canon Law. It seems certain, however, that even those authors who hold this position would limit its application to the cases in which such action was permitted before the Code, namely, in instances in which the seduction had been committed by means of a promise to contract marriage and to cases in which the seducer was unable to make a financial settlement.[114]

In spite of the opinion here outlined, the authors in a majority fashion hold that under the provisions of the Code of Canon Law the judge is never justified in absolutely imposing the order to contract marriage. These authors hold that the judge must give the culprit the alternative either of marrying or of endowing the woman:

> CAPPELLO: . . . iudex solum ius habet exigendi *vel* matrimonium *vel* dotationem. . . .[115]

> BOUSCAREN-ELLIS: . . . the payment of compensatory or punitive damages is a choice to which the culprit is justly entitled.[116]

> VERMEERSCH: . . . cum nunc nulla actio datur ad exigendum ipsum matrimonium, iniustus dicendus est omnis metus ad matrimonium obtinendum incussus. . . .[117]

> NOLDIN-SCHMITT: . . . iudex solum ius habet exigendi aut matrimonium aut dotationem. . . .[118]

> ROTA: . . . iniuste . . . quoad modum . . . iudex ageret qui stupratori absolute puellam violatam uxorem ducere imponeret, cum fas eidem stupratori sit eamdem simpliciter dotare.[119]

---

[114] Cf. *supra*, pp. 93-95, notes 117-125.

[115] *De Sacramentis*, V, p. 591, n. 607.

[116] *Commentary*, p. 509.

[117] *Theologia Moralis*, III, n. 735.

[118] *Summa Theologiae Moralis*, II, n. 634; n. 469.

[119] S.R.R., *Romana, Nullitatis Matrimonii*, 9 maii 1933, coram R.P.D. Iulio Grazioli, Dec. XXXV, n. 4—*S.R.R. Dec.*, XXV (1933), 298; cf. also Dossetti, *La Violenza nel Matrimonio*, p. 304, n. 105; Jemolo, *Il Matrimonio nel Diritto Canonico*, p. 224, n. 118, note 1.

The reasons upon which this opinion is based are cogent. Under the pre-Code law the ecclesiastical judge could take the most stringent possible action against a seducer who had seduced a woman in consequence of his promise to marry her. Such a promise to contract marriage is no longer binding even in conscience under the provisions of canon 1017. Therefore, even in this extreme case the judge is no longer justified in imposing absolutely upon a seducer the order to contract marriage, and, if he is not permitted to do so in this case, he is not permitted to do so in any case.

However, since marriage enjoys the favor of the law, and, since according to canon 1014 every marriage must, in the face of a doubt, be held to be valid, if an ecclesiastical judge were to bind a seducer to contract marriage under threat of severe penalties in cases in which the seducer had promised to marry the woman and in cases in which the seducer was unable to endow the woman, the action would have to be considered just and the marriage valid.

Aside from these two extreme cases, the justice of the action of an ecclesiastical judge would receive its determination from the obligations of the seducer in conscience, from the loss actually suffered by the woman, from the woman's relative culpability, from the possibility of scandal, and from other similar considerations as discussed above.[120]

Generally such cases are not tried in the ecclesiastical courts. With reference to such matters Ordinaries are thus admonished by the Code:

> *In delictis mixti fori Ordinarii regulariter ne procedant cum reus laicus est et civilis magistratus, in reum animadvertens, publico bono satis consulit.*[121]

It remains, therefore, to examine the question of the justice and injustice of coercion when employed in the secular courts against a seducer. This question will be treated briefly in the following pages.

---

[120] Cf. *supra*, pp. 129-132, § 4-§ 7.

[121] Canon 1933, § 3; cf. also canon 2198.

§ 9. *Just and Unjust Coercion in the Secular Courts*[122]

Since sex crimes are offenses against the civil as well as against the spiritual order, the State has the right to legislate against them and to pass judgment upon such cases according to the statutes which are lawfully enacted.[123] It should be noted with Sangmeister that some European authors have misunderstood the laws of the United States concerning seduction and rape, and consequently their observations on these laws must be subjected to careful scrutiny.[124] In every case in which an ecclesiastical tribunal is called upon to evaluate the justice of coercive measures used upon a seducer through recourse to the secular courts a legal expert should be consulted. The laws vary from state to state, and the information contained in manuals could easily lead to false conclusions. Here, accordingly, no effort will be made to analyze the laws of the forty-eight states, nor will any specific references be made to manuals, though these have been cited in note 122 above. Here simply the general principles governing such cases will be briefly discussed.

---

[122] This dissertation does not discuss the relative applicability of Canon and Secular Law in the marriages of *unbaptized* persons. On this point cf. William J. Goldsmith, *The Competence of Church and State over Marriage—Disputed Points,* The Catholic University of America Canon Law Studies, n. 197 (Washington, D. C.: The Catholic University of America Press, 1944). Neither does it discuss the laws of the several jurisdictions of the United States of America on coercion or duress in marriage. Concerning these laws cf. Culver B. Alford, *Jus Matrimoniale Comparatum* (Romae: Anonima Libreria Cattolica Italiana—New York: Kenedy, 1938); Geoffrey May, *Marriage Laws and Decisions in the United States* (New York: Russell Sage Foundation, 1929). Concerning the laws of the several states on *bastardy* cf. Chester G. Vernier, *American Family Laws* (5 vols., Stanford University, California: Stanford University Press, 1931-1938), Vol. IV, *Parent and Child* (1936). Concerning the laws on seduction and rape cf. Justin Miller, *Handbook of Criminal Law,* Hornbook Series (St. Paul, Minn.: West Publishing Co., 1934).

[123] Cf. Sangmeister, *Force and Fear,* p. 114; Gasparri, *De Matrimonio,* II, n. 853; Cappello, *De Sacramentis,* V, p. 590, n. 607; Jemolo, *Il Matrimonio nel Diritto Canonico,* p. 224, n. 118, note 1; Dossetti, *La Violenza nel Matrimonio,* p. 305, n. 105.

[124] Sangmeister, *Force and Fear,* pp. 114-115.

The office of the judge is *to apply* the law as it is written, not to make it. The judge, therefore, may use discretionary powers only to the extent that this is permitted by the law. The substantial justice of the action of a judge, therefore, is determined by the statutes and by the accepted construction that has been placed upon them in the courts. Besides the question of the substantial justice, the question of procedural justice must be considered.[125] This involves the difficult questions of jurisdiction, charges, indictment, arrest, extradition, counsel and evidence. Here, too, ecclesiastical courts should consult a legal expert in order to ascertain if any injustice has been committed.

In most instances in which action is taken against a seducer in the secular courts the charges will be based upon the *bastardy, rape* or *seduction* laws. A brief note concerning each of these is, therefore, in order.

The definitions of these crimes will depend upon the respective laws of the several jurisdictions. These laws admit only strict interpretation; a person cannot be found guilty of a given crime in view of having committed an offense which closely resembles that crime.

In secular law, so-called *common law rape* corresponds in a general way with canonical *stuprum* in the strictest sense of the term:[126] it is carnal knowledge of a woman through the use *of force* or grave fear.

In secular law the term *seduction* is used to designate carnal knowledge of a woman by use of fraud, deceit, promises, persuasion: it corresponds in a general way, therefore, to canonical *stuprum* in the strict and in the less strict senses of the term.[127] *Statutory rape* in secular law, on the other hand, is a fiction of the law: it is carnal knowledge of a woman who is under a certain age and younger than the man who has relations with her. Because of the element of age, the law considers her as being incapable of consenting to the act, and consequently the crime is committed even though the woman gives full moral consent. Rape, both common law and statutory, and seduction are *crimes*.

---

[125] Cf. *supra*, pp. 112-115; 120-122.

[126] Cf. *supra*, p. 128, n. 1.

[127] Cf. *supra*, p. 128, nn. 2-3.

Bastardy is treated as a crime in some jurisdictions while in others it is not. The general purpose of bastardy proceedings is simply to determine paternity and to provide for the sustenance of the child. Penalties may also be inflicted in those jurisdictions which consider *bastardy* as a crime.

In cases of rape, seduction or bastardy the law may provide that the judge can suspend his sentence if the seducer wishes to marry the woman.

The following observations may assist the canonist in determining the justice and injustice of action before a secular judge, and the consequent justice and injustice of fear that may arise from such action:

1. If a competent judge finds a man guilty when in fact the man did not commit the crime *with which he is charged,* the action is unjust *quoad substantiam.*[128]

2. If the law specifically provides that a man guilty of *stuprum* (rape, seduction, bastardy) must either marry the woman or be severely punished, and the judge advises the culprit that he must either "marry or be punished," the action of the judge is *just.* This is true even though *Canon Law* in the same case would require that the seducer be given the alternative to marry, *or endow,* or be punished.[129] Some authors seem to take exception to this with their contention that the seducer *is always* entitled to the alternative either of marrying *or of endowing* the woman.[130] How-

[128] Cf. *supra,* p. 118, n. 1, note 63.

[129] Dossetti, *La Violenza nel Matrimonio,* p. 316, n. 110, note 1; Cappello, *De Sacramentis,* V, p. 590, n. 607; Gasparri, *De Matrimonio,* II, n. 853; Jemolo, *Il Matrimonio nel Diritto Canonico,* p. 224, n. 118; Coronata, *De Sacramentis,* III, p. 635, n. 472; S.R.R., *Nullitatis Matrimonii,* 22 dec. 1934, coram R.P.D. Henrico Quattrocolo, Dec. XCV, n. 11—*S.R.R. Dec.,* XXVI (1934), 800; S.R.R., *Nullitatis Matrimonii,* 31 mart. 1933, coram R.P.D. Iulio Grazioli, Dec. XXI, n. 3—*S.R.R Dec.,* XXV (1933), 165-166; S.R.R., *Panormitana, Nullitatis Matrimonii,* 11 maii 1931, coram R.P.D. Iulio Grazioli, Dec. XXII, n. 5—*S.R.R. Dec.,* XXIII (1931), 181-182; S.R.R., *Angelorum et S. Didaci, Nullitatis Matrimonii,* 4 ian. 1934, coram R.P.D. Guillelmo Heard, Dec. I, n. 2—*S.R.R. Dec.,* XXVI (1934), 1-11; S.R.R., *Parisien., Nullitatis Matrimonii,* 13 apr. 1939, coram Exc.mo P.D. Iulio Grazioli, Decano, Dec. XXII, n. 2—*S.R.R. Dec.,* XXXI (1939), 193-194.

[130] Cf., e.g., Noldin-Schmitt, *Summa Theologiae Moralis,* III, n. 634; Bouscaren-Ellis, *Commentary,* p. 509; Vermeersch, *Theologia Moralis,* III, n. 735.

ever, to take this position would seem to be an unwarranted extension of the rules of canonical jurisprudence into the secular courts. There is nothing in the natural law which forbids legitimate authority to give a seducer only the alternative of marrying the woman or of being punished, as the Church did in certain cases before the Code. Since the seducer's obligation in conscience is either *to marry* or *to endow,* there seems to be no sound reason why legitimate public authority, even that of the State, could not establish by law that only one of these alternatives would obtain.

3. On the other hand, if the law provided that a seducer's sentence would be suspended if he *either* married the woman *or* endowed her, and a judge, unauthorized by law so to do, would bind the seducer simply to marry the woman or to accept the penalties provided in the law, such an action would be unjust. Some authors would call this an injustice *quoad substantiam,* others would call it an injustice *quoad modum.*[131]

4. If a seducer were found guilty according to law, and the law left it to the discretion of the judge to offer the seducer the alternative of marriage or endowment, or to offer him merely the alternative of marriage as a condition for suspending the sentence to penalties, the judge could not be accused of injustice if he bound the man simply either to marriage or to the acceptance of the penalties provided in the law.

5. A final case presents special difficulties. Suppose that in a given case it were quite evident that if a seducer married the woman it would cause grave scandal, or that the marriage would almost certainly end in failure. In this case, would it be just for a judge, according to the provisions of the law, to sentence a seducer to severe penalties with the provision that this sentence would be suspended only upon condition that the seducer *marry the woman?* In this case, if the man is guilty of the crime and has been found guilty in court, the action of the judge in sentencing him to severe penalties *is certainly just.* If the judge specifically points out to the culprit that the sentence will be suspended if the seducer marries the woman, he is only doing what the law provides. The law would be an unwise law if it permitted a man to marry in order to avoid

---

[131] Cf. *supra,* p. 118, notes 64 and 65.

penalties in a case in which the marriage would cause scandal or in which the marriage is almost certainly doomed to failure; nevertheless it seems that the responsibility for this *rests with the seducer.* The law is made for the generality of cases. If in a particular case marriage would cause scandal or seems to be foredoomed to failure, it is the seducer's obligation to accept the penalties which have been inflicted upon him. The action of the judge in calling to the attention of the seducer the provision that the penalties would be suspended if the seducer married the woman could scarcely be called unjust.

But if in this same case the law left it to the discretion of the judge to suspend sentence if the seducer consented *either* to marry *or* to endow the woman, and the judge were to insist upon the alternative of marriage in the face of probable scandal or a probable unsuccessful marriage, his action would be unjust.

§ 10. *The Justice and the Injustice of Action by Private Persons; Threats of Accusation*

1. A private person has every right to use persuasion to bring another to fulfill the payment of his debts. However, no private person has the right to threaten or to inflict harm or penalties upon another, even though the threatened penalties are the same as those which lawful public authority could apply. If a private person threatened to punish or actually punished an *innocent* person whom he had charged with seduction, the action would be unjust *quoad substantiam.*[132] If a private person threatened to punish or actually punished another who was truly guilty of seduction with punishment other than that which lawful public authority would inflict, some authors would call this unjust *quoad substantiam*[133] while others would call it unjust *quoad modum.*[134] If a private person threatened to punish or actually punished a person guilty of seduction with the same penalties which would be applied by lawful public authority, the action would be unjust *quoad modum.*[135]

---

[132] Cf. *supra,* p. 118, n. 1, note 63.
[133] Cf. *supra,* p. 118, n. 2, note 64.
[134] *Supra, ibidem,* note 65.
[135] Cf. *supra,* p. 122, n. 4, note 75.

2. The justice and injustice of the threats of accusing another to public authority is a more complex problem. To evaluate the justice of a threat to lodge an accusation several factors must be considered: a. the right of the accuser to prefer charges; b. the existence of the crime with which the accused will be charged; c. the jurisdiction of the court before which the charges will be made; d. the penalties which this court will inflict if the accused is found guilty; e. the alternative provided in the law as conditions for the possible suspension of penalties; f. the condition or conditions proposed to the accused by the accuser as alternatives to the threatened lodging of charges.

3. *The right of the accuser to prefer charges.* Since the suppression of crime is in the interest of the common good, it is generally admitted that every member of a given society has the right to accuse a criminal of his crime, though the procedure for making such an accusation differs according to the several jurisdictions. However, every person has the natural right to his good reputation, and, therefore, the natural law itself requires that a person must have some reasonable assurance that a crime has been committed and that *this* person committed it before he has the right to accuse this person. To violate this fundamental rule is certainly an injustice.[136]

4. *The existence of the crime.* To accuse or to threaten to accuse another of a crime that has *not been committed* is an objective, material injustice *quoad substantiam,* even though the party who threatens the accusation does so in good faith.[137]

5. *The jurisdiction of the court.* To accuse or to threaten to accuse a person guilty of a crime to a court which has no jurisdiction over the accused is an injustice *quoad modum.*[138]

---

[136] Cf. S.R.R., *Angelorum et S. Didaci, Nullitatis Matrimonii,* 4 ian. 1934, coram R.P.D. Guillelmo Heard, Dec. I, n. 6—*S.R.R. Dec.,* XXVI (1934), 6, where cognizance is taken of this rule in a concrete case. Also note the caution enjoined by canon 1946, § 2, n. 3.

[137] Cf. *supra,* p. 118, n. 1, note 63; p. 120, § 4, note 68; Sangmeister, *Force and Fear,* p. 120, note 150; De Smet, *De Sponsalibus et Matrimonio,* p. 472, n. 538, note 3.

[138] S.R.R., *Nullitatis Matrimonii,* 21 oct. 1946, coram R.P.D. (Francisco) Brennan—apud *Il Diritto Ecclesiastico,* LVII (1946), 339.

6. *The condition or conditions proposed by the accuser.* Threats of accusing another are generally made under a condition: "either you marry the woman, or I will accuse you," or "either marry or endow the woman, or I will accuse you." It is in the evaluation of the justice of threats made under such conditions that difficulties arise.

a. The Rota and the authors are generally content to state that it is just to threaten a seducer with accusation unless he *either marries or endows the woman.*[139]

b. On the other hand, certain decisions seem to hold that the threat to accuse under the simple condition that the seducer must *marry or be accused* is just.[140]

c. The two positions can be reconciled. It has been seen above that the ecclesiastical judge generally must give the seducer the alternative either of marrying, or of endowing the woman or of accepting canonical penalties. In two cases however, namely, when the seduction was accomplished by means of a promise to contract marriage, and when the seducer is unable to endow the woman, some authors permit that the judge impose *marriage* as the only alternative to penalties.[141] It has also been seen that the laws of some secular jurisdictions may permit the judge to suspend sentence only upon the condition that the seducer *marry* the woman, while other laws may permit the judge to suspend sentence if the seducer *either* marries the woman *or* endows her.

Now, if a person who threatens to accuse another of seduction were permitted to threaten accusation *unless the seducer married* the woman, while the court to which the accusation would be made was required to offer the seducer the alternative *either* of marrying the woman *or* of endowing her, then more authority would be given to a private person than is given to the court itself. In other

---

[139] Sangmeister, *Force and Fear,* pp. 117-118; De Smet, *De Sponsalibus et Matrimonio,* p. 472, n. 538; Vermeersch-Creusen, *Epitome,* II, p. 264, n. 375; Coronata, *De Sacramentis,* III, p. 635, n. 472; S.R.R., *Nullitatis Matrimonii,* 22 dec. 1934, coram R.P.D. Henrico Quattrocolo, Dec. XCV, n. 11—*S.R.R. Dec.,* XXVI (1934), 800.

[140] S.R.R., *Nullitatis Matrimonii,* 21 oct. 1946, coram R.P.D. (Francisco) Brennan—apud *Il Diritto Ecclesiastico* LVII (1946), 339; S.R.R., *Angelorum et S. Didaci, Nullitatis Matrimonii,* 10 nov. 1934, coram R.P.D. Andrea Jullien, Dec. LXXXV, n. 2—*S.R.R. Dec.,* XXVI (1934), 728.

[141] Cf. *supra,* pp. 134-137, notes 108-120.

words, it seems reasonable to conclude that the justice of the threats of accusing a seducer under an alternative must be judged in terms of the *alternative* to which the seducer will be subjected by the court when action is taken upon the accusation.

ARTICLE VII. THE QUALIFICATION: *A Quo Ut Quis Se Liberet, Eligere Cogatur Matrimonium*

§ 1. *The Problem*

It is universally agreed that the clause *a quo ut quis se liberet, cogatur eligere matrimonium* was substituted in the wording of canon 1087 for the references which pre-Code jurisprudence had made to the intention of the person inflicting fear upon another.[142] However, when it comes to determining the meaning of the phrase more definitely, the authors are divided. As will be seen below: 1. some hold that the phrase is verified only in cases in which the person inflicting the fear has the *intention of causing marriage* (*metus directe incussus*); 2. others hold that the phrase is verified both when the fear is *directe incussus* and also whenever the victim of the fear is placed in such objective circumstances by the agent causing the fear that he is personally convinced that marriage is the only escape (the *unicum effugium*) from an unjust harm or evil regardless of the intention of the agent inflicting the fear. Concerning this dispute, Sangmeister concluded in 1932:

> Since the opinion . . . which requires a directly inflicted fear enjoys at least extrinsic probability, a marriage in which there is any positive doubt on this point could not be declared null and void until the Holy See makes some definite declaration.[143]

The particular interest here will be to examine the evolution of opinion on this point since 1932.

§ 2. *Opinion of Those Who Hold That Only "Metus Directe Incussus" Invalidates Marriage*

In a rather exhaustive article on this topic written in 1932 Wyszynski lists the following authors as holding that only *metus*

[142] Cf. *supra*, pp. 71-75, note 31-46.

[143] *Force and Fear*, p. 136.

directe incussus invalidates marriage: Noldin-Schmitt, Tanquerey, Prümmer, De Smet, Vlaming, Leitner, Blat, Fourneret, Wernz-Vidal, Knecht, Hilling, and Bouaert. He also lists twelve Rota decisions as expressing this view.[144] Though Wyszynski lists De Smet as holding this opinion, De Smet clearly teaches that there may be exceptions to this rule.[145] For this reason, no doubt, Roberti lists De Smet among the authors who hold that fear can invalidate marriage though it be only *indirecte incussus*.[146]

More recently the position which requires *metus directe incussus* has been vigorously defended by Fedele. Fedele bases his argument on these two points: 1. if the person inflicting the fear does not intend to cause the giving of matrimonial consent by the victim, then the determination of matrimonial consent is *ab intrinseco;* 2. because the fear is *ab intrinseco* it cannot be said to be *iniuste incussus*.[147] When pressed to justify this position, Fedele answered that the purpose of canon 1087 was to suppress injustice peculiar to matrimonial coercion rather than to protect the freedom of matrimonial consent.[148]

Vidal, insisting on the words *ob* and *cogatur eligere* in canon 1087, defends his position by declaring that the fear must be the *cause* of the marriage in order to invalidate it, and that the fear which is not *directe incussus* is the mere occasion and not the cause of the marriage.[149]

If to the foregoing arguments one add the consideration that *metus directe incussus* was postulated by the majority of the authors prior to the Code, then the full strength of the position which postulates a *metus directe incussus* becomes manifest.

---

[144] Wyszynski, "Utrum Metus Indirecte Incussus Dirimere Possit Matrimonium," *Jus Pontificium,* XII (1932), 59-60. Cf. also Sangmeister, *Force and Fear,* p. 131.

[145] *De Sponsalibus et Matrimonio,* p. 471, n. 537.

[146] Roberti, "De Metu Indirecto quoad Negotia Iuridica praesertim Matrimonium," *Apollinaris,* XI (1938), 558.

[147] Fedele, *Vizi del Consenso Matrimoniale,* p. 31*.

[148] *Op. cit.,* pp. 57-58. For a refutation of this cf. *supra,* pp. 101-103, notes 1-13.

[149] *Ius Canonicum,* V, n. 501.

Payen, Dossetti and Regatillo must also be listed among the more recent authors who have insisted that only a *metus directe incussus* certainly invalidates the marriage. Payen adds the note that there will hardly ever be a case in which marriage is the *unicum effugium* from fear unless the fear had been *directe incussus.*[150] Dossetti adds a distinctive note which is purely accidental in character when he insists that the fear may have been inflicted *from the beginning* for some purpose other than that of causing marriage, but that, *at least for a moment* before the victim gives matrimonial consent, it must be *the intention of the agent* to cause that consent.[151] Regatillo adds a final argument by means of his appeal to the decisions of the Rota:

> Neque in collectione *Rotae Romanae Decisiones* usque ad a. 1937 inclusive invenimus unam sententiam nullitatis *ex capite metus indirecti. . . .*[152]

The validity of all these arguments will be considered in turn in the following pages. For the moment cognizance must be taken of those Rota decisions which defend the position that only a *metus directe incussus* invalidates marriage. There are a number of Rota decisions which explicitly defend this opinion.[153] It is to be noted that any argument based upon the jurisprudence of the Roman Rota will depend almost exclusively upon decisions *coram Grazioli.*

---

[150] *De Matrimonio,* II, n. 1686.

[151] *La Violenza nel Matrimonio,* p. 208.

[152] *Ius Sacramentarium,* II, p. 333, n. 501 C.

[153] S.R.R., *Lublinen., Nullitatis Matrimonii,* 25 nov. 1924 coram R.P.D. Iulio Grazioli, Dec. XLV, n. 2—*S.R.R. Dec.,* XVI (1924), 396; S.R.R., *Transilvanien., Nullitatis Matrimonii,* 27 mart. 1931, coram R.P.D. Iulio Grazioli, Dec. XIII, n. 5—*S.R.R. Dec.,* XXIII (1931), 103; S.R.R., *Nullitatis Matrimonii,* 2 dec. 1935, coram R.P.D. Iulio Grazioli, Dec. LXXXIV, n. 5—*S.R.R. Dec.,* XXVII (1935), 623; S.R.R., *Nullitatis Matrimonii,* 8 aug. 1938, coram Exc.mo P.D. Iulio Grazioli, Decano, Dec. LIX, n. 2—*S.R.R. Dec.,* XXX (1938), 534; S.R.R., *Romana, Nullitatis Matrimonii,* 15 mart. 1933, coram R.P.D. Stanislao Janasik, Dec. XVIII, n. 2—*S.R.R. Dec.,* XXV (1933), 143.

§ 3. *Refutation of the Arguments Proposed in Support of the Opinion Which Requires "Metus Directe Incussus"*

1. Fear can be *ab extrinseco* without being *directe incussus.* Fedele's argument is that unless the fear is inflicted with the intention of causing marriage it is *ab intrinseco.*[154] This is true if one considers only the formulated orientation of the fear: in other words, if an agent inflicts fear for some purpose other than marriage, and *the victim sees* that marriage is the only escape from the impending harm or danger, the formulated *nexus* between the fear and the danger is *ab intrinseco.* However, to insist that *this nexus* must also be *ab extrinseco* is simply begging the question. The canon says only *ob metum ab extrinseco;* it does not say *ob metum cuius nexus cum matrimonio est ab extrinseco.* If an agent tells a victim that he is going to shoot him because he hates him, this fear is *ab extrinseco,* and, as far as origin is concerned this is all that the canon requires.[155]

2. Fear can be unjust without being *directe incussus.* Fedele argues that unless fear is caused *with the intention* of extorting matrimonial consent it is not unjust.[156] It is true that it is not unjust *qua coactio matrimonialis,* but again the argument is based on a *petitio principii.* The canon says *ob metum iniuste incussum,* it does not say *ob metum iniustum quantum praecise ordinatur ad cogendum consensum matrimonialem.* An agent can tell an innocent man that he is going to charge him with murder in order to keep someone else from being suspected, and the action is unjust *quoad substantiam.* All that the canon says is that the fear must be *iniuste incussus.* To require that this injustice consist precisely in the intention of the agent who is determined to *cause marriage* is simply reading into the canon words that are not there.

3. Fear can be the cause of marriage even though it is not *directe incussus.* Vidal taught that if the fear is not inflicted for the

---

[154] *Vizi del Consenso Matrimoniale,* p. 31*.

[155] For a thorough refutation of this and the other arguments of Fedele cf. Pietro Agostino D'Avack, "Sul Metus Consultus nel Codex Juris Canonici," *Studi di Storia e Diritto in Onore di Enrico Besta per il XL Anno del Suo Insegnamento* (4 vols., Milano: Dott. A. Giuffre, 1937-1939), III, 243-276.

[156] *Vizi del Consenso Matrimoniale,* p. 31*.

purpose of causing marriage, then it is the mere *occasion* and not the cause of marriage as is required by canon 1087. This argument is refuted in a Rota decision which stands not merely on extrinsic authority but also on the basis of internal logic. The Rota's argument, therefore, is here quoted at some length:

> *Causa* nempe dicitur id quod natura sua producit effectum, seu quam natura sua sequitur effectus; dum *occasio,* licet aliquid conferat ut effectus sequatur, tamen non natura sua in eum tendit, quia illum non continet totum virtute sua. Tum vero, praeeunte canone, dicemus matrimonium contractum *ob* metum, seu metum fuisse *causam* matrimonii, cum metum passus in talibus obiectivis circumstantiis versetur ob eum qui metum infert, ut ab extrinseco coniiciatur in alternativum "aut hoc, gravem nempe metum, aut matrimonium."[157]

In other words, when the objective circumstances indicate to the victim that marriage is the only escape from a harm or evil that an adverse agent has brought to bear upon him, that *harm or evil* is the objective cause of the marriage. To require that the harm or evil be also the intentional, formal cause of the marriage in the mind of the agent is to beg the question.

4. No conclusive argument can be drawn from the practice of the Rota. Regatillo (in 1946) stated that he had not found any decision of the Rota down to the year 1937 inclusive which held that fear *indirecte incussus* could invalidate marriage.[158] However, a decision which was issued in 1922 concerning a marriage which took place before the Code stated the following: *nihilque refert, quod metus directe an indirecte influat in matrimonii consensum.*[159] Furthermore, in 1938 the Rota ruled:

> Iure Codicis, nullum est matrimonium, tum si metus gravis sit directe incussus ad extorquendum consensum

---

[157] S.R.R., *Nullitatis Matrimonii,* 11 maii 1926, coram R.P.D. Ubaldo Mannucci, Dec. XXIII, n. 2—*S.R.R. Dec.,* XVIII (1926), 175-176.

[158] *Ius Sacramentarium,* II, n. 333, n. 501 C.

[159] S.R.R., *Nullitatis Matrimonii,* 9 ian. 1922, coram R.P.D. Iosepho Florczak, Dec. I, n. 3—*S.R.R. Dec.,* XIV (1922), 2-3.

> matrimonialem, tum si ad hoc non sit directe incussus. . . .[160]

These two examples are given here simply in direct refutation, to show the inadequacy of Regatillo's statement as a comprehensive claim in the matter. The full import of the jurisprudence of the Rota will be examined in the subsequent pages.

5. The argument that appeals to the opinion which was held by the majority of the authors before the Code will also be studied in the following pages.

§ 4. *The Opinion of Those Who Do Not Require That the Fear Be "Directe Incussus"*

Since 1932 there has been a definite tendency among the authors and the decisions of the Rota in favor of the opinion which does not require the fear to be *directe incussus* in order to invalidate marriage. It is to be noted from the beginning that this opinion does not state simply that a *metus indirecte incussus* suffices to invalidate marriage. This opinion *adds* that marriage must be the *unicum effugium* in order to avoid the threatened harm or evil. This opinion holds that canon 1087 does not look so much to the intention of the agent who causes the fear, but that it looks rather to the necessity in which the fear places the victim. Those who oppose this opinion are too easily inclined to make the question simply one of *metus directe incussus vs. metus indirecte incussus* which, of course would be a false over-simplification of the issue.

In the 1932 edition of his work *De Matrimonio* Cardinal Gasparri revealed the discussion of the Pontifical Commission which prepared the Code on the clause *a quo ut quis se liberet, eligere cogatur matrimonium.*[161] The text is of prime importance and, therefore, will be quoted at length:

> Antiquo iure gravis erat hac de re controversia. Gravissimi enim AA. putabant metum gravem . . . non irritare

[160] S.R.R., *Nullitatis Matrimonii,* 20 iul. 1938, coram R.P.D. Caesare Pecorari, Dec. XLVIII, n. 5—*S.R.R. Dec.,* XXX (1938), 438. As this case did not appear in print until 1946, one may assume that it was not available when Regatillo wrote in that year.

[161] *Op. cit.,* II, n. 856.

> matrimonium, nisi esset directus ad extorquendum consensum matrimonialem; sed alii non minus graves DD. id negabant, inter quos Schmalz., lib. IV, disp. I, n. 398 seq., et De Lugo, *De iust. et iur.*, disp. XXII, n. 175, seq. Ut legitur in actis praeparatoriis ad Codicem, examini Consultorum propositus fuerat canon primae sententiae favens: § 1. *Nullum quoque est matrimonium initum ob metum gravem ab extrinseco et iniuste incussum in ordine ad extorquendum consensum matrimonialem.* Praeses Commissionis recoluit gravem, quae in subiecta materia aderat, controversiam inter canonistas; et P. Palmieri proposuit ut formula, quae in suo voto erat quaeque utramque sententiam comprehendit, acceptaretur: *Metus debet esse ab extrinseco, iniuste incussus, a quo ut quis se liberet, eligere cogatur matrimonium,* quae reipsa acceptata fuit. Hinc iure Codicis nullum est matrimonium tum si metus gravis sit directe incussus ad extorquendum consensum matrimonialem, tum si ad hoc non sit directe incussus, sed pars persuasum habeat se ab eo liberare non posse, nisi matrimonium contrahat. Proinde iure Codicis matrimonium est certe invalidum in casibus qui sequuntur: 1. Si Titius aggreditur Caiam ut eam interficiat: Caia, ut mortem effugiat, offert nuptias; Titius acceptat; 2. Si pater Titium, stupratorem filiae suae Annae, vult interficere ad vindictam criminis et offensae; Titius ut sese leberet, nuptias proponit cum Anna; pater acceptat; 3. Si mulier infirma, cum medicus curationem ex officio et iustitia debitam eidem denegaverit ex odio, ignavia, aliave causa, promittit matrimonium eidem vel eius filio, ut sic medicus ad praestandam curationem inducatur; medicus assentitur; et ita porro in similibus casibus.[162]

Three things appear clearly from this statement: 1. the Commission rejected the formula which required absolutely that the fear be *directe incussus;* 2. the Commission did not select a formula which stated simply that *metus indirecte incussus* suffices; 3. the formula of the Code was selected as embracing both *metus directe incussus* and *metus indirecte incussus,* and Cardinal Gasparri explained that if consideration is to be given to *metus indirecte insussus* the victim must be convinced that marriage is the only means open to him for escaping from the harm or evil with which he is threatened.

[162] *Op. cit., loc. cit.*

Now the question arises: what authority must be attached to this statement? The Rota answers this question in one decision as follows:

> E.mus Gasparri in exponenda hac re non considerandus est ut merus Doctor privatus utcumque gravis, cuius opinioni contradicere liceat sicuti cuilibet alii Auctori, sed potius ut Praeses Commissionis Pontificiae ad redigendum novum Codicem Iuris Canonici institutae.[163]

However, Payen is not satisfied with this explanation. He states:

> De *mente* scriptorum nos docet C. Gasparri. Sed *verba,* quae ad hanc mentem *exprimendam* adhibuerunt, non videntur ita clara ut *omne dubium* expellant, et controversiam dirimant.[164]

Payen seems to involve himself in a vicious circle. He says that the words which the codifiers of the Code selected are not so clear as to clear away *all doubt.* He says that Cardinal Gasparri explained the mind of the codifiers in selecting these words. Then he goes back to the words themselves and insists on their dubious meaning. Words themselves are not going to change by being explained and any lack of clarity in them certainly cannot be better explained than by the person who speaks or writes them.

Cardinal Gasparri's explanation has proved sufficient for the majority of the current authors:

> VERMEERSCH-CREUSEN: Cum autem doceamur Codicis verba electa fuisse, positive reiecto textu qui requireret "metum incussum ad extorquendum consensum" . . . disputationi locus iam non est.[165]

> BOUSCAREN-ELLIS: We cannot read into a canon words which are not there, especially when we know that they were explicitly rejected.[166]

[163] S.R.R., *Lincien., Nullitatis Matrimonii,* 5 dec. 1933, coram R.P.D. Arcturo Wynen, Dec. LXXII, n. 3—*S.R.R. Dec.,* XXV (1933), 608-609.

[164] *De Matrimonio,* II, n. 1686, pp. 85-86, note 6.

[165] *Epitome,* II, p. 264, n. 376.

[166] *Commentary,* pp. 508-509.

> HEYLEN: sententia asserens non requiri metum directe incussum ad extorquendum consensum . . . nunc certa est. . . .[167]

As far as the decisions of the Rota are concerned, it must be admitted that in the years immediately after the promulgation of the Code of Canon Law most of them favored the view that only *metus directe incussus* invalidates marriage. However, one has an entirely inadequate view of the jurisprudence of the Rota if one restricts oneself to an examination of the early decisions. The vast majority of the decisions, so numerous as to make citation impracticable, simply advert to the clause *a quo ut quis se liberet, eligere cogatur matrimonium* without further comment. But over and above this there are numerous decisions which insist that a *metus directe incussus* is not required. These decisions leave little doubt that the Rota, at least on many occasions, considered the clause *a quo ut quis se liberet, eligere cogatur matrimonium* as looking to the necessity of the victim and not necessarily at the motive of the agent of the fear:

> Ut igitur probetur matrimonium irritum ex capite metus, demonstrari debet nupturientem matrimonio tantummodo consensisse ad evitandum aliquod grave malum, a causa libera iniuste procedens, quod sibi persuasum habuit vere imminere, et quod alio modo quam matrimonio effugere non potuit.[168]

---

[167] *Tractatus de Matrimonio* (9. ed., Mechliniae: H. Dessain, 1945), p. 221; cf. also Sangmeister, *Force and Fear*, pp. 127, 134; De Smet, *De Sponsalibus et Matrimonio*, p. 471, n. 537; Sipos, *Enchiridion*, pp. 602-603; Wyszynski, "Utrum Metus Indirecte Incussus Dirimere Possit Matrimonium," *Jus Pontificium*, XII (1932), 62; Roberti, "De Metu Indirecto quoad Negotia Iuridica praesertim Matrimonium," *Apollinaris*, XI (1938), 560; Cappello, *De Sacramentis*, V, 592, n. 607; Chelodi-Ciprotti, *De Matrimonio*, p. 144, n. 118; Coronata, *De Sacramentis*, III, p. 641, n. 479; *ibidem*, p. 645, n. 481; Jemolo, *Il Matrimonio nel Diritto Canonico*, p. 226, n. 119; Vermeersch, *Theologia Moralis*, III, n. 735.

[168] S.R.R., *Westmonasterien., Nullitatis Matrimonii*, 25 iul. 1932, coram R.P.D. Guillelmo Heard, Dec. XXXVII, n. 3—*S.R.R. Dec.*, XXIV (1932), 350. Cf. also S.R.R., *Nullitatis Matrimonii*, 12 dec. 1925, coram R.P.D. Andrea Jullien, Dec. L, n. 2—*S.R.R. Dec.*, XVII (1925), 401; S.R.R., *Nullitatis Matrimonii*, 11 maii 1926, coram R.P.D. Ubaldo Mannucci, Dec.

Practical Summary

1. Since 1932 the following authors have continued to hold that only *metus directe incussus* invalidates marriage: Fedele, Vidal, Payen, Regatillo, Dossetti. Their chief argument is, necessarily, that *metus directe incussus* was postulated by the majority of the pre-Code authors and that it is not perfectly evident that the Code departed from this position.

2. Today, the majority of the authors hold that *metus indirecte incussus* invalidates marriage if the fear places its victim in such circumstances that he is convinced that marriage is the *unicum effugium* for him to avoid the harm or evil with which he is threatened. This position is taken by: Gasparri, Vermeersch-Creusen, Bouscaren-Ellis, Heylen, Sangmeister, Sipos, Roberti, Cappello, Chelodi-Ciprotti, Coronata and Jemolo, and is held in at least thirteen Rota decisions issued between the years 1932-1939.

3. Even those authors who still hold that *metus directe incussus* is required of fear in order that it invalidate marriage would logically be forced to admit that marriage is invalidated though the agent of fear begins his aggression with some other motive, but, at least for a moment before the marriage takes place, insists

XXII, n. 2—*S.R.R. Dec.,* XVIII (1926), 175-176; S.R.R., *Transilvanien., Nullitatis Matrimonii,* 6 aug. 1929, coram R.P.D. Arcturo Wynen, Dec. XLVI, n. 2—*S.R.R. Dec.,* XXI (1929), 386, S.R.R., *Scepusien., Nullitatis Matrimonii,* 4 apr. 1930, coram R.P.D. Iulio Grazioli, Dec. XVII, n. 5—*S.R.R. Dec.,* XXII (1930), 204-205; S.R.R., *Romana, Nullitatis Matrimonii,* 9 maii 1933, coram R.P.D. Iulio Grazioli, Dec. XXXV, n. 4—*S.R.R. Dec.,* XXV (1933), 298; S.R.R., *Lincien., Nullitatis Matrimonii,* 5 dec. 1933, coram R.P.D. Arcturo Wynen, Dec. LXXII, nn. 3-4—*S.R.R. Dec.,* XXV (1933), 608-610; S.R.R., *Versalien., Nullitatis Matrimonii,* 7 iun. 1934, coram R.P.D. Guillelmo Heard, Dec. XLI, n. 2—*S.R.R. Dec.,* XXVI (1934) 357; S.R.R., *Neapolitana, Nullitatis Matrimonii,* 9 iul. 1936, coram R.P.D. Stanislao Janasik, Dec. XLIX, n. 2—*S.R.R. Dec.,* XXVIII (1936), 458; S.R.R., *Romana, Nullitatis Matrimonii,* 22 dec. 1937, coram R.P.D. Andrea Jullien, Dec. LXXIX, n. 2—*S.R.R. Dec.,* XXIX (1937), 783; S.R.R., *Nullitatis Matrimonii,* 20 iul. 1938, coram R.P.D. Caesare Pecorari, Dec. XLVIII, n. 5—*S.R.R. Dec.,* XXX (1938), 438; S.R.R., *Romana, Nullitatis Matrimonii,* 30 nov. 1938, coram R.P.D. Henrico Quattrocolo, Dec. LXX, n. 3—*S.R.R. Dec.,* XXX (1938), 641; S.R.R., *Romana, Nullitatis Matrimonii,* 13 maii 1939, coram R.P.D. Guillelmo Heard, Dec. XXXII, n. 2—*S.R.R. Dec.,* XXXI (1939), 293.

that the victim enter marriage as a means of escape from the impending harm or evil.

4. Likewise, the stoutest defenders of the necessity of *metus directe incussus* are willing to admit that, if there is doubt about the intention of the agent of the fear, then a court can reasonably formulate a *presumptio hominis* that the fear was *directe incussus* if the fear placed the victim in circumstances in which marriage was the *unicum effugium* from the threatened harm or evil.[169]

5. The extreme case is had when it is certain that the agent of the fear did not intend to cause the victim to enter marriage. This writer is of the opinion that even in this case a decision of *constat de nullitate matrimonii* can be given if it is clear that the fear placed the victim in such circumstances that he prudently judged that marriage was the *unicum effugium* open to him in order to escape the impending harm or evil. The reasons for this conclusion are as follows:

a. *Leges ecclesiasticae intelligendae sunt secundum propriam verborum significationem* (canon 18) and the clause *a quo ut quis se liberet, eligere cogatur matrimonium* is completely and properly verified in this sense.

b. It is useless to appeal to canon 6, n. 4, because Cardinal Gasparri has stated definitely that the Pontifical Commission selected the wording of canon 1087 precisely as a rejection of the former majority opinion which required *metus directe incussus.*

c. The vast majority of authors who have written since 1932 hold to this interpretation; the Rota has stated this position repeatedly in its decisions; the arguments of those who still require a *metus directe incussus* are refuted so completely as to deprive them of any solidly probable canonical basis.

6. If it is objected that the recently published canons on marriage for the Oriental Churches require *metus . . . incussus ad extor-*

---

[169] Cf., e.g., Regatillo, *Ius Sacramentarium,* II, p. 334, n. 501 E; Fedele, *Vizi del Consenso Matrimoniale,* p. 39*; S.R.R., *Nullitatis Matrimonii,* 2 iul. 1918, coram R.P.D. Petro Rossetti, Dec. III, n. 15—*S.R.R. Dec.,* X (1926), 67, where this opinion is attributed to Reiffenstuel.

quendum consensum[170] the objection can be completely answered as follows:

a. These canons apply only to the Oriental Churches.

b. They have modified or changed the Latin discipline on a number of points: the impediment of disparity of cult applies to *all* marriages of persons one of whom is baptized and the other not baptized (canon 60); the *tractus longior* is not used exclusively in computing consanguinity, but all persons involved are reckoned in the computation (canon 66); sponsors in baptism contract spiritual relationship with *the parents* of the person who is baptized (canon 70); marriage is invalid if contracted under any condition whatsoever (canon 83), etc.

---

[170] *Acta Apostolicae Sedis, Commentarium Officiale* (Romae, 1909—), XXXI (12 mart. 1949), p. 106, canon 78.

CHAPTER IX

THE SOURCE OF THE INVALIDATING EFFECTS OF FORCE-FEAR UPON MARRIAGE

Since the publication of the Code of Canon Law opinion has remained divided concerning the source of the invalidating effects of force-fear upon marriage.

Among others, Gasparri,[1] Chelodi-Ciprotti,[2] Vermeersch-Creusen,[3] Sipos[4] and several decisions of the Rota[5] favor the view that force-fear as described in canon 1087 invalidate marriage only in virtue of the positive legislation of the Church. If this is true, it follows that canon 1087 affects only the marriages of baptized persons. It remains possible and even more probable, however, that unbaptized persons are affected by the statutes of the secular jurisdiction to which they belong. This question is beyond the scope of this thesis.

In defense of this view the arguments of the pre-Code authors are simply repeated.[6]

On the other hand, Wernz-Vidal,[7] Coronata,[8] Cappello[9] and at

[1] *De Matrimonio,* II, n. 841.

[2] *De Matrimonio,* p. 120, n. 146.

[3] *Epitome,* II, p. 265, n. 376.

[4] *Enchiridion,* p. 603.

[5] S.R.R., *Nullitatis Matrimonii,* 13 apr. 1936, coram Exc.mo P.D. Iulio Grazioli, Decano, Dec. XLVIII, n. 4—*S.R.R. Dec.,* XXVIII (1936), 452; S.R.R., *Kielcen., Nullitatis Matrimonii,* 21 ian. 1937, coram Exc.mo P.D. Iulio Grazioli, Decano, Dec. VI, n. 3—*S.R.R. Dec.,* XXIX (1937), 40; S.R.R., *Iannen., Nullitatis Matrimonii,* 3 dec. 1938, coram R.P.D. Stanislao Janasik, Dec. LXXIII, n. 2—*S.R.R. Dec.,* XXX (1938), 671; S.R.R., *Posnanien., Nullitatis Matrimonii,* 25 ian. 1939, coram R.P.D. Henrico Quattrocolo, Dec. VI, n. 2—*S.R.R. Dec.,* XXXI (1939), 52; S.R.R., *Parisien., Nullitatis Matrimonii,* 13 apr. 1939, coram Exc.mo P.D. Iulio Grazioli, Decano, Dec. XXII, n. 2—*S.R.R. Dec.,* XXXI (1939), 193.

[6] Cf. *supra,* pp. 62-63, nn. 1-2; pp. 95-98.

[7] *Ius Canonicum,* V, n. 502.

[8] *De Sacramentis,* III, pp. 643-645, n. 480.

[9] *De Sacramentis,* V, p. 593, n. 609.

least one decision of the Rota[10] defend the position that force-fear, as described in canon 1087, invalidate marriage in consequence of the natural law and antecedently to any positive legislation. The arguments as proposed present nothing that has not already been suggested by pre-Code authors.[11] Authors who defend this position almost invariably appeal to the authority of Saint Thomas, but significantly enough they do not quote any text to support their appeal.[12]

Finally, some authors and Rota decisions propose a middle solution, namely, that force-fear invalidate marriage on a legal basis which is founded or rooted in the natural law but determined and specified in the positive law.[13]

OBSERVATIONS

1. Perhaps the reason why this dispute has continued for so many centuries is that force-fear, as described in canon 1087, invalidate marriage *at times* in consequence of the natural law, and *at other times* in consequence of the positive law.

2. The question as here raised does not relate to the source of the invalidating effects of absolute or physical force. All agree that physical force invalidates marriage in consequence of the natural law. The question here concerns only such force-fear as do not destroy the freedom of the victim: the victim *consents to marriage* by means of an act which is voluntary *simpliciter* but involuntary *secundum quid.*

3. It cannot be denied that in times past matrimonial consent which was the effect of force-fear *was not* invalidated in certain

[10] S.R.R., *Nili Aequatorialis, Nullitatis Matrimonii,* 8 aug. 1936, coram R.P.D. Henrico Quattrocolo, Dec. XLI, n. 3—*S.R.R. Dec.,* XXVIII (1936), 584.

[11] Cf. *supra,* p. 61, notes 9-14; p. 96.

[12] For another evaluation of the position of Saint Thomas on this question, cf. *supra,* pp. 54-58, notes 14-31.

[13] Sangmeister, *Force and Fear,* pp. 162-163; De Smet, *De Sponsalibus et Matrimonio,* p. 469, n. 535; Gasparri, *De Matrimonio,* II, n. 841; Wernz-Vidal, *Ius Canonicum,* V, n. 502; S.R.R., *Nullitatis Matrimonii,* 3 dec. 1930, coram R.P.D. Arcturo Wynen, Dec. LVIII, n. 2—*S.R.R. Dec.,* XXII (1930), 641; S.R.R., *Mediolanen., Nullitatis Matrimonii,* 15 mart. 1939, coram R.P.D. Henrico Caiazzo, Dec. XVIII, n. 4—*S.R.R. Dec.,* XXXI (1939), 149.

cases in which today it would certainly be invalidated. Cases of coercion after *dolus*,[14] broken espousals,[15] and certain instances in which the *bonum pacis* demanded a certain marriage[16] are instances in point. There can be no doubt, therefore, that today marriage is invalidated *in these cases* solely in consequence of the positive law of the Church.

4. Over and above these special cases, there remain a whole gamut of possible cases falling within the range of the provisions of canon 1087. At the top of this range are cases of coercion which fall just short of absolute force: the victim consents, but the voluntary element is at the lowest possible intensity. At the bottom of this range are cases which only slightly exceed *metus levis,* but which do qualify as being *metus gravis.* Within these two extremes it seems possible to distinguish between instances in which fear invalidates in virtue of the natural law and other instances in which fear invalidates only in virtue of the positive law.

5. In cases in which the fear overcomes an antipathy to marriage which is of such intensity as to render impossible the attainment of the primary end of marriage, which is the procreation and education of offspring, the marriage is invalid in virtue of the natural law.

6. In cases in which the fear overcomes an antipathy to marriage which is not of such intensity as to render the primary end of marriage impossible of attainment, the marriage is invalid only in consequence simply of the Church's own positive law, which in canon 1087 specifies and applies as a conclusion that which is in harmony with the principles of the natural law.

7. The conclusions drawn in nn. 5-6 seem to flow naturally from the principles enunciated by Saint Thomas Aquinas.[17]

AD MAIOREM DEI GLORIAM
ANIMARUMQUE SALUTEM

---

[14] Cf. *supra,* p. 48, note 79.

[15] Cf. *supra,* pp. 36-38, note 40-50; p. 84, n. 5, note 76.

[16] Cf. *supra,* p. 49, note 80.

[17] Cf. *supra,* pp. 54-58, notes 14-31.

CONCLUSIONS

1. The purpose of the legislator in enacting canon 1087 was: a. to protect the full freedom of matrimonial consent; b. to preclude the unhappy results usually attendant upon coerced marriages; c. to restrain injustice (pp. 101-104).

2. Canon 1087 more probably contemplates only *conditional force* which, in its ultimate effect, is identical with *fear.* This effect is a *voluntary act* on the part of the victim giving matrimonial consent, which would not have been given except for an impending harm or evil (pp. 104-109).

3. It is now certain that the phrase *iniuste incussus* in canon 1087 embraces not only *metus iniustus quoad substantiam* but also *metus iniustus quoad modum tantum* (pp. 112-123).

4. It is more probable that an ecclesiastical judge cannot justly coerce a seducer *to marry,* to the neglect of the alternative of *endowing the woman.* However, some hold that an ecclesiastical judge can require *marriage* of a seducer under threat of canonical penalties: a. if the seduction had been made possible by a promise to marry; b. if the seducer is unable to endow the woman (pp. 127-137).

5. The justice of coercion by a secular judge must be estimated in terms of the provisions of the secular law (pp. 138-142).

6. The justice of coercion by private persons who threaten a seducer with accusation before a court must be estimated in terms: a. of the right of the accuser to prefer charges; b. of the guilt of the accused; c. of the jurisdiction of the court before which the charges will be made; d. of the alternatives to which the accused has a right if he is brought into court (pp. 142-145).

7. In consequence of the clause, *a quo ut quis se liberet, cogatur eligere matrimonium,* marriage is invalidated by a fear which puts the victim into such a position that he prudently judges that marriage is the *unicum effugium* from the impending harm or evil. The canon thus looks rather to the circumstances into which the fear thrusts the victim than to the intention of the

agent of the fear. The opinion of those few authors who hold that only *metus directe incussus* invalidates marriage seems to be devoid of solid probability (pp. 145-156).

8. Fear invalidates marriage in consequence of the natural law if it of sufficient intensity to overcome an antipathy to marriage which is so great as to render impossible the procreation and education of offspring. Fear invalidates marriage in consequence of the positive law if it only of sufficient intensity to overcome an antipathy to marriage which leaves intact the possibility of the accomplishment of the primary end of marriage (pp. 157-159).

BIBLIOGRAPHY

Sources

Acta Apostolicae Sedis, Commentarium Officiale, Romae, 1909—.

Augustinus, Antonius, *Antiquae Collectiones Decretalium,* Iliriae, 1571.

Corpus Iuris Canonici, ed. Lipsiensis secunda, 2 vols., post Aemilii Ludovici Richteri curas instruxit Aemilius Friedberg, 1879-1881; ed. Anastatice repetita, Lipsiae, Tauchnitz, 1928.

Corpus Iuris Civilis, 3 vols., Berolini, 1928-1929; Vol. I, *Institutiones,* ed. stereotypa quinta decima, recognovit Theodorus Mommsen, retractavit Paulus Krueger, 1928; Vol. II, *Codex Iustinianus,* ed. stereotypa decima, recognovit et retractavit Paulus Krueger, 1929.

Cironius, Innocentius, *Compilatio V,* Tolosae, 1645.

Decretales Gregorii IX una cum glossis, Romae, 1582.

Codex Iuris Canonici Pii X Pontificis Maximi iussu digestus Benedicti Papae XV auctoritate promulgatus, Romae, Typis Polyglottis Vaticanis, 1917.

Decretum Gratiani una cum glossis, 2 vols., Venetiis, 1605.

Digesta Iustiniani Augusti, 2 vols., recognovit, adsumpto in operis societatem Paulo Kruegero, Th. Mommsen, Berolini, apud Weidmannos, 1870.

Jaffé, Philippus, *Regesta Pontificum Romanorum ab condita Ecclesia ad annum post Christum natum MCXCVIII,* 2. ed., 2 toms. in 1 vol., correctam et auctam auspiciis Gulielmi Wattenbach curaverunt F. Kaltenbrunner, P. Ewald, S. Löwenfeld, Lipsiae, 1885-1888.

Potthast, August, *Regesta Pontificum Romanorum, MCXCVIII ad MCCCIX,* 2 vols., Berolini, 1874-1875.

Sacrae Romanae Rotae Decisiones seu Sententiae . . . quae prodierunt anno 1909—, Romae, Typis Polyglottis Vaticanis, 1912—.

Schroeder, H. J., *Canons and Decrees of the Council of Trent,* St. Louis-London, Herder, 1941.

Thesaurus Resolutionum Sacrae Congregationis Concilii, 167 vols., Urbini et Romae, 1718-1908.

Thiel, A., *Epistolae Romanorum Pontificum Genuinae et quae ad eos scriptae sunt A Hilario usque ad S. Hormisdam,* Brunsbergae, 1868.

Reference Works

Alford, Culver B., *Jus Matrimoniale Comparatum,* Romae, Anonima Libreria Cattolica Italiana-New York, Kenedy, 1938.

Alphonsus M. de Ligorio, St., *Theologia Moralis,* 4 toms., ed. Gaudé, Romae, Typis Polyglottis Vaticanis, 1905-1912.

Barbosa, Augustinus, *Collectanea in Ius Pontificium,* 6 toms., Ludguni, 1656.

Berardi, Carolus Sebastianus, *Gratiani Canones Genuini ab Apocryphis Discreti,* 4 vols., Venetiis, 1777.

Biondi, Biondo, *Istituzioni di Diritto Romano,* Milano, A. Giuffre, 1946.

Bouscaren, T. Lincoln-Ellis, Adam C., *Canon Law, a Text and Commentary,* 2nd printing, Milwaukee, The Bruce Publishing Company, 1948.

Cangardel, Louis, *Le Consentement des Epoux au Mariage,* Paris, Libraire du Recueil Sirey, 1934.

Cappello, Felix M., *Tractatus Canonico-Moralis de Sacramentis,* 5 vols., Vol. III, 5. ed., *De Matrimonio,* Augustae Taurinorum-Romae, Domus Editorialis Marietti, 1947.

Chelodi, Ioannes, *Ius Canonicum de Matrimonio,* 5. ed., recognita et aucta a Pio Ciprotti, Vicenza, Società Anonima Tipografica Editrice, 1947.

Coronata, Matthaeus Conte a, *De Sacramentis,* 3 vols., Taurini-Romae, Domus Editorialis Marietti, Vol. I, 1943; Vol. II, 1945; Vol. III, 1946.

D'Annibale, Iosephus Cardinalis, *Summula Theologiae Moralis,* 5. ed., 4 vols., Romae, 1908-1909.

Dauvillier, Jean, *Le Mariage dans le Droit Classique de l'Eglise, depuis le Décret de Gratien (1140), jusqu'à la Mort de Clement V (1314),* Paris, Libraire du Recueil Sirey, 1933.

De Becker, Julius, *De Sponsalibus et Matrimonio Praelectiones Canonicae,* 2. ed., Lovanii, 1903.

De Lugo, Joannes, *Opera Omnia,* 4 toms., in 2 vols., Venetiis, 1718.

De Smet, Al., *Tractatus Theologico-Canonicus de Sponsalibus et Matrimonio,* 4. ed., inde a Codice altera, Brugis, Car. Beyaert, 1927.

Dictionnaire de Théologie Catholique, 15 vols. in 30, Paris, Mabillion-Marletta, 1903—.

Dossetti, Giuseppe, *La Violenza nel Matrimonio in Diritto Canonico,* Milano, Società Editrice "Vita e Pensiero," 1943.

Esmein, A., *Le Mariage en Droit Canonique,* 2 vols., Vol. I, 2. ed., mise à jour par R. Généstal, Paris, Librairie du Recueil Sirey, 1929.

Fagnanus, Prosper, *Commentaria in Quinque Libros Decretalium,* 4 vols., Venetiis, 1696.

Fair, Bartholomew Francis L., *The Inpediment of Abduction,* The Catholic University of America Canon Law Studies, n. 194, Washington, D. C., The Catholic University of America Press, 1944.

Fedele, Pio, *Contributi alla Teoria Canonistica dei Vizi del Consenso Matrimoniale,* Firenze, Casa Editrice del Dottore Carlo Cya, 1940.

Ferraris, Lucius, *Prompta Bibliotheca Canonica, Iuridica, Moralis, Theologica nec non Ascetica, Polemica, Rubricistica, Historica,* 9 toms., Romae, 1885-1899.

Gasparri, P., *Tractatus Canonicus de Matrimonio,* 2 vols., 3. ed., Parisiis, 1904.

———, *Tractatus Canonicus de Matrimonio,* ed. nova ad mentem Codicis I.C., Civitate Vaticana, 2 vols., Typis Polyglottis Vaticanis, 1932.

Giacchi, Orio, *La Violenza nel Negozio Giuridico Canonico,* Milano, Giuffre, 1937.

Goldsmith, William J., *The Competence of Church and State over Marriage—Disputed Points,* The Catholic University of America Canon Law Studies, n. 197, Washington, D. C., The Catholic University of America Press, 1944.

Gonzalez-Tellez, Emanuel, *Commentaria Perpetua in Singulos Textus Quinque Librorum Decretalium Gregorii IX,* 5 toms., Lugduni, 1576.

Heylen, V., *Tractatus de Matrimonio,* 9. ed., Mechliniae, H. Dessain, 1945,

Hostiensis (Henricus de Segusio), *Commentaria in Quinque Decretalium Libros,* 2 vols., Venetiis, 1581.

Jemolo, A. C., *Il Matrimonio nel Diritto Canonico,* Milano, Casa Editrice Dottor Francesco Vallardi, 1941.

Joannes, Andreae, *In VI Libros Decretalium Novella Commentaria,* 6 vols., Venetiis, 1581.

Kuttner, Stephan, *Kanonistische Schuldlehre von Gratian bis auf die Dekretalen Gregors IX, Studi e Testi n.* 64, Città del Vaticano, Biblioteca Apostolica Vaticana, 1935.

———, *Repertorium der Kanonistik (1140-1234), Studi e Testi, n.* 71 Città del Vaticano, Biblioteca Apostolica Vaticana, 1937.

Laymann, Paulus, *Theologia Moralis,* Venetiis, 1630.

Leage, R. W., *Roman Private Law,* 2. ed. by C. H. Ziegler, London, Macmillan, 1942.

Le Bras, C., "Mariage à l'Epoque Carolingienne"—*Dictionnaire* de Théologie Catholique, Paris, Mabillion-Marletta, 1903—, tome 9, 2 partie, col. 2118 sq.

Lottin, Odon, *Le Droit Naturel chez Saint Thomas d'Aquin et ses Predecesseurs,* 2. ed., Bruges, Charles Beyaert, 1931.

May, Geoffrey, *Marriage Laws and Decisions in the United States,* New York, Russell Sage Foundation, 1929.

Merkelbach, Benedictus Henricus, *Summa Theologiae Moralis,* 3 vols., 3. ed., Parisiis, Typis Desclée de Brouwer et Soc., 1938-1939.

Miller, Justin, *Handbook of Criminal Law,* Hornbook Series, St. Paul, Minn., West Publishing Co., 1934.

Noldin, H.-Schmitt, A., *Summa Theologiae Moralis,* 3 vols., Oeniponte-Lipsiae, Sumptibus et Typis Feliciana Rauch, Vol. I, 27. ed., 1940; Vol. II, 27. ed., 1941; Vol. III, 26. ed., 1941.

———, *Complementum de Sexto Praecepto et de Usu Matrimonii,* 31. ed., 1940.

Panormitanus (Nicolaus de Tudeschis), *Commentaria in Quinque Libros Decretalium,* 5 vols., Venetiis, 1588.

Payen, G., *De Matrimonio in Missionibus ac Potissimum in Sinis Tractatus Practicus et Casus,* 3 vols., 2. ed., Zi-ka-wei, in Typographia T'ou-sè-wè, 1935-1936.

Pirhing, Ernricus, *Jus Canonicum in V Libros Decretalium,* 4 toms., Dilingae, 1722.

Radin, Max, *Handbook of Roman Law,* Hornbook Series, Saint Paul, West Publishing Co., 1927.

Rebello, Fernandus, *De Obligationibus Iustitiae, Religionis, et Caritatis,* Lugduni, 1608.

Regatillo, Eduardus F., *Ius Sacramentarium,* 2 vols., Santander, Sal Terrae, 1945-1946.

Reiffenstuel, Anacletus, *Jus Canonicum Universum,* 6 toms., Romae, 1831-1834.

Sanchez, Thomas, *De Sancto Matrimonii Sacramento,* 3 toms., Antverpiae, 1626.

Sangmeister, Joseph V., *Force and Fear as Precluding Matrimonial Consent,* The Catholic University of America Canon Law Studies, n. 80, Washington, D. C., The Catholic University of America, 1932.

Schmalzgrueber, Franciscus, *Jus Ecclesiasticum Universum,* 5 toms. in 12, Romae, 1843-1844.

Singer, Heinrich, *Die Summa Decretorum des Magister Rufinus,* Paderborn, 1902.

Sipos, Stephanus, *Enchiridion Iuris Canonici,* 3. ed., Pécs, ex Typographia "Haladás R.T.," 1936.

Soto, Dominicus, *Commentariorum in Quartum Sententiarum Tomus Secundus,* Venetiis, 1584.

Studi di Storia e Diritto in Onore di Enrico Besta per il XL Anno del Suo Insegnamento, 4 vols., Milano, Dott. A. Giuffre, Editore, 1937-1939.

Sylvester Prierias, *Summae Sylvestrinae Quae Summa Summorum merito Nuncupantur,* 2 vols., Venetiis, 1901.

Thomas Aquinas, St., *Opera Omnia,* 34 vols., ed. L. Vivès, Parisiis, 1871-1880; Vol. IX, 1873, *Commentum in Quattuor Libros Sententiarum Magistri Petri Lombardi,* in III.

———, *Opera Omnia iussu impensaque Leonis XIII, P.M. edita,* 15 toms., Romae, ex Typographia Polyglotta, 1882—; Tom. XII, 1906, *Summa, Suppl.* III.

———, *Summa Theologica,* 6 toms., Taurini, Marietti, 1932.

Van Hove, A., *Commentarium Lovaniense in Codicem Iuris Canonici,* Vol. I, Tom. I, *Prolegomena,* 2. ed., Mechliniae-Romae, H. Dessain, 1945.

Vermeersch, Arthurus, *Theologia Moralis, Principia, Responsa, Consilia,* 4 vols., 3. ed., Romae, Pont. Università Gregoriana, Vol. I, 1933; Vol. II, 1937; Vol. III, after 1935; Vol. IV, 1933.

Vermeersch, A,-Creusen, J., *Epitome Iuris Canonici,* 3 vols., Mechliniae-Romae, H. Dessain; Vol. II, 6. ed., 1940; Vol. III, 6. ed., 1946.

Vernier, Chester G., *American Family Laws,* 5 vols., Stanford University, California, Stanford University Press, 1931-1938.

Wernz, Franciscus X., *Ius Decretalium,* 6 toms., Romae; Tom. I, 2. ed., 1905; Tom. II, 1899; Tom. III, 1901; Tom. IV, 1904; Tom. V, 1914; Tom. VI, 1913.

Wernz, Franciscus Xav.-Vidal, Petrus, *Ius Canonicum,* 7 vols. in 8, Vol. V, *Ius Matrimoniale,* 3. ed. a Philippo Aguirre recognita, Romae, apud aedes Universitatis Gregorianae, 1946.

Periodicals

Apollinaris, Romae, 1928—.
English Historical Review, The, London, 1886—.
Jurist, The, Washington, D. C., 1941—.
Jus Pontificium, Romae, 1921-1940.
Il Diritto Ecclesiastico, Romae, 1889—.

Articles

Allers, Rudolph, "Some Medico-Psychological Remarks on Canons 1068, 1081, and 1087," *The Jurist*, IV (1944), 351-380.

D'Avack, Pietro Agostino, "Sul Metus Consultus nel Codex Juris Canonici," *Studi in Onore di Besta* (cf. *supra*), III, 243-276.

Kuttner, S.-Smalley, Beryl, "The *Glossa Ordinaria* to the Gregorian Decretals," *The English Historical Review*, IX (1945), 97-105.

Roberti, Franciscus, "De Metu Indirecto quoad Negotia Iuridica praesertim Matrimonium," *Apollinaris*, X (1938), 557-561.

Wyszynski, M., "Utrum Metus Indirecte Incussus Dirimere Possit Matrimonium," *Jus Pontificium*, X (1930), 193-200; XI (1931), 42-51; XII (1932), 43-52 and 122-127; XII (1933), 52-63.

ABBREVIATIONS

Bibliotheca—Ferraris, *Prompta Bibliotheca Canonica, Iuridica, Moralis, Theologica, nec non Ascetica, Polemica, Rubricistica, Historica.*

Fagnanus—*Commentaria in Quinque Libros Decretalium.*

Gonzalez-Tellez—*Commentaria Perpetua in Singulos Textu Quinque Librorum Decretalium Gregorii IX.*

Hostiensis—*Commentaria in Quinque Decretalium Libros.*

Jaffé—*Regesta Pontificum Romanorum ab condita Ecclesia ad annum post Christum natum MCXCVIII*, ed. 2.

Joannes Andreae—*In VI Libros Decretalium Novella Commentaria.*

Kanonistische Schuldlehre—Kuttner, *Kanonistische Schuldlehre von Gratian bis auf die Dekretalen Gregors IX.*

Panormitanus—*Commentaria in Quinque Libros Decretalium.*

Pirhing,—*Jus Canonicum in V Libros Decretalium.*

Potthast—*Regesta Pontificum Romanorum, MCXCVIII ad MCCCIV.*

Rebello—*De Obligationibus Iustitiae, Religiosus, et Caritatis.*

S.C.C., *Thesaurus*—*Thesaurus Resolutionum Sacrae Congregationis Concilii.*

S.R.R. Dec.—*Sacrae Romanae Rotae Decisiones seu Sententiae.*

BIOGRAPHICAL NOTE

Josiah George Chatham was born in Vicksburg, Mississippi, on June 20, 1914. He attended the parochial schools of Saint Paul's parish, Vicksburg. His classical studies were made under the Benedictine Fathers at Saint Joseph's Seminary, Saint Benedict, Louisiana. In the fall of 1934 he entered the North American College in Rome, where he was ordained on July 30, 1939. He received the degrees of Bachelor of Philosophy in 1936, Bachelor of Theology in 1938, and Licentiate of Theology in 1940 from the Pontifical Gregorian University, Rome, Italy. Returning to the United States in May of 1940, he was assigned by the Bishop of Natchez to the Church of the Immaculate Heart of Mary in Greenwood, Mississippi. He worked as an assistant in that parish and its attached missions until November, 1942. From December, 1942, until May, 1945, he was a Chaplain in the Army of the United States. In October of 1946 he entered the Graduate School of Canon Law at the Catholic University of America, Washington, D. C. He received the degree of Bachelor of Canon Law in June, 1947. Returning to the University after an interruption during which he served in the Curia of the Diocese of Natchez, he received the degree of Licentiate in Canon Law in 1950. He is officialis of the Tribunal of the Diocese of Natchez.

ALPHABETICAL INDEX

AUTHORS AND TRIBUNALS

Albertus, 34
Alford, 138
Allers, 106
Alphonsus, St., 66, 78, 81, 82, 83, 85, 86, 89, 90, 91, 92, 94, 95
Ambrose, St., 12
Antonius de Butrio, 41
Augustine, St., 11

Ballerini, A., 72
Barbosa, 67, 69, 72, 78, 84, 85, 89, 90, 93, 96
Bazianus, 3
Benencasa, 30, 31, 39
Berardus, 11
Bernard of Pavia, 19, 28, 29
Biondi, 4
Blat, 146
Bouaert, 146
Bouscaren-Ellis, 104, 107, 114, 118, 122, 136, 140, 152, 154

Cangardel, 114
Cappello, 107, 121, 125, 136, 138, 140, 153, 154, 157
Chelodi-Ciprotti, 107, 108, 114, 121, 122, 153, 154, 157
Cironius, 16
Coronata, 102, 107, 109, 114, 117, 121, 122, 123, 125, 135, 140, 144, 153, 154, 157

Damasus, 40-41
D'Annibale, 70, 72, 79, 80, 81, 92, 95
Dauvillier, 12, 15
D'Avack, 148
DeAngelis, 72
DeBecker, 66
DeLugo, 67, 69, 73, 78, 79, 80, 81, 82, 83, 84, 85, 96, 116, 151
DeSmet, 72, 108, 113, 143, 144, 146, 153, 158
Dossetti, 5, 13, 39, 41, 42, 107, 130, 132, 138, 140, 147, 152, 154

Esmein-Génestal, 3, 11, 12, 15

Fagnanus, 67, 90
Fair, 15
Faventenius, 15, 27, 33
Fedele, 102, 146, 148, 154
Feiji, 72
Ferraris, 66, 70, 72, 78, 87, 91, 93, 94, 95
Fourneret, 146

Gasparri, 15, 67, 71, 72, 78, 79, 81, 82, 84, 86, 95, 96, 102, 107, 109, 117, 118, 120, 121, 122, 138, 140, 150-151, 152, 154, 155, 157, 158
Génestal—Cf. "Esmein-Génestal"
Giacchi, 5
Gilbertus, 34
Glossa Ordinaria, to the Decree of Gratian, 28, 29, 34-35, 36, 45, 46, 48, 77
Glossa Ordinaria, to the Gregorian Decretals, 23, 28, 29, 35, 37, 39. 41, 42, 49, 77
Goffredus de Trano, 40-42
Goldsmith, 138
Gonzalez Tellez, 66, 69, 72, 78. 84. 85, 88, 95
Grandclaude, 73
Gratian, 9 ff.
Gury, 72

Heiner, 72
Heylen, 153, 154
Hilling, 146
Hostiensis, 28, 29, 33, 37, 39, 41, 47
Huguccio, 27, 34

Jaffé, 10 ff.
Jemolo, 102, 108, 118, 121, 123, 124, 125, 138, 140, 153, 154
Joannes Andreae, 29, 30, 31, 34, 37, 39, 41, 49
Joannes Teutonicus, 30, 34, 39
Justinian, 3 ff.

Knecht, 146
Kugler, 72
Kutschker, 72
Kuttner, 3, 15, 16, 27, 30, 31, 33, 34, 39, 40
Kuttner-Smalley, 23

Laurentius, 72
Laymann, 67, 69, 72, 78, 82, 96
Leage, 8
LeBras, 10
Lehmkuhl, 72
Leitner, 72, 146
Lottin, 55, 56

May, 138
Merkelbach, 103, 107, 127, 128, 129, 130, 131, 132
Miller, 138
Mommsen, 4
München, 72

Noldin-Schmitt, 102, 107, 108, 127, 128, 129, 130, 136, 140, 146

Palmeiri, 73, 151
Paludanus, 62
Panormitanus, 28, 29, 30, 31, 35, 38, 40, 42, 45, 48, 49
Paucapalea, 11
Paul, St., 9
Payen, 107, 108, 113, 117, 121, 132, 147, 152, 154
Phillips, 73
Pirhing, 67, 69, 72, 78, 82, 84, 85, 87, 88, 89, 90, 91, 93, 94, 96
Ploch, 73
Pomponius, 7
Potthast, 16 ff.
Prümmer, 146

Radin, 8
Raymond of Pennafort, St., 44
Rebello, 67, 68, 72, 77, 95
Regatillo, 107, 114, 117, 121, 147, 149, 154, 155
Reiffenstuel, 67, 72, 78, 84, 88, 89, 90, 91, 93, 94, 95
Ricardus, 62
Roberti, 22, 146, 153, 154
Rotae, Sacrae, Romanae—Decisiones seu Sententiae, 70, 71, 74, 75, 79, 80, 81, 82, 83, 84, 85, 86, 90, 91, 92, 93, 94, 95, 102, 103, 111. 112, 114, 115, 116, 119, 121, 122, 124, 125, 135, 136, 140, 143, 144, 146, 147, 149, 150, 152, 153, 154, 155, 157, 158
Rufinus, 15, 27, 31, 33, 39

Salmanticenses, 72
Sanchez, 67, 68, 72, 76, 78, 80, 82, 83, 84, 85, 86, 96, 102, 120
Sangmeister, 4, 11, 15, 102, 108, 113, 117, 118, 120, 121, 122, 127, 130, 131, 132, 138, 143, 144, 145, 154, 158
Santi, 72
Scherer, 72
Schmalzgrueber, 67, 70, 73, 81, 82, 83, 84, 85, 86, 87, 88, 89, 90, 91, 92, 93, 94, 96, 151
Schroeder, 15
Schulte, 72
Scotus, 60
Sicardus, 27
Simon, 15, 33
Singer, 33
Sipos, 107, 108, 113, 153, 154, 157
Soto, 42, 57-58, 59-65, 71, 77, 78
Stephanus, 33
Sylvester Prierias, 63

Tancred, 3
Tanquerey, 146
Thesaurus Resolutionum Sacrae Congregationis Concilii, 71, 74, 81, 82, 85, 90, 92, 93
Thiel, 10
Thomas Aquinas, St., 51-58, 101, 158
Tournely, 95

Ulpianus, 4

Van Hove, 3, 9, 11, 16
Veracruz, 80
Vermeersch, 101, 107, 127, 128, 129, 130, 131, 136, 140, 153
Vermeersch-Creusen, 102, 103, 108. 113, 118, 121, 127, 134, 144, 152, 154, 157
Vernier, 138
Vlaming, 146

Wernz, 67, 78, 83, 96
Wernz-Vidal, 107, 108, 114, 118, 125, 146, 149, 154, 157, 158
Wiestner, 73
Wyszynski, 22, 72, 73, 145-146, 153

Zabarella, 42

General

Abduction,—cf. also "Raptus,"
  defined, 14
  identified with coercion, 14-15, 19
  as a distinct impediment, 14, 29

Bastardy, 139-142

Coercion, — cf. "Fear," "Metus," "Force"
Compilationes Antiquae, — cf. "Decretals"
Consent, matrimonial,
 of the essence of marriage, 4, 16, 43
Corpus Iuris Canonici, 9, 16 ff.
Corpus Iuris Civilis, 3, 4
Culpa praecedens, 7, 8, 13, 30, 31

Decretals, 16 ff.
 law on force-fear, 17 ff.
Decretum Gratiani, 9 ff.
Deuteronomy, Book of, 53

Espousals,—cf. also "Obligation to marry"
 types of, 22
 in the Code of Canon Law, 126-127
Exodus, Book of, 24

Fear,—cf. also "Metus," "Force"
 casual relationship with resulting marriage, 6, 21
 caused by private persons, 85, 118, 122-125, 142-145
 defined, 5, 27-28, 50-52, 58-59, 65, 104-108
 directe incussus, 71-75, 115-117, 145-150
 extrinsic origin of, 6, 21, 63, 65, 104
 gravity of, 6, 20
 indirecte incussus, 21-22, 71-75, 115-117, 150-156
 injustice of, 6, 22, 39-43, 63-65, 76-95, 112-145
 injustice of, in the courts, 42-43, 85, 93-94, 118, 121-122, 126-127, 133-142
 injustice of, *quoad modum,* 40-41, 63-64, 65, 76-77, 79-81, 84, 85, 110, 112-115, 120-123, 124, 139, 141, 142, 143
 injustice of, *quoad substantiam,* 76-77, 79-81, 84, 85, 110, 112-115, 117-119, 121, 124, 140, 141, 142, 143
 intention of agent inflicting, 64, 65, 71, 76, 77, 78, 86, 111, 115-117, 145-156
 reverential, 82-83, 86, 118-119, 123-124
 when only materially unjust, can still invalidate marriage, 120

Force,—cf. also "Fear," "Metus"
 absolute (physical or passive), 5, 27, 43, 58, 66, 68, 105-106, 109
 absolute — eliminated from treatment under force-fear, 29-30, 52, 58, 66, 108-109
 absolute — treated in context of doctrine on force-fear, 67
 defined, 4, 52, 58-59, 65, 104-108
 identified with fear, 5, 29, 52, 58, 66, 67-68
Freedom, matrimonial, 4, 9, 11, 16, 17, 101-104, 116
 limitations upon, 10-12, 18,—cf. also "Obligation to marry"

Injustice of fear,—cf. entries under "Fear"

Liberty, matrimonial,—cf. "Freedom, matrimonial"
Lothair, II, King of Lorraine, 10

Meaux, Council of, 14 note 29
Metus,—cf. "Fear," "Force"
 metus iustus, not to be confused with *metus iniuste incussus,* 30-39, 58-59

Obligation to marry
 alternative obligation generally arises from seduction, 24-25, 36, 92-93, 128-129, 140, 141
 ex contractu, 8, 12, 22-23, 30, 36-38, 53, 84, 126-127
 ex delicto, 8, 12, 13, 15, 23-25, 30-36, 53, 84, 86-95, 127-145
 in connection with bastardy, 139-142
 in connection with rape, 139-142
 no alternative permitted seducer under certain circumstances, 93-95, 130-131 (132-133)
 no obligation to marry *ex contractu* in the Code of Canon Law, 110
Orientals, new canons on marriage for, 155-156

Palea, 10, 11, 18
Popes,
 Alexander, III, 17, 18, 19, 20, 21
 Honorius, III, 20, 21
 Hormisdas, 10, 18
 Innocent, III, 19
 Lucius, III, 17, 23
 Nicholas, I, 10, 18
 Urban, II, 10

Pregnancy, cases of force-fear in, 123, 124

Rape, common law, 139-142
Rape, statutory, 139-142
Raptus,—cf. also "Abduction"
  as a distinct impediment, 14, 29
  defined, 14
  identified with force-fear, 14-15
Ratio canonica of canon 1087, 101-104, 115-120
Restitutio in integrum, 4, 6, 30
Roman Law, 3 ff.
  influence upon Canon Law, 3, 13, 19, 40

Sancho, King of Aragon, 10
Seduction,—cf. also "Stuprum"
  action against seducer in ecclesiastical courts, 133-137
  action against seducer in secular courts, 138-142
  as source of obligation to marry, 24, 31, 34, 36,—cf. also "Obligation to marry"
  circumstances under which seducer has alternative of either marrying or endowing the woman, 24-25, 36, 92-93, 133
  circumstances under which seducer has modified obligation to woman, 131-132
  circumstances under which seducer has no alternative except to marry the woman, 93-95, 130-131 (132-133)
  circumstances under which seducer has no obligation to woman, 89-92, 129
  circumstances under which seducer is unable to endow woman, 132-133
  defined, 13-14, 87-88, 127-128
  penalties for in the Code of Canon Law, 110, 134
  presumptions against the woman in cases of, 89
  presumptions in favor of the woman in cases of, 34, 36, 88-89
  with insincere promise to marry, 94, 130-131
  with sincere promise to marry, 93, 130-131, 133
Sex crimes, 138-142
Source of invalidity
  natural law theory, 44-48, 60-62, 96, 157-159
  positive law theory, 12, 25-26, 44-50, 62-63, 96-98, 157-159
Sponsalia,—cf. "Espousals"
Stuprum,—cf. also "Seduction"
  defined, 13-14, 87-88, 127-128
Suicide, as constituting a source of force-fear, 124

Trent, Council of, 15, 30, 65

Ubaldus, 11, 15

Vis,—cf. "Force," "Fear," "Metus"

CANON LAW STUDIES*

1. Freriks, Rev. Celestine A., C.PP.S., J.C.D., Religious Congregations in Their External Relations, 121 pp. 1916.
2. Galliher, Rev. Daniel M., O.P., J.C.D., Canonical Elections, 117 pp., 1917.
3. Borkowski, Rev. Aurelius L., O.F.M., J.C.D., De Confraternibus Ecclesiasticis, 136 pp., 1918.
4. Castillo, Rev. Cayo, J.C.D., Disertacion Historico-Canonica sobre la Potestad del Cabildo en Sede Vacante o Impedida del Vicario Capitular, 99 pp., 1919 (1918).
5. Kubelbeck, Rev. William J., S.T.B., J.C.D., The Sacred Penitentiaria and Its Relation to Faculties of Ordinaries and Priests, 129 pp., 1918.
6. Petrovits, Rev. Joseph, J.C., S.T.D., J.C.D., The New Church Law on Matrimony, X-461 pp., 1919.
7. Hickey, Rev. John J., S.T.B., J.C.D., Irregularities and Simple Impediments in the New Code of Canon Law, 100 pp., 1920.
8. Klekotka, Rev. Peter J., S.T.B., J.C.D., Diocesan Consultors, 179 pp., 1920.
9. Wanenmacher, Rev. Francis, J.C.D., The Evidence in Ecclesiastical Procedure Affecting the Marriage Bond, 1920 (Printed 1935).
10. Golden, Rev. Henry Francis, J.C.D., Parochial Benefices in the New Code, IV-119 pp., 1921 (Printed 1925).
11. Koudelka, Rev. Charles J., J.C.D., Pastors, Their Rights and Duties According to the New Code of Canon Law, 211 pp., 1921.
12. Melo, Rev. Antonius, O.F.M., J.C.D., De Exemptione Regularium, X-188 pp., 1921.
13. Schaaf, Rev. Valentine Theodore, O.F.M., S.T.B., J.C.D., The Cloister, X-180 pp., 1921.
14. Burke, Rev. Thomas Joseph, S.T.D., J.C.D., Competence in Ecclesiastical Tribunals, IV-117 pp., 1922.
15. Leech, Rev. George Leo, J.C.D., A Comparative Study of the Constitution "Apostolicae Sedis" and the "Codex Juris Canonici," 179 pp., 1922.
16. Motry, Rev. Hubert Louis, S.T.D., J.C.D., Diocesan Faculties According to the Code of Canon Law, II-167 pp., 1922.
17. Murphy, Rev. George Lawrence, J.C.D., Delinquencies and Penalties in the Administration and the Reception of the Sacraments, IV-121 pp., 1923.

***All published numbers are available from the Catholic University of America Press, 620 Michigan Avenue, N.E., Washington 17, D. C., except the following: Nos. 1-114 inclusive, 115, 118, 120, 122, 123, 136, 153, 162, 182 and 198. But the following numbers, now reissued, are obtainable from *The Jurist*, The Catholic University of America, Washington 17, D. C., namely: Nos. 5, 7, 11, 17, 18, 19, 26, 28, 30, 31, 34, 42, 44, 51, 52 and 61.**

18. O'Reilly, Rev. John Anthony, S.T.B., J.C.D., Ecclesiastical Sepulture in the New Code of Canon Law, II-129 pp., 1923.
19. Michalicka, Rev. Wenceslas Cyrill, O.S.B., J.C.D., Judicial Procedure in Dismissal of Clerical Exempt Religious, 107 pp., 1923.
20. Dargin, Rev. Edward Vincent, S.T.B., J.C.D., Reserved Cases According to the Code of Canon Law, IV-103 pp., 1924.
21. Godfrey, Rev. John A., S.T.B., J.C.D., The Right of Patronage According to the Code of Canon Law, 153 pp., 1924.
22. Hagedorn, Rev. Francis Edward, J.C.D., General Legislation on Indulgences, II-154 pp., 1924.
23. King, Rev. James Ignatius, J.C.D., The Administration of the Sacraments to Dying Non-Catholics, V-141 pp., 1924.
24. Winslow, Rev. Francis Joseph, O.F.M., J.C.D., Vicars and Prefects Apostolic, IV-149 pp., 1924.
25. Correa, Rev. Jose Servelion, S.T.L., J.C.D., La Potestad Legislativa de la Iglesia Catolica, IV-127 pp., 1925.
26. Dugan, Rev. Henry Francis, A.M., J.C.D., The Judiciary Department of the Diocesan Curia, 87 pp., 1925.
27. Keller, Rev. Charles Frederick, S.T.B., J.C.D., Mass Stipends, 167 pp., 1925.
28. Paschang, Rev. John Linus, J.C.D., The Sacramentals According to the Code of Canon Law, 129 pp., 1925.
29. Piontek, Rev. Cyrillus, O.F.M., S.T.B., J.C.D., De Indulto Exclaustrationis necnon Saecularizationis, XIII-289 pp., 1925.
30. Kearney, Rev. Richard Joseph, S.T.B., J.C.D., Sponsors at Baptism According to the Code of Canon Law, IV-127 pp., 1925.
31. Bartlett, Rev. Chester Joseph, A.M., LL.B., J.C.D., The Tenure of Parochial Property in the United States of America, V-108 pp., 1926.
32. Kilker, Rev. Adrian Jerome, J.C.D., Extreme Unction, V-425 pp., 1926.
33. McCormick, Rev. Robert Emmett, J.C.D., Confessors of Religious, VIII-266 pp., 1926.
34. Miller, Rev. Newton Thomas, J.C.D., Founded Masses According to the Code of Canon Law, VII-93 pp., 1926.
35. Roelker, Rev. Edward G., S.T.D., J.C.D., Principles of Privilege According to the Code of Canon Law, XI-166 pp., 1926.
36. Bakalarczyk, Rev. Richardus, M.I.C., J.U.D., De Novitiatu, VIII-208 pp., 1927.
37. Pizzuti, Rev. Lawrence, O.F.M., J.U.L., De Parochis Religiosis, 1927. (Not Printed.)
38. Bliley, Rev. Nicholas Martin, O.S.B., J.C.D., Altars According to the Code of Canon Law, XIX-132 pp., 1927.
39. Brown, Mr. Brendan Francis, A.B., LL.M., J.U.D., The Canonical Juristic Personality with Special Reference to its Status in the United States of America, V-212 pp., 1927.

40. Cavanaugh, Rev. William Thomas, C.P., J.U.D., The Reservation of the Blessed Sacrament, VIII-101 pp., 1927.
41. Doheny, Rev. William J., C.S.C., A.B., J.C.D., Church Property: Modes of Acquisition, X-118 pp., 1927.
42. Feldhaus, Rev. Aloysius H., C.PP.S., J.C.D., Oratories, IV-141 pp., 1927.
43. Kelly, Rev. James Patrick, A.B., J.C.D., The Jurisdiction of the Simple Confessor, X-208 pp., 1927.
44. Neuberger, Rev. Nicholas J., J.C.D., Canon 6 or the Relation of the Codex Iuris Canonici to the Preceding Legislation, V-95 pp., 1927.
45. O'Keefe, Rev. Gerald Michael, J.C.D., Matrimonial Dispensations, Powers of Bishops, Priests, and Confessors, VIII-232 pp., 1927.
46. Quigley, Rev. Joseph A. M., A.B., J.C.D., Condemned Societies, 139 pp., 1927.
47. Zaplotnik, Rev. Johannes Leo, J.C.D., De Vicariis Foraneis, X-142 pp., 1927.
48. Duskie, Rev. John Aloysius, A.B., J.C.D., The Canonical Status of the Orientals in the United States, VIII-196 pp., 1928.
49. Hyland, Rev. Francis Edward, J.C.D., Excommunication, Its Nature, Historical Development and Effects, VIII-181 pp., 1928.
50. Reimann, Rev. Gerald Joseph, O.M.C., J.C.D., The Third Order Secular of Saint Francis, 201 pp., 1928.
51. Schenk, Rev. Francis J., J.C.D., The Matrimonial Impediments of Mixed Religion and Disparity of Cult, XVI-318 pp., 1929.
52. Coady, Rev. John Joseph, S.T.D., J.U.D., A.M., The Appointment of Pastors, VIII-150 pp., 1929.
53. Kay, Rev. Thomas Henry, J.C.D., Competence in Matrimonial Procedure, VIII-164 pp., 1929.
54. Turner, Rev. Sidney Joseph, C.P., J.U. D., The Vow of Poverty, XLIX-217 pp., 1929.
55. Kearney, Rev. Raymond A., A.B., S.T.D., J.C.D., The Principles of Delegation, VII-149 pp., 1929.
56. Conran, Rev. Edward James, A.B., J.C.D., The Interdict, V-163 pp., 1930.
57. O'Neill, Rev. William H., J.C.D., Papal Rescripts of Favor, VII-218 pp., 1930.
58. Bastnagel, Rev. Clement Vincent, J.U.D., The Appointment of Parochial Adjutants and Assistants, XV-257 pp., 1930.
59. Ferry, Rev. William A., A.B., J.C.D., Stole Fees, V-136 pp., 1930.
60. Costello, Rev. John Michael, A.B., J.C.D., Domicile and Quasi-Domicile, VII-201 pp., 1930.
61. Kremer, Rev. Michael Nicholas, A.B., S.T.B., J.C.D., Church Support in the United States, VI-136 pp., 1930.
62. Angulo, Rev. Luis, C.M., J.C.D., Legislation de la Iglesia sobre la intencion en la application de la Santa Misa, VII-104 pp., 1931.

63. Frey, Rev. Wolfgang Norbert, O.S.B., A.B., J.C.D., The Act of Religious Profession, VIII-174 pp., 1931.
64. Roberts, Rev. James Brendan, A.B., J.C.D., The Banns of Marriage, XIV-140 pp., 1931.
65. Ryder, Rev. Raymond Aloysius, A.B., J.C.D., Simony, IX-151 pp., 1931.
66. Campagna, Rev. Angelo, Ph.D., J.U.D., Il Vicario Generale del Vescovo, VII-205, pp., 1931.
67. Cox, Rev. Joseph Godfrey, A.B., J.C.D., The Administration of Seminaries, VI-124 pp., 1931.
68. Gregory, Rev. Donald J., J.U.D., The Pauline Privilege, XV-165 pp., 1931.
69. Donohue, Rev. John F., J.C.D., The Impediment of Crime, VII-110 pp., 1931.
70. Dooley, Rev. Eugene A., O.M.I., J.C.D., Church Law on Sacred Relics, IX-143 pp., 1931.
71. Orth, Rev. Clement Raymond, O.M.C., J.C.D., The Approbation of Religious Institutes, 171 pp., 1931.
72. Pernicone, Rev. Joseph M., A.B., J.C.D., The Ecclesiastical Prohibition of Books, XII-267 pp., 1932.
73. Clinton, Rev. Connell, A.B., J.C.D., The Paschal Precept, IX-108 pp., 1932.
74. Donnelly, Rev. Francis B., A.M., S.T.L., J.C.D., The Diocesan Synod, VIII-125 pp., 1932.
75. Torrente, Rev. Camilo, C.M.F., J.C.D., Las Procesiones Sagradas, V-145 pp., 1932.
76. Murphy, Rev. Edwin J., C.PP.S., J.C.D., Suspension Ex Informata Conscientia, XI-122 pp., 1932.
77. MacKenzie, Rev. Eric F., A.M., S.T.L., J.C.D., The Delict of Heresy in its Commission, Penalization, Absolution, VII-124 pp., 1932.
78. Lyons, Rev. Avitus E., S.T.B., J.C.D., The Collegiate Tribunal of First Instance, XI-147 pp., 1932.
79. Connolly, Rev. Thomas A., J.C.D., Appeals, XI-195 pp., 1932.
80. Sangmeister, Rev. Joseph V., A.B., J.C.D., Force and Fear as Precluding Matrimonial Consent, V-211 pp., 1932.
81. Jaeger, Rev. Leo A., A.B., J.C.D., The Administration of Vacant and Quasi-Vacant Episcopal Sees in the United States, IX-229 pp., 1932.
82. Rimlinger, Rev. Herbert T., J.C.D., Error Invalidating Matrimonial Consent, VII-79 pp., 1932.
83. Barrett, Rev. John D. M., S.S., J.C.D., A Comparative Study of the Councils of Baltimore and the Code of Canon Law, IX-223 pp., 1932.
84. Carberry, Rev. John J., Ph.D., S.T.D., J.C.D., The Juridical Form of Marriage, X-177 pp., 1934.
85. Dolan, Rev. John L., A.B., J.C.D., The Defensor Vinculi, XII-157 pp., 1934.

86. HANNAN, REV. JEROME D., A.M., S.T.D., LL.B., J.C.D., The Canon Law of Wills, IX-517 pp., 1934.
87. LEMIEUX, REV. DELISE A., A.M., J.C.D., The Sentence in Ecclesiastical Procedure, IX-131 pp., 1934.
88. O'ROURKE, REV. JAMES J., A.B., J.C.D., Parish Registers, VII-109 pp., 1934.
89. TIMLIN, REV. BARTHOLOMEW, O.F.M., A.M., J.C.D., Conditional Matrimonial Consent, X-381 pp., 1934.
90. WAHL, REV. FRANCIS X., A.B., J.C.D., The Matrimonial Impediments of Consanguinity and Affinity, VI-125 pp., 1934.
91. WHITE, REV. ROBERT J., A.B., LL.B., S.T.B., J.C.D., Canonical Ante-Nuptial Promises and the Civil Law, VI-152 pp., 1934.
92. HERRERA, REV. ANTONIO PARRA, O.C.D., J.C.D., Legislacion Ecclesiastica sobra el Ayuno y la Abstinencia, XI-191 pp., 1935.
93. KENNEDY, REV. EDWIN J., J.C.D., The Special Matrimonial Process in Cases of Evident Nullity, X-165 pp., 1935.
94. MANNING, REV. JOHN J., A.B., J.C.D., Presumption of Law in Matrimonial Procedure, XI-111 pp., 1935.
95. MOEDER, REV. JOHN M., J.C.D., The Proper Bishop for Ordination and Dismissorial Letters, VII-135 pp., 1935.
96. O'MARA, REV. WILLIAM A., A.B., J.C.D., Canonical Causes for Matrimonial Dispensations, IX-155 pp., 1935.
97. REILLY, REV. PETER, J.C.D., Residence of Pastors, IX-81 pp., 1935.
98. SMITH, REV. MARINER T., O.P., S.T.Lr., J.C.D., The Penal Law for Religious, VIII-169 pp., 1935.
99. WHALEN, REV. DONALD W., A.M., J.C.D., The Value of Testimonial Evidence in Matrimonial Procedure, XIII-297 pp., 1935.
100. CLEARY, REV. JOSEPH F., J.C.D., Canonical Limitations on the Alienation of Church Property, VIII-141 pp., 1936.
101. GLYNN, REV. JOHN C., J.C.D., The Promoter of Justice, XX-337 pp., 1936.
102. BRENNAN, REV. JAMES H., S.S., M.A., S.T.B., J.C.D., The Simple Convalidation of Marriage, VI-135 pp., 1937.
103. BRUNINI, REV. JOSEPH BERNARD, J.C.D., The Clerical Obligations of Canons 139 and 142, X-121 pp., 1937.
104. CONNOR, REV. MAURICE, A.B., J.C.D., The Administrative Removal of Pastors, VIII-159 pp., 1937.
105. GUILFOYLE, REV. MERLIN JOSEPH, J.C.D., Custom, XI-144 pp., 1937.
106. HUGHES, REV. JAMES AUSTIN, A.B., A.M., J.C.D., Witnesses in Criminal Trials of Clerics, IX-140 pp., 1937.
107. JANSEN, REV. RAYMOND J., A.B., S.T.L., J.C.D., Canonical Provisions for Catechetical Instruction, VII-153 pp., 1937.
108. KEALY, REV. JOHN JAMES, A.B., J.C.D., The Introductory Libellus in Church Court Procedure, XI-121 pp., 1937.

109. McManus, Rev. James Edward, C.SS.R., J.C.D., The Administration of Temporal Goods in Religious Institutes, XVI-196 pp., 1937.
110. Moriarty, Rev. Eugene James, J.C.D., Oaths in Ecclesiastical Courts, X-115 pp., 1937.
111. Rainer, Reg. Eligius George, C.SS.R., J.C.D., Suspension of Clerics, XVII-249 pp., 1937.
112. Reilly, Rev. Thomas F., C.SS.R., J.C.D., Visitation of Religious, VI-195 pp., 1938.
113. Moriarty, Rev. Francis E., C.SS.R., J.C.D., The Extraordinary Absolution from Censures, XV-334 pp., 1938.
114. Connolly, Rev. Nicholas P., J.C.D., The Canonical Erection of Parishes, X-132 pp., 1938.
115. Donovan, Rev. James Joseph, J.C.D., The Pastor's Obligation in Prenuptial Investigation, XII-322 pp., 1938.
116. Harrigan, Rev. Robert J., M.A., S.T.B., J.C.D., The Radical Sanation of Invalid Marriages, VIII-208 pp., 1938.
117. Boffa, Rev. Conrad Humbert, J.C.D., Canonical Provisions for Catholic Schools, VII-211 pp., 1939.
118. Parsons, Rev. Anscar John, O.M.Cap., J.C.D., Canonical Elections, XII-236 pp., 1939.
119. Reilly, Rev. Edward Michael, A.B., J.C.D., The General Norms of Dispensation, XII-156 pp., 1939.
120. Ryan, Rev. Gerald Aloysius, A.B., J.C.D., Principles of Episcopal Jurisdiction, XII-172 pp., 1939.
121. Burton, Rev. Francis James, C.S.C., A.B., J.C.D., A Commentary on Canon 1125, X-222 pp., 1940.
122. Miaskiewicz, Rev. Francis Sigismund, J.C.D., Supplied Jurisdiction According to Canon 209, XII-340 pp., 1940.
123. Rice, Rev. Patrick William, A.B., J.C.D., Proof of Death in Prenuptial Investigation, VIII-156 pp., 1940.
124. Anglin, Rev. Thomas Francis, M.S., J.C.D., The Eucharistic Fast, VIII-183 pp., 1941.
125. Coleman, Rev. John Jerome, J.C.D., The Minister of Confirmation, VI-153 pp., 1941.
126. Downs, Rev. John Emmanuel, A.B., J.C.D., The Concept of Clerical Immunity, XI-163 pp., 1941.
127. Esswein, Rev. Anthony Albert, J.C.D., Extrajudicial Penal Powers of Ecclesiastical Superiors, X-144 pp., 1941.
128. Farrell, Rev. Benjamin Francis, M.A., S.T.L., J.C.D., The Rights and Duties of the Local Ordinary Regarding Congregations of Women Religious of Pontifical Approval, V-195 pp., 1941.
129. Feeney, Rev. Thomas John, A.B., S.T.L., J.C.D., Restitutio in Integrum, VI-169 pp., 1941.
130. Findlay, Rev. Stephen William, O.S.B., A.B., J.C.D., Canonical Norms Governing the Deposition and Degradation of Clerics, XVII-279 pp., 1941.

131. GOODWINE, REV. JOHN, A.B., S.T.L., J.C.D., The Right of the Church to Acquire Property, VIII-119 pp., 1941.
132. HESTON, REV. EDWARD LOUIS, C.S.C., PH.D., S.T.D., J.C.D., The Alienation of Church Property in the United States, XII-222 pp., 1941.
133. HOGAN, REV. JAMES JOHN, A.B., S.T.L., J.C.D., Judicial Advocates and Procurators, XIII-200 pp., 1941.
134. KEALY, REV. THOMAS M., A.B., LITT.B., J.C.D., Dowry of Women Religious, IX-152 pp., 1941.
135. KEENE, REV. MICHAEL JAMES, O.S.B., J.C.D., Religious Ordinaries and Canon 198, V-164 pp., 1941 (printed 1942).
136. KERIN, REV. CHARLES A., S.S., M.A., S.T.B., J.C.D., The Privation of Christian Burial, XVI-279 pp., 1941.
137. LOUIS, REV. WILLIAM FRANCIS, M.A., J.C.D., Diocesan Archives, X-101 pp., 1941.
138. MCDEVITT, REV. GILBERT JOSEPH, A.B., J.C.D., Legitimacy and Legitimation, X-247 pp., 1941.
139. MCDONOUGH, REV. THOMAS JOSEPH, A.B., J.C.D., Apostolic Administrators, X-217 pp., 1941.
140. MEIER, REV. CARL ANTHONY, A.B., J.C.D., Penal Administrative Procedure Against Negligent Pastors, XI-240 pp., 1941.
141. SCHMIDT, REV. JOHN ROGG, A.B., J.C.D., The Principles of Authentic Interpretation in Canon 17 of the Code of Canon Law, XII-331 pp., 1941.
142. SLAFKOSKY, REV. ANDREW LEONARD, A.B., J.C.D., The Canonical Episcopal Visitation of the Diocese, X-197 pp., 1941.
143. SWOBODA, REV. INNOCENT ROBERT, O.F.M., J.C.D., Ignorance in Relation to the Imputability of Delicts, IX-271 pp., 1941.
144. DUBÉ, REV. ARTHUR JOSEPH, A.B., J.C.D., The General Principles for the Reckoning of Time in Canon Law, VIII-299 pp., 1941.
145. MCBRIDE, REV. JAMES T., A.B., J.C.D., Incardination and Excardination of Seculars, XX-585 pp., 1941.
146. KRÓL, REV. JOHN T., J.C.D., The Defendant in Ecclesiastical Trials, XII-207 pp., 1942.
147. COMYNS, REV. JOSEPH J., C.SS.R., A.B., J.C.D., Papal and Episcopal Administration of Church Property, XIV-155 pp., 1942.
148. BARRY, REV. GARRETT FRANCIS, O.M.I., J.C.D., Violation of the Cloister, XII-260 pp., 1942.
149. BOLDUC, REV. GATIEN, C.S.V., A.B., S.T.L., J.C.D., Les Études dans les Religious Cléricales, VIII-155 pp., 1942.
150. BOYLE, REV. DAVID JOHN, M.A., J.C.D., The Juridic Effects of Moral Certitude on Pre-Nuptial Guarantees, XII-188 pp., 1942.
151. CANAVAN, REV. WALTER JOSEPH, M.A., LITT.D., J.C.D., The Profession of Faith, XII-143 pp., 1942.
152. DESROCHERS, REV. BRUNO, A.B., PH.L., S.T.B., J.C.D., Le Premier Concile Plénier de Québec et le Code de Droit Canonique, XIV-186 pp., 1942.

153. Dillon, Rev. Robert Edward, A.B., J.C.D., Common Law Marriage, X-148 pp., 1942.
154. Dodwell, Rev. Edward John, Ph.D., S.T.B., J.C.D., The Time and Place for the Celebration of Marriage, X-156 pp., 1942.
155. Donnellan, Rev. Thomas Andrew, A.B., J.C.D., The Obligation of the Missa pro Populo, VII-131 pp., 1942.
156. Eltz, Rev. Louis Anthony, A.B., J.C.D., Cooperation in Crime, XII-208 pp., 1942.
157. Gass, Rev. Sylvester Francis, M.A., J.C.D., Ecclesiastical Pensions, XI-206 pp., 1942.
158. Guiniven, Rev. John Joseph, C.SS.R., J.C.D., The Precept of Hearing Mass, XIV-188 pp., 1942.
159. Gulczynski, Rev. John Theophilus, J.C.D., The Desecration and Violation of Churches, X-126 pp., 1942.
160. Hammill, Rev. John Leo, M.A., J.C.D., The Obligations of the Traveler According to Canon 14, VIII-204 pp., 1942.
161. Haydt, Rev. John Joseph, A.B., J.C.D., Reserved Benefices, XI-148 pp., 1942.
162. Huser, Rev. Roger John, O.F.M., A.B., J.C.D., The Crime of Abortion in Canon Law, XII-187 pp., 1942.
163. Kearney, Rev. Francis Patrick, A.B., S.T.L., J.C.D., The Principles of Canon Law 1127, X-162 pp., 1942.
164. Linahen, Rev. Leo James, S.T.L., J.C.D., De Absolutione Complicis in Peccato Turpi, V-114 pp., 1942.
165. McCloskey, Rev. Joseph Aloysius, A.B., J.C.D., The Subject of Ecclesiastical Law According to Canon 12, XVII-246 pp., 1942 (printed 1943).
166. O'Neill, Rev. Francis Joseph, C.SS.R., J.C.D., The Dismissal of Religious in Temporary Vows, XIII-220 pp., 1942.
167. Prince, Rev. John Edward, A.B., S.T.B., J.C.D., The Diocesan Chancellor, X-136 pp., 1942.
168. Riesner, Rev. Albert Joseph, C.SS.R., J.C.D., Apostates and Fugitives from Religious Institutes, IX-168 pp., 1942.
169. Stenger, Rev. Joseph Bernard, J.C.D., The Mortgaging of Church Property, 186 pp., 1942.
170. Waldron, Rev. Joseph Francis, A.B., J.C.D., The Minister of Baptism, XII-197 pp., 1942.
171. Willett, Rev. Robert Albert, J.C.D., The Probative Value of Documents in Ecclesiastical Trials, X-124 pp., 1942.
172. Woeber, Rev. Edward Martin, M.A., J.C.D., The Interpellations, XII-161 pp., 1942.
173. Benko, Rev. Matthew Aloysius, O.S.B., M.A., J.C.D., The Abbot *Nullius,* XVI-148 pp., 1943.
174. Christ, Rev. Joseph James, M.A., S.T.L., J.C.D., Dispensation from Vindicative Penalties, XIV-285 pp., 1943.
175. Clancy, Rev. Patrick M. J., O.P., A.B., S.T.Lr., J.C.D., The Local Religious Superior, X-229 pp., 1943.

176. Clarke, Rev. Thomas James, J.C.D., Parish Societies, XII-147 pp., 1943.
177. Connolly, Rev. John Patrick, S.T.L., J.C.D., Synodical Examiners and Parish Priest Consultors, X-223 pp., 1943.
178. Drumm, Rev. William Martin, A.B., J.C.D., Hospital Chaplains, XII-175 pp., 1943.
179. Flanagan, Rev. Bernard Joseph, A.B., S.T.L., J.C.D., The Canonical Erection of Religious Houses, X-147 pp., 1943.
180. Kelleher, Rev. Stephen Joseph, A.B., S.T.B., J.C.D., Discussions with Non-Catholics: Canonical Legislation, X-93 pp., 1943.
181. Lewis, Rev. Gordian, C.P., J.C.D., Chapters in Religious Institutes, XII-169 pp., 1943.
182. Marx, Rev. Adolph, J.C.D., The Declaration of Nullity of Marriages Contracted Outside the Church, X-151 pp., 1943.
183. Matulenas, Rev. Raymond Anthony, O.S.B., A.B., J.C.D., Communication, a Source of Privileges, VII-225 pp., 1943.
184. O'Leary, Rev. Charles Gerard, C.SS.R., J.C.D., Religious Dismissed After Perpetual Profession, X-213 pp., 1943.
185. Power, Rev. Cornelius Michael, J.C.D., The Blessing of Cemeteries, XII-231 pp., 1943.
186. Shuhler, Rev. Ralph Vincent, O.S.A., J.C.D., Privileges of Religious to Absolve and Dispense, XII-195 pp., 1943.
187. Ziolkowski, Rev. Thaddeus Stanislaus, A.B., J.C.D., The Consecration and Blessing of Churches, XII-151 pp., 1943.
188. Heneghan, Rev. John Joseph, S.T.D., J.C.D., The Marriages of Unworthy Catholics: Canons 1065 and 1066, XVI-213 pp., 1944.
189. Carroll, Rev. Coleman Francis, M.A., S.T.L., J.C.L., Charitable Institutions.
190. Ciesluk, Rev. Joseph Edward, Ph.B., S.T.L., J.C.D., National Parishes in the United States, VI-178 pp., 1944.
191. Coburn, Rev. Vincent Paul, A.B., J.C.D., Marriages of Conscience, XII-172 pp., 1944.
192. Connors, Rev. Charles Paul, C.S.Sp., A.B., J.C.D., Extra-Judicial Procurators in the Code of Canon Law, X-94 pp., 1944.
193. Coyle, Rev. Paul Raymond, A.B., J.C.D., Judicial Exceptions, X-142 pp., 1944.
194. Fair, Rev. Bartholomew Francis, A.B., S.T.L., J.C.D., The Impediment of Abduction, XII-122 pp., 1944.
195. Gallagher, Rev. Thomas Raphael, O.P., A.B., S.T.Lr., J.C.D., The Examination of the Qualities of the Ordinand, X-166 pp., 1944.
196. Gannon, Rev. John Mark, S.T.L., J.C.D., The Interstices Required for the Promotion to Orders, XII-100 pp., 1944.
197. Goldsmith, Rev. J. William, B.C.S., S.T.L., J.C.D., The Competence of Church and State Over Marriages—Disputed Points, X-128 pp., 1944.

198. Goodwine, Rev. Joseph Gerard, A.B., S.T.B., J.C.D., The Reception of Converts, XIV-326 pp., 1944.
199. Kowalski, Rev. Romuald Eugene, O.F.M., A.B., J.C.D., Sustenance of Religious Houses of Regulars, X-174 pp., 1944.
200. McCoy, Rev. Alan Edward, O.F.M., J.C.D., Force and Fear in Relation to Delictual Imputability and Penal Responsibility, XII-160 pp., 1944.
201. McDevitt, Rev. Vincent John, Ph.B., S.T.L., J.C.L., Perjury.
202. Martin, Rev. Thomas Owen, Ph.D., S.T.D., J.C.D., Adverse Possession, Prescription and Limitation of Actions: The Canonical "Praescriptio," XX-208 pp., 1944.
203. Miklosovic, Rev. Paul John, A.B., J.C.L., Attempted Marriages and Their Consequent Juridic Effects.
204. Mundy, Rev. Thomas Maurice, A.B., S.T.L., J.C.D., The Union of Parishes, X-164 pp. 1944.
205. O'Dea, Rev. John Coyle, A.B., J.C.D., The Matrimonial Impediment of Nonage, VIII-126 pp., 1944.
206. Olalia, Rev. Alexander Ayson, S.T.L., J.C.D., A Comparative Study of the Christian Constitution of States and the Constitution of the Philippine Commonwealth, XII-136 pp., 1944.
207. Poisson, Rev. Pierre-Marie, C.S.C., A.B., Ph.L., Th.L., J.C.L., Droits Patrimoniaux des Maisons et des Eglises Religieuses.
208. Stadalnikas, Rev. Casimir Joseph, M.I.C., J.C.D., Reservation of Censures, X-141 pp., 1944.
209. Sullivan, Rev. Eugene Henry, S.T.L., J.C.D., Proof of the Reception of the Sacraments, X-165 pp., 1944.
210. Vaughan, Rev. William Edward, J.C.D., Constitutions for Diocesan Courts, X-200 pp., 1944.
211. Paro, Rev. Gino, S.T.D., J.C.D., The Right of Papal Legation, X-221 pp., 1944 (printed 1947).
212. Balzer, Rev. Ralph Francis, C.P., J.C.D., The Computation of Time in a Canonical Novitiate, X-227 pp., 1945.
213. Dougherty, Rev. John Whelan, A.B., S.T.L., J.C.D., De Inquisitione Speciali, XII-195 pp., 1945.
214. Dziob, Rev. Michael Walter, J.C.D., The Sacred Congregation for the Oriental Church, XII-181 pp., 1945.
215. Eidenschink, Rev. John Albert, O.S.B., B.A., J.C.D., The Election of Bishops in the Letters of Pope Gregory the Great, VIII-200 pp., 1945.
216. Gill, Rev. Nicholas, C.P., J.C.D., The Spiritual Prefect in Clerical Religious Houses of Study, X-140 pp., 1945.
217. Hynes, Rev. Harry Gerard, S.T.L., J.C.D., The Privileges of Cardinals, XII-183 pp., 1945.
218. McDevitt, Rev. Gerald Vincent, S.T.L., J.C.D., The Renunciation of an Ecclesiastical Office, XIV-179 pp., 1945.

219. MANNING, REV. JOSEPH LEROY, J.C.D., The Free Conferral of Offices, VII-116 pp., 1945.
220. MEYER, REV. LOUIS G., O.S.B., A.B., S.T.B., J.C.D., Alms-gathering by Religious, XII-163 pp., 1945.
221. O'DONNELL, REV. CLETUS FRANCIS, M.A., J.C.D., The Marriage of Minors, XII-268 pp., 1945.
222. PRUNSKIS, REV. JOSEPH, J.C.D., Comparative Law, Ecclesiastical and Civil, in Lithuanian Concordat, X-161 pp., 1945.
223. SWEENEY, REV. FRANCIS PATRICK, C.SS.R., J.C.D., The Reduction of Clerics to the Lay State, X-199 pp., 1945.
224. VOGELPOHL, REV. HENRY JOHN, J.C.D., The Simple Impediments to Holy Orders, XVI-190 pp., 1945.
225. BROCKHAUS, REV. THOMAS AQUINAS, O.S.B., J.C.D., Religious who are known as *Conversi,* X-127 pp., 1945.
226. GRIESE, REV. ORVILLE NICHOLAS, S.T.D., J.C.D., The Marriage Contract and the Procreation of Offspring, XVI-224 pp., 1946.
227. BOUDREAUX, REV. WARREN LOUIS, J.C.D., The *"ab acatholicis nati"* of Canon 1099, § 2, XII-110 pp., 1946.
228. BOWE, REV. THOMAS JOSEPH, A.B., J.C.D., Religious Superioresses, VIII-206 pp., 1946.
229. DIEDERICHS, REV. MICHAEL FERDINAND, S.C.J., J.C.D., The Jurisdiction of the Latin Ordinaries over their Oriental Subjects, XIV-153 pp., 1946.
230. DINGMAN, REV. MAURICE JOHN, A.B., S.T.L., J.C.L., The Plaintiff in Contentious Trials.
231. FRISON, REV. BASIL, C.M.F., M.MUS., J.C.D., The Retroactivity of Law, X-221 pp., 1946.
232. CALVIN, REV. WILLIAM ANTHONY, M.A., J.C.D., The Administrative Transfer of Pastors, XII-288 pp., 1946.
233. GORACY, REV. JOSEPH C., J.C.L., The Diriment Matrimonial Impediment of Major Orders.
234. HALE, REV. JOSEPH FRANCIS, M.A., S.T.L., J.C.D., The Pastor of Burial, X-247 pp., 1946 (printed 1949).
235. HENRY, REV. JOSEPH ARTHUR, A.B., J.C.D., The Mass and Holy Communion: Interritual Law, XII-138 pp., 1946.
236. LINENBERGER, REV. HERBERT, C.PP.S., J.C.D., The False Denunciation of an Innocent Confessor, VIII-205 pp., 1946 (1949).
237. LOWRY, REV. JAMES MARTIN, A.B., J.C.D., Dispensation from Private Vows, XII-266 pp., 1946.
238. LYNCH, REV. GEORGE EDWARD, A.B., S.T.L., J.C.D., Coadjutors and Auxiliaries of Bishops, X-107 pp., 1946 (printed 1947).
239. LYNCH, REV. TIMOTHY, M.S.SS.T., J.C.D., Contracts between Bishops and Religious Congregations, XIII-232 pp., 1946.
240. MCCLUNN, REV. JUSTIN DAVID, A.B., S.T.L., J.C.D., Administrative Recourse, VII-142 pp., 1946.

241. Lohmuller, Rev. Martin Nicholas, A.B., J.C.D., The Promulgation of Law, XII-140 pp., 1947.
242. McGrath, Rev. James, A.B., J.C.D., The Privilege of the Canon, XII-156 pp., 1946.
243. Marbach, Rev. Joseph Francis, A.B., J.C.D., Marriage Legislation for the Catholics of the Oriental Rites in the United States and Canada, XIV-314 pp., 1946.
244. Shimkus, Rev. Bernard Aloysius, A.B., J.C.L., The Determination and Transfer of Rite.
245. Smith, Rev. Vincent Michael, A.B., S.T.L., J.C.L., Ignorance Affecting Matrimonial Consent.
246. Wachtrle, Rev. Paul Anthony, A.B., J.C.L., The Baptism of the Children of Non-Catholics.
247. Crotty, Rev. Matthew Michael, J.C.D., The Recipient of First Holy Communion, X-142 pp., 1947.
248. Eagleton, Rev. George, J.C.D., The Quinquennial Faculties, Formula IV, XIV-199 pp., 1947 (printed 1948).
249. Gibbons, Rev. Marion Leo, C.M., J.C.L., Domicile of the Wife Unlawfully Separated from Her Husband, XIV-171 pp., 1947.
250. Kelly, Rev. Bernard M., S.T.L., J.C.D., The Functions Reserved to Pastors, XII-141 pp., 1947.
251. Kilcullen, Rev. Thomas J., LL.M., J.C.D., The Collegiate Moral Person as Party Litigant, X-150 pp., 1947.
252. Lafontaine, Rev. Germaine Joseph, W.F., J.C.D., Relations Canoniques entre le Missionaire et Ses Superieurs, X-117 pp., 1947.
253. Lane, Rev. Loras Thomas, A.B., S.T.L., J.C.D., Matrimonial Procedure in the Ordinary Court of Second Instance, XVI-184 pp., 1947.
254. Lover, Rev. James Francis, C.Ss.R., J.C.D., The Master of Novices, X-168 pp., 1947.
255. McNicholas, Rev. Timothy Joseph, J.C.D., The *Septimae Manus* Witness, XII-133 pp., 1947 (printed 1949).
256. Marositz, Rev. Joseph John, M.S.C., J.C.D., Obligations and Privileges of Religious Promoted to the Episcopal or Cardinalitial Dignities, XII-180 pp., 1947.
257. Murphy, Rev. Francis Joseph, J.C.D., Legislative Powers of the Provincial Council, XII-158 pp., 1947.
258. O'Brien, Rev. Romaeus William, O.Carm., J.C.D., The Provincial Superior in Religious Orders of Men, X-294 pp., 1947.
259. Pfaller, Rev. Benedict Anthony, O.S.B., J.C.D., *The ipso facto* Effected Dismissal of Religious, XII-225 pp., 1947.
260. Popek, Rev. Alphonse Sylvester, J.C.D., The Rights and Obligations of Metropolitans, XX-460 pp., 1947.
261. Ristuccia, Rev. Bernard Joseph, C.M., J.C.D., Quasi-Religious, XVI-318 pp., 1947 (printed 1949).
262. Sonntag, Rev. Nathaniel Louis, O.F.M.Cap., J.C.D., Censorship of Special Classes of Books, XII-147 pp., 1947.

263. Stadler, Rev. Joseph Nicholas, J.C.D., Frequent Holy Communion, X-158 pp., 1947.
264. Szal, Rev. Ignatius Joseph, J.C.D., The Communication of Catholics with Schismatics, XII-217 pp., 1947.
265. Wagner, Rev. Urban S., O.F.M., Conv., J.C.D., Parochial Substitute Vicars and Supplying Priests, IX-126 pp., 1947.
266. Quinn, Rev. Joseph, M.A., J.C.D., Documents Required for the Reception of Orders, XIV-207 pp., 1948.
267. Bennington, Rev. James Clement, A.B., J.C.L., The Recipient of Confirmation.
268. Blaher, Rev. Damian Joseph, O.F.M., A.B., J.C.D., The Ordinary Processes in Causes of Beatification and Canonization, XVI-290 pp., 1948 (printed 1949).
269. Clune, Rev. Robert Bell, B.A., J.C.D., The Judicial Interrogation of the Parties, XII-142 pp., 1948.
270. Courtemanche, Rev. Basil F., B.A., J.C.D., The Total Simulation of Matrimonial Consent, XX-120 pp., 1948.
271. Dlouhy, Rev. Maur John, O.S.B., A.B., J.C.L., The Ordination of Exempt Religious.
272. Donovan, Rev. John Thomas, Ph.B., S.T.L., J.C.D., The Clerical Obligation of Canons 138 and 140, XII-209 pp., 1948.
273. Freking, Rev. Frederick W., A.B., S.T.B., J.C.D., The Canonical Installation of Pastors, XII-210 pp., 1948.
274. Fulton, Rev. Thomas B., J.C.D., Prenuptial Investigation, XII-190 pp., 1948.
275. Godley, Rev. James P., J.C.D., Time and Place for the Celebration of Mass, X-206 pp., 1948 (printed 1949).
276. Kane, Rev. Thomas A., A.B., B.S., J.C.D., Jurisdiction of the Patriarchs of the Major Sees in Antiquity and in the Middle Ages, XII-111 pp., 1948 (printed 1949).
277. Kennedy, Rev. Andrew A., J.C.L., The Annual Pastoral Report to the Local Ordinary.
278. Konrad, Rev. Joseph George, J.C.D., Transfer of Religious to Another Community, VIII-284 pp., 1948 (printed 1949).
279. Kress, Rev. Alphonse, J.C.L., Contumacy in Ecclesiastical Trials.
280. McCartney, Rev. Marcellus Anthony, O.F.M., M.A., J.C.D., Faculties of Regular Confessors, XII-164 pp., 1948 (printed 1949).
281. McCaslin, Rev. Edward Patrick, M.A., S.T.L., J.C.L., The Division of Parishes.
282. McElroy, Rev. Francis J., A.B., J.C.L., The Privileges of Bishops.
283. Quinn, Rev. Stephen, M.S.SS.T., J.C.D., Relation Between the Local Ordinary and Religious of Diocesan Approval, XII-153 pp., 1948 (printed 1949).
284. Schneider, Rev. Edelhard Louis, S.D.S., B.A., J.C.L., The Status of Secularized Ex-Religious Clerics, X-155 pp., 1948.

285. THOMPSON, CHESTER J., A.B., J.C.L., The Simple Removal from Office.
286. O'BRIEN, REV. KENNETH R., A.B., J.C.D., The Nature of Support of Diocesan Priests in the United States, XVI-162 pp., 1949.
287. METZ, REV. JOHN E., S.T.L., J.C.D., The Recording Judge in the Ecclesiastical Collegiate Tribunal, X-130 pp., 1949.
288. REINHARDT, REV. MARION J., S.T.L., J.C.D., The Rogatory Commission, XIII-182 pp., 1949.
289. ORTEGA UHIUK, REV. JUAN, S.J., J.C.L., De Delicto Sollicitationis.
290. CASEY, REV. JAMES V., J.C.D., A Study of Canon 2222 § 1, XII-127 pp., 1949.
291. ALLGEIER, REV. JOSEPH L., J.C.D., The Canonical Obligation of Preaching in Parish Churches, X-115 pp., 1949 (printed 1950).
292. CAHILL, REV. DANIEL R., J.C.D., The Custody of the Holy Eucharist, XVI-178 pp., 1949 (printed 1950).
293. CARR, REV. AIDEN, O.F.M., CARM., S.T.D., J.C.L., Vocation to the Priesthood: Its Canonical Concept.
294. KNOPKE, REV. ROCH F., O.F.M., J.C.D., Reverential Fear in Matrimonial Cases in Asiatic Countries: Rota Cases, XII-112 pp., 1949.
295. LAVELLE, REV. HOWARD D., J.C.D., The Obligation of Holding Sacred Missions in Parishes, XVI-142 pp., 1949.
296. MICKELLS, REV. ANTHONY B., J.C.L., The Constitutive Elements of Parishes.
297. NOONE, REV. JOHN J., J.C.D., Nullity in Judicial Acts, X-147 pp., 1949 (printed 1950).
298. SHEEHAN, REV. DANIEL E., J.C.L., The Minister of Holy Communion.
299. STATKUS, REV. FRANCIS J., J.C.L., The Minister of the Last Sacraments.
300. COOK, REV. JOHN P., J.C.D., Ecclesiastical Communities and Their Ability to Induce Legal Customs, XII-152 pp., 1949 (printed 1950).
301. FAZZALARO, REV. FRANCIS J., J.C.D., The Place for the Hearing of Confessions, X-150 pp., 1949 (printed 1950).
302. HANNAN, REV. PHILIP M., J.C.D., The Canonical Concept of *congrua sustentatio* for the Secular Clergy, XII-237 pp., 1949 (printed 1950).
303. QUINN, REV. HUGH G., S.T.L., J.C.L., The Particular Penal Precept.
304. GALLAGHER, REV. JOHN F., J.C.L., The Matrimonial Impediment of Public Propriety.
305. WELSH, REV. THOMAS J., J.C.L., The Use of the Portable Altar.
306. WATERS, REV. JOSEPH L., S.S.J., J.C.L., The Probation in Societies of Quasi-Religious.
307. REGAN, REV. MICHAEL J., J.C.L., Canon 16.
308. BYRNE, REV. HARRY J., J.C.L., Investment of Church Funds.
309. GALLAGHER, REV. THOMAS V., J.C.L., The Rejection of Judicial Witnesses and Testimony.
310. CHATHAM, REV. JOSIAH G., PH.B., S.T.L., J.C.L., Force and Fear as Invalidating Marriage: the Element of Injustice, XIV-183 pp., 1950.
311. BROWN, REV. JAMES VICTOR, O.R.S.A., J.C.L., The Invalidating Effects of Force, Fear, and Fraud Upon the Canonical Novitiate.

312. Duerr, Rev. Charles J., B.A., J.C.L., The Judicial Notary.
313. Gonzalez, Rev. Francisco J., O.S.A., J.C.L., De Parocho Religioso Eiusque Superiore Locali.
314. Hannon, Rev. James J., J.C.L., Holy Viaticum.
315. Sadlowski, Rev. Erwin L., J.C.L., The Sacred Furnishings of Churches.
316. Sego, Rev. Arthur A., J.C.L., Dispensation From the Interpellations.
317. Waterhouse, Rev. John M., J.C.L., The Power of the Local Ordinary to Impose a Matrimonial Ban.
318. Frein, Rev. Eugene B., J.C.L., The Discretionary Power of the Defender of the Matrimonial Bond.
319. Carton, Rev. George A., J.C.L., The Time Factor in the Gaining of Indulgences.
320. Walsh, Rev. John J., C.S.Sp., J.C.L., The Jurisdiction of the Interritual Confessor in the United States and Canada.
321. Unterkoefler, Rev. Ernest L., S.T.L., J.C.L., The Presiding Judge in Matrimonial Causes of First Instance.

www.ingramcontent.com/pod-product-compliance
Lightning Source LLC
LaVergne TN
LVHW050237080826
844660LV00012B/548

* 9 7 8 0 8 1 3 2 2 4 8 5 5 *